Emergence of Kurdish Nationalism

Patricia J. Bunch

Abstract

This book delves into the intriguing concept of Kurdism and its emergence during the first half of the nineteenth century. Focusing on the foundations, origins, and evolution of Kurdish nationalism, which stems from Kurdism, the study investigates the interplay between the Ottoman Empire and the three Kurdish emirates of Soran, Botan, and Baban during this critical period.

Warm relations between the Ottomans and the Kurds endured until the advent of the New Order (Nizami Cedit) under the rule of Sultan Selim III (1789-1807) and Sultan Mahmud II (1808-1839). Subsequent modernization and administrative reforms, known as the Tanzimat (1839-1876), consolidated central power in the hands of the Sultan, leading to the abolition of local authorities, including the Kurdish semi-autonomous emirates. In response, the Kurds vehemently resisted the imposition of direct Ottoman rule, perceiving the Ottomans as an unwelcome "other." This pivotal moment marked the flourishing of Kurdism as an ideology, reawakening Kurdish consciousness concerning politics, language, and literature.

Central to the development of Kurdism were Kurdish Melas (Islamic scholars), popular poets, and folkloric poets in the Soran, Botan, and Baban emirates. These intellectuals played a major role in articulating Kurdish cultural politics through literary expression. The study draws from diverse literary sources to analyze the political rule of Kurdish mirs (princes) and the role of Kurdish intellectuals in shaping language and cultural politics within the Kurdish emirates during the first half of the nineteenth century. It demonstrates how the adoption of Kurdism enabled the Kurds to assert their identity as a distinct community with a unique historical legacy.

As Kurdism took root, it sowed the seeds of Kurdish nationalism, which gained momentum in the late nineteenth century through events such as the Kurdish revolt of 1880 led by Sheikh Ubeydullah Nehri, the establishment of the first Kurdish newspaper in 1897, and the burgeoning literary works of the period. This nationalistic sentiment continued to mature throughout the twentieth century.

Through meticulous historical analysis and exploration of literary sources, this book offers a comprehensive understanding of the trajectory of Kurdism and its pivotal role in the formation of Kurdish nationalism during the dynamic first half of the nineteenth century. It sheds light on how the concept of Kurdism became a cornerstone for Kurdish identity, emboldening the Kurds to assert their claims to autonomy and to their emirates. Moreover, it provides valuable insights into the intricate relationship between nationalism, identity, and cultural expression in the context of an empire undergoing profound transformation.

Table of Contents

Chapter Three: The Role of Kurdish Language and Literature in identity formation before the 19th century — 62

Acknowledgment

I would like to express my heartfelt gratitude to all those who have contributed to the completion of this book, "Kurdism and Kurdish Nationalism: A Historical Study of the First Half of the Nineteenth Century." Without their unwavering support, guidance, and encouragement, this endeavor would not have been possible.

First and foremost, I extend my deepest appreciation to my thesis advisor and mentor, [Advisor's Name], for their invaluable expertise, patience, and constant encouragement throughout the research process. Their insightful feedback and scholarly guidance have been instrumental in shaping the content and direction of this work.

I am also profoundly grateful to the members of my thesis committee, [Committee Member 1], [Committee Member 2], and [Committee Member 3], for their constructive critiques and thoughtful insights that have enriched this study.

I wish to extend my sincere thanks to the librarians, archivists, and staff at various institutions and libraries who provided access to the historical documents and literary sources crucial for this research. Their assistance was pivotal in gathering the primary materials that underpin the foundations of this study.

I am indebted to the Kurdish communities, scholars, and intellectuals who generously shared their knowledge and perspectives on the subject matter. Their passion for preserving and promoting Kurdish culture and history has been an inspiration.

To my family and friends, thank you for your unwavering support, understanding, and encouragement. Your belief in me kept me motivated during the challenging times of this undertaking.

I would like to extend my appreciation to the reviewers and editors whose valuable feedback helped refine the manuscript and enhance its clarity.

Finally, I am grateful to the open-access academic community and the various institutions whose funding and resources facilitated the research and publication of this book.

To all those mentioned above and to anyone whose contributions might have inadvertently been omitted, please accept my sincerest thanks. Your support has been immeasurable, and I am honored to have had you by my side on this academic journey.

With utmost gratitude,

[Patricia J. Bunch]

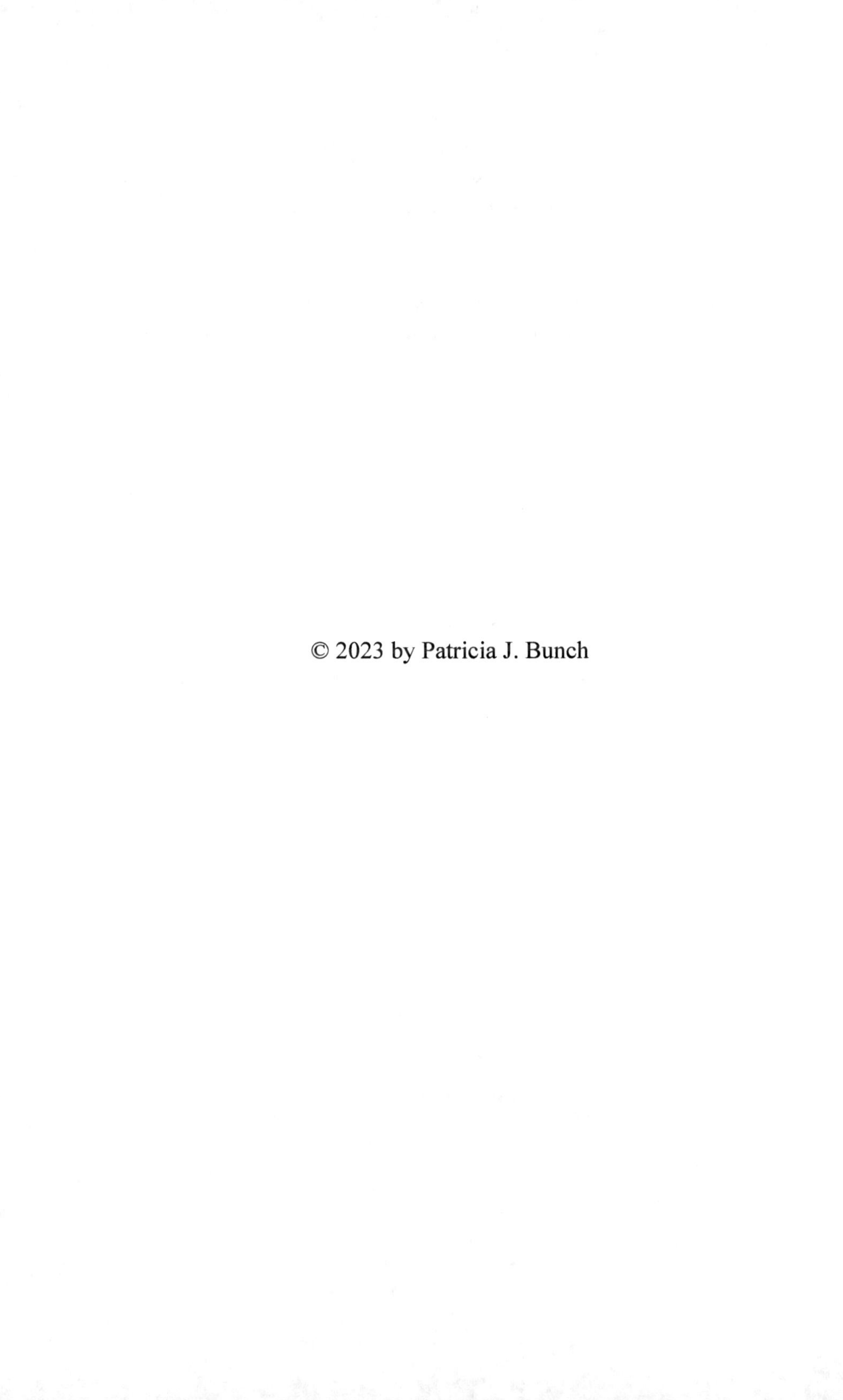

Note on Transliteration and Translation

One of the difficulties faced writing in English is, challenging original words spelled in Arabic script. To provide uniformity, this thesis has tried to establish a consistent pattern in spelling Kurdish, Ottoman, and Arabic and Persian words. Therefore, regardless of origin, all Kurdish proper names are rendered in romanized form.

Kurds in Iraqi and Iranian Kurdistan generally write Kurdish in Arabic script. The best way to transliterate Kurdish into English is a matter for debate. There is more than one system but in this study the romanization scheme originally developed by Jeladet Bedirkhan for writing Kurmanjî and Sorani is followed.

The list below indicates how written romanized Kurdish should be pronounced:

a ..... as in the English "far", for instance the Kurdish word "*Naz*"

e ..... as in the English "baker", for instance the Kurdish word "*Seywan*"

ê ..... as in the English "text", for in Kurdish word "*dê*"

ç ..... as in the English "teacher", for in Kurdish word "*çaw*"

î ..... as in the English "deal", for in Kurdish word "*sîr*"

Í ...... as in the English "feel", for in Kurdish word "*dil*"

ő ..... as in the English "ball", for in Kurdish word "*gővar*"

ř ..... as in the English "red", for in Kurdish word "*řaw*"

ş ..... as in the English "she", for in Kurdish word "*şaş*"

û ..... as in the English "foot", for in Kurdish word "*jûr*"

x ..... as in the English "sheikh", for in Kurdish word "*Xanî*"

Abbreviations

FO	Foreign Office
IOR	Indian Office Record
TBL	The British Library
TNA	The National Archive
WO	War Office

Chapter One: Introduction

1.1 Introduction: The Scope and Purpose of the Study

The last thirty years have seen a remarkable growth in the number of works dealing with the Kurds, Kurdistan and Kurdishness.[1] A new generation of scholars has examined the history of the Kurds and their national movements resulting in considerable discussion around the controversial origins and formation of Kurdism in the late nineteenth and early twentieth centuries. At the beginning of the nineteenth century, a new relationship was developing between the Kurdish emirates and the Ottoman Empire. Events during the first half of that period led to a deterioration in the relationship between the central administration and the Kurds. This led to the destruction of all remaining Kurdish emirates. In turn within this historical context, it will be argued, Kurdism was born. These events have rarely been the sustained focus of historical literature. Yet almost from the inception of post-Second World War historiography, their importance has been noted. Elphinston wrote in 1946 that:

> "the assistance given by the Kurds to the Ottoman Army in its fight against the Persians secured for them a privileged and autonomous position within the Ottoman Empire...history tells of no serious trouble between the Kurds and the Turkish Government until 1826, when the modernising policy of Sultan Mahmud II began to antagonize the feudal chiefs and led to the insurrection of 1830...led by two families."[2]

The history of the Kurdish principalities and their downfall in the first half of the nineteenth century has received far less attention than other periods in Kurdish history. This thesis attempts to analyse the background, context, issues and events that led to the development of Kurdism during the reform of the Ottoman Empire, when national movements emerged amongst the diverse peoples within that empire. It could be argued that Kurdism developed out of self-awareness, with language, literature, and administration all being used to advance

---

1For a recent overview see; *Power, ideology, knowledge - deconstructing Kurdish Studies*. Edited by Clémence Scalbert and Marie Le Ray European Journal of Turkish Studies, 5 | 2006 : Power, ideology, knowledge - deconstructing Kurdish Studies http://ejts.revues.org/index777.html#tocto2n1. Also Martin van Bruinessen; The Kurdish Question: Whose Question, Whose Answers? http://www.kurdishacademy.org/?q=node/144

[2] Elphinston, William Graham (1946). "The Kurdish Question", *International Affairs*, Vol. XXII, p. 93. An important paper on the period has recently appeared Eppel, M., (March 2008). *The Demise of the Kurdish Emirates: The Impact of Ottoman Reforms and International Relations on Kurdistan during the First half of the Nineteenth Century;* Middle Eastern Studies, Vol. 44, No. 2.

the concept of Kurdishness. The works of those few scholars who have considered this will be explored.

However, in the first half of the nineteenth century, the Ottoman Empire during Sultan Selim III (1789-1807) started to introduce "Nizam-i Cedid" (New Order), mainly to reform the Ottoman army. Ottoman officials became aware that they were much behind the progress of the West, and that therefore, army reform was necessary and there was a need to create new institutions. Although Selim did not succeed, the seeds of reform spread, supporting the eventual establishment of the new Ottoman army during the era of Sultan Mahmud II (1808-1839) who aimed to destroy the Janissaries, the old Ottoman army, in June and July 1826. All this led to a wider Modern Ottoman Reform "Tanzimat in Turkish" (1839-1876).[3]

One of the aims of these reforms was to destroy the local rule in the Balkans and in other parts of the empire, including Kurdistan. The nationalist aim in the Balkans, and to some extent the resistance in Kurdistan, contributed to ending Ottoman rule. The process of ending Kurdish self-rule took a long time and the Ottomans had to destroy the Kurdish emirates within Ottoman boundaries. This Ottoman attack prompted the Kurds to realise that the Ottomans desired an end to Kurdish self-rule. In resisting the Ottomans, Kurdish self-awareness deepened amongst Kurdish officials, poets and scholars, leading to ongoing development of Kurdish language and literature. This developing Kurdish self-awareness, in the first half of the nineteenth century, in the three Kurdish emirates of Soran, Botan and Baban indicates that the Kurds had their own notion of identity and understood that as Kurds they should govern their own affairs and have the right to develop their culture, language and literature.

This study aims to explore how Kurdism developed and came into being during the time of the three Kurdish emirates Soran, Botan and Baban in the first half of the nineteenth century. This study focuses upon Kurdish political activists, emirate officials, poets and scholars who promoted the Kurdish language, literature, customs, and Kurdish self-awareness in this period.

---

[3] For more details see Shaw, Stanford J. and Shaw, Ezel K (2002). History of the Ottoman Empire and Modern Turkey, Volume II, Cambridge, Cambridge University Press, pp. 1-171. Zurcher, Erik J (1998). *Turkey a Modern History*, I. B. Tauris & Co Ltd, pp. 32-74.

1.2 Definitions and classifications

Kurdism, as a term, is a combination of the word "Kurd" identifying a national group of this name, and the suffix "ism". The Oxford English Dictionary defines -ism as "[... used generically ...] A form of doctrine, theory, or practice having, or claiming to have, a distinctive character or relation: chiefly used disparagingly, and sometimes with implied reference to schism."[4] For example, Basheer M. Nafi describes Arabism in its first manifestations within the Ottoman Empire as being like Islamism "reflecting a cultural expression of an Arab sense of identity and a discourse of political opposition."[5]

Kurdism, as the term is used here, describes the idea, process, state and theory of Kurdish identity and its materialization in terms of historical events and transformations. Elements of Kurdism include a sense of distinctive identity relative to 'an other' (the Turks, Arabs and Persians), the use of Kurdish language in communication, literature and political institutions, a defence or celebration of Kurdish customs and way of life, a consciousness of national solidarity and aspirations to freedom and self-rule. Here it could be said that Kurdism used to signify the early period of Kurdish nationalism, or the period of proto-nationalism. Therefore, Kurdism never called for establishing a Kurdish state.

The term Kurdism is used in this thesis to denote a self-consciousness and awareness of being a Kurd, and part of a wider group of other Kurds. Yet, for the purpose of this thesis it is necessary to define the term '*Kurdist*' as a person who identified his or her own ethnicity as "Kurdish" and who promotes and expresses thoughts regarding the identity of the Kurds as a generalized term for the people living in the geographical area of the Middle East that has been known historically as 'Kurdistan'. In this sense both terms, Kurdism and Kurdist, indicate concepts of proto-nationalism and pro-active nationalism. In other words, Kurdism is not Kurdish nationalism, and Kurdist is not nationalist. Kurdism as proto-nationalism is some sort of local feeling or springing from regional or local political communities. It will be argued that there was a sense of Kurdishness amongst people in this area prior to the

---

[4] Simpson, J. A. J. and Weiner E. S. C. (1989). *The Oxford English Dictionary*, prepared by Second Edition, Volume VIII, Clarendon Press, Oxford, p. 112.
[5] Nafi, Basheer M. (1998). *Arabism, Islamism and the Palestine Question 1908-1914 A Political History*, Garnet Publishing Limited, Ithaca, p. 5.

Ubeydullah Revolt of the late nineteenth century, particularly so in those areas known as 'Emirates' in the first half of the nineteenth century.

In considering how Kurdish intellectuals expressed Kurdism in the early twentieth century, it is interesting to note that in 1910, a group of Kurdish students in the High Institute for Agriculture established the first Kurdish Student Society *Hêvi* [Hope] in Istanbul.[6] The first important step that the society took was to publish *Govari Řoji Kurd* [Kurdish Sun Magazine] in 1913. *Řoji Kurd* enjoyed great credit among Kurdish intellectuals across Kurdistan. Kurdish writers, poets and politicians from Silêmanî, Diarbekir, Wan, Mehabad, Arabgir, Kirkuk, Dirsim, and Kharput, held the magazine in high esteem. They advocated for a Kurdism which would support the recognition of Kurds within the Ottoman Empire, promoting Kurdish self-awareness through spreading political thought. In the editorial article, the board of the magazine admitted that through history, Kurds held both swords and land, but that "sword and land …must be in the hands of wise people who have received high education, knowledge and self-awareness."[7] Furthermore, society tended to emphasise cultural identity in order to lift treachery and injustice.[8] Here, it is clear that the editorial board were aware of their identity as Kurds.

In an article by Babanzade Ismael Haqqi (1876-1914) entitled *Musulmanliq u Kurdlak* [Islamism and Kurdism], the writer created a new ideology of Kurdism and presented it as a "road map" for the Kurdish question. Babanzade wrote about nations and languages, emphasising the significant role of language in Kurdism. Babanzade stated "language is an element for the revival of a nation and its production." Further, he sought to develop a constitution and program built on two principles: "Islamism and recognition of nations such as Arabs, Turks, Kurds and Persians."[9] Furthermore, Babanzade believed in both Islamism and Kurdism and that "Islam should be in the interests of Kurdism". He saw that a strengthening of the Kurds' sense of Islam would "benefit both Islamism and Kurdism."[10]

A colleague of Babanzade and contributor to *Řoji Kurd,* Abdullah Jewdet (1869-1932), refused the traditional Ottoman opinion about nations and nationalism. He fully understood

---

[6] Sharif, Dr Abdulsattar Tahir (1989). *Al-Jam'iyat wa al-munazzamat wa al-ahzab al-Kurdiya fi nisf qarin 1908-1957*, Arabic text, *Kurdish societies, organizations and parties in a half century 1908-1958*, Dar al-hurriy press, Baghdad, p. 37.
[7] *Govari Řoji Kurd* (1913). Our Aim, No. 1, June 1913, p. 2.
[8] Ibid, p.3.
[9] Babanzade, Ismael Haqqi (1913). "Musulmanliq u Kurdlak", Turkish and Kurdish magazine, Islamism and Kurdism, *Řoji Kurd*, No. 1, 6th July 1913, p. 5. This magazine has been republished by Jin Centre, Silemani, 2005.
[10] Ibid, p.7.

the new situation of the Ottoman Empire and the change in the thinking of Ottoman and Kurdish intellectuals. Abdullah Jewdet frankly spoke about Kurdish rights, emphasising "now is a time of nations; no powerful state on earth could deny this thought and this path. There is no way to reject public common sense, if we want unity amongst people from different ethnic groups, we must recognise the difference between them, and we should have enough encouragement to differentiate among them according to social science."[11] Abdullah Jewdet continues to express an agenda of Kurdism, stating that "Kurds want to study in their language and write their history, they want to understand their identity better in order to reach a stage of greater visibility."[12] Jedwet was here making a statement about Kurdish identity, stating that Kurds should advance through studying Kurdish history and Kurdish language and through demonstrating to others that Kurds have the ability to recognize themselves as Kurds.

The terms Kurdism and Kurdist have been used by the historian of the Hamidiye, Janet Klein, to describe the idea of Kurdish nationalism in the minds of some Kurdish activists of the late Ottoman Empire who saw themselves as members of the Ottoman multi-nation state.[13] She did not attempt to describe Kurdism in general, yet concluded that the Kurdish nationalist movement "was neither unified nor linear." She therefore described the Kurdism of the late Ottoman Empire as "… tinted with varying shades of meaning for different groups."[14] Klein stresses that "the idea of imperial disintegration and nationalism were *inherently* intertwined and, by extension, that a separate and nationalist state was the dominant goal of ethnic leaders."[15]

Denise Natali uses the term *Kurdayeti* to delineate Kurdism in a much wider sense than her predecessors. She suggests that "national identity becomes ethnicized [with] the similarities and variations in its manifestation [changing] across space and time … part of a repertoire of identities based on the nature of the political space in each state."[16] Whilst nationalism and *Kurdayeti* are not the same, and it is necessary to differentiate between the two, Natali's insight needs to be borne in mind in the context of this thesis as such factors have affected the

---

[11] Jewdet, Abdullah (1913). "Ittihad Yuli", The way of united, ibid, p. 9.
[12] Ibid.
[13] Klein, Janet (2007). "Kurdish Nationalists and non-nationalist Kurdists: rethinking minority nationalism and the dissolution of the Ottoman Empire", 1908-1909, *Nations and Nationalism*, Volume 13, Number, p. 135.
[14] Ibid, p 137
[15] Ibid, p. 136.
[16] Natali, Denise (2005). *The Kurds and the State*, Syracuse, pp. xvii-xviii; See also her review of Ozoğlu; *Ottoman Kurds and Emergent Kurdish Nationalism*, Critical Middle Eastern Studies, 13(3), Fall 2004, p. 384.

Kurds throughout their history, not just in the twentieth century. Nationalism and '*Kurdayeti*' may not be entirely synonymous, but both are factors in the shaping of Kurdish consciousness in the period under consideration.

Hakan Ozoğlu also employed the term "Kurdism" to refer to Kurdish political thought before the period of nationalism.[17] For Ozoğlu, the key elements of Kurdism were Kurdish language, history, and culture. Ozoğlu used the term "Kurdism" to refer to an intellectual and cultural movement promoting curiosity about Kurdish language, history, and culture."[18] In other words, Ozoğlu held that Kurdism is the thought of Kurdish activists and intellectuals to revive and use Kurdish language, history and culture from a pre-nationalism period to promote Kurdish consciousness. Indeed, arguably, Kurdish language, history, and culture distinguish Kurds from Turks, Arabs, Persians and others. It is through Kurdish language, history, and culture that Kurds feel able to sustain their continuity.

As the Kurds have failed to establish their own nation-state, their national identity as well as nationalism has remained a matter of debate and much controversy. It goes without saying, that a Kurdish nation-state would have greatly contributed to settling most of the basic issues related to identity and power: the process of the nationalisation of the culture, standardisation of the language, setting up national institutions and structures, formation of a national archive and library etc. In the absence of the vital factor of self-determination, the political as well as cultural issues relating to the Kurds remain complex and controversial, attracting the attention of academics of diverse persuasions, think-tanks and international political institutions and circles.[19]

During this period, Kurdism did not fully grow into political nationalism. Nationalism like any other aspect of human development, had stages of growth. It is therefore vital to understand and distinguish between periods of nationalism. To fully discuss this, we must also offer a proper definition of nationalism. According to Ernest Gellner, nationalism "is a political principle 'which holds that the political and national unit should be congruent'… a theory of political legitimacy."[20] To help us understand the concept of Kurdism during the

---

[17] Ozoğlu, Hakan (2004). *Kurdish Notables and the Ottoman State*, State University of New York Press, Albany, p. 70.
[18] Ibid, footnote no. 1 of chapter 4, p. 143.
[19] There are many centres in Europe for Kurdish studies such as: *Royal Institute for International Affairs, Royal Geographical Society, and Royal Asiatic Society*, other centres are in Moscow, Leningrad, Paris, International Crisis Group.
[20] Gellner, cited in Smith, Anthony D. (1998). *Nationalism and Modernism*, Routledge, London and New York, p. 29.

first half of the nineteenth century, we can make use of the distinctions drawn by Miroslav Hroch between three phases A, B, C during the progress of national movements.

According to his paradigm, Phase A depends on "the energies of the activists were above all devoted to scholarly enquiry into and dissemination of an awareness of the linguistic, culture, social and sometimes historical attributes of the non-dominant group"[21] in national consciousness amongst an ethnic group. Hroch emphasized that in this stage the non-dominant group in general is not "pressing specifically national demands to remedy deficits (some did not even believe their group could develop into a nation)."[22] In a second stage or Phase B, a wider collection of activists appear in political campaigns to mobilize "as many of their ethnic group as possible" to gather and take part in awakening the people to create a future nation. Finally, in Phase C, nationalist activists manage that "a full social structure could come into being, and that the movement differentiated out into conservative-clerical, liberal and democratic wings, each with own program."[23] For Hobsbawm, Phase C is the most important one, when "nationalist programmes acquire mass support, or at least some of the mass support that nationalists always claim they represent."[24] It shall be argued that the first period of Kurdism or Phase A (by Miroslav Hroch's analysis) occurred in the first half of the nineteenth century when a Kurdish consciousness appeared among both politicians and intellectuals.

In this sense, it is understood that Kurdism is a proto-national sentiment. As Hosbawm states, this can involve "supra-local forms of popular identification which go beyond those circumscribing the actual spaces in which people passed most of their lives."[25] This might apply to Kurds before the Ottomans became their official rulers, when they were able to function apart from the direct rule of the central power. Under the Ottoman Empire, Kurds lived with other peoples in large territories where no common polity existed, but where Kurds were able to preserve a sense of self-awareness. This may be understood as proto-national Kurdish sentiment.[26] However, it is clear that Kurdism itself as proto-nationalism, during the three Kurdish emirates in the first half of the nineteenth century, never called for the creation

---

[21] Hroch, Miroslav (1993). "From National Movement to the Fully-formed Nation: the nation-building precess in Europe", *New Left Review*, 198/1993, pp. 6-7. That Hroch's analysis is littered with historical error does not wholly disqualify his general analysis from offering a useful framework. See his comments on Flemish nationalism at p.12

[22] Ibid. p. 7.

[23] Ibid.

[24] Hobsbawm, Ernest, J. (2004). *Nations and Nationalism since 1780: Programme, Myth, Reality*, Cambridge University Press Cambridge, p. 12.

[25] Ibid, p. 46.

[26] Ibid, p. 64.

of a Kurdish state. It seems that Kurds were aware that either they did not have enough resources to establish a state, or that they purposely wished to live within the Ottoman Empire but under their own rule. As Hobsbawm comments, "the mere setting up of a state is not sufficient in itself to create a nation."[27]

Therefore, according to Phase A of Hroch, Kurdism reflected a sense of Kurdish self-awareness and was a major factor in supporting the Kurdish emirates against Ottoman influence in Kurdistan. It may be argued that "the character and role of those active in it [Kurdism], and the degree of national consciousness emergent in the ethnic group at large"[28] laid the foundations of Kurdish nationalism in later periods, and paved the way for the emergence of Kurdish poets, writers and politicians. These years witnessed the earliest forms and expressions of Kurdish nationalism exemplified by both poets and politicians. Men such as Sayyid Ubeydullah of Nahri, Haji Qadir Koyi, Bedirkhan's sons, Sayyid Abdulqadir of Nahri, Sheikh Mahmud Hafid and others, all became symbols representing Kurdism.

In the introductory chapter of this thesis, the historical development of Kurdism in the three emirates of Soran, Botan and Baban in the first half of the nineteenth century that is from 1800-1850, will be sketched out. In order to have a systematic approach to the complexity of the issues and conditions that precipitated the emergence and development of Kurdism in that period, the following will be explored:

1. The historical (internal and external) context of the emergence of Kurdism in the first half of the nineteenth century. Here the focus will be mainly on the factors that frustrated, necessitated or facilitated the emergence of a sense of distinctive Kurdish identity and destiny.

2. The modality of Kurdism: the different ways in which Kurdish identity began to express itself in the face of other ethnic groups or external dangers and hostile environments will be dealt with. This will include the political processes of the emergence of Kurdish emirates and the way these impacted upon a Kurdish sense of identity. The cultural manifestations of this process especially in poetry will also be explored.

---

[27] Ibid, p. 78.
[28] Hroch, Miroslav (1993). Op. cit, p. 6.

3. The successes and failures of Kurdism in that period in the assistance and development of Kurdish nationalism will be evaluated.

The past few decades have seen an increase in the number of scholars who have written about Kurdish history and Kurdish movements.[29] A new generation of scholars has examined the history of the Kurds and their national movement.[30] These scholars share a primary concern of dealing with the origins and beginning of the formation of Kurdism and for this purpose they often focus on the events of the nineteenth and early twentieth centuries. In fact, for the majority the early twentieth century is the historical focal point, while a tiny minority such as Wadie Jwaideh and Robert Olson prefer to associate the birth of Kurdism with events that developed in the late nineteenth century.[31]

1.3 The theoretical context

As most of the major scholars of Kurdish nationalism have approached the issues of Kurdish identity and nationalism in the context of the relationship between nationalism and modernity, in the Western sense of the word, this study will focus upon the development of Kurdish identity and Kurdish self-awareness in the first half of nineteenth century on the big narrative that sees Kurdism as a product of modernity. It shall be argued that this popular modernist narrative of Kurdism has become so dominant that it may block other narratives from forming.

1.4 The problem of Modernity

The problem of the affinity between modernity and Kurdism is easy to state but very difficult to define. Abbas Vali states plainly it "is a product of modernity."[32] What really does this general and abstract statement mean? Abbas Vali further asserts that: "Modernity is an

---

[29] See note 1.

[30] For example: Wadie Jwaideh (2006). *Kurdish National Movement: its Origins and Development*, Syracuse University Press, Syracuse, New York. Robert Olson (1989). *The Emergence of Kurdish Nationalism and the Sheikh Said Rebellion*, 1880- 1925, University of Texas Press, Austin. Amir Hassanpour (1992). *Nationalism and Language in Kurdistan 1918-1985*, Mellen Research University Press, San Francisco. van Bruinessen, Martin (1992). *Agha, Shaikh and State: The Social and Political Structure of Kurdistan*, Zed Books Ltd, London and New York. Hakan Ozoğlu (2004). *Kurdish Notables and the Ottoman State*, State University of New York Press, Albany, New York. Natali, Denise (2005). *The Kurds and the State*, Syracuse University Press, Syracuse. David Romano (2006). *The Kurdish Nationalist Movement*, Cambridge University Press, Cambridge. Jabar, F. A., & Dawod, H. (2006). *The Kurds: Nationalism and Politics*, Saqi Books, London, and others.

[31] See Jwaideh and Olson.

[32] Vali, Abbas (1998). "The Kurds and Their Others: Fragmented Identity and Fragmented Politics", *Comparative Studies of South Asia, Africa and the Middle East*, Vol. XVIII, No. 2, p. 82.

elusive concept, remaining ambiguous despite its wide currency in contemporary post-Marxist and post-liberal discourses. This ambiguity is largely due to the association of the concept with the philosophical foundations of post-structuralism and post-modernism, which are diverse and heterogeneous."[33]

It is now commonplace for the concept of modernity to be associated with a specific historical development in the West. This development provided a base for what is defined as 'modern society' and, indeed, this notion also meant, until recently, 'industrial society'. However, again this notion begs some very important questions. Although all the early 'protagonists' were agreed that something unique and important happened during the industrial revolution, they were by no means in agreement about, what, precisely, it was. They defined this historical development in different ways and therefore provided different accounts of what they had observed. Provided that all that was required was a notion to define this historical development, and a descriptive term to explain the relationships between individual people, terms like 'modern society', 'industrial society and 'post-modern' society gained great importance. We are aware now that there is no such object as 'modern society', or 'traditional society', with an existence completely separated from individual peoples and certainly not one that could be seen or touched; however, there is always a set of social forces "exerted by people over one another and over themselves."[34] Depending on how people define these social forces, the notion of modern society and modernity can equally be interpreted as industrialism, capitalism, urbanism, and even post-modernism.

First, there is a unique interpretation of Kurdism that is articulated mainly by Abbas Vali. Vali sees Kurdism as mainly or entirely the result of the advance of modernity in the region and views Kurdism as a defensive catch-up reaction to Iranian nationalism. A second group includes various accounts of modernisation theory, cultural narrations and post-structuralism accounts. Most of these argue that Kurdism was shaped by the socio-economic and political changes which occurred in the region and had a great impact on Kurdish society. They argue that Kurdism was an overtly political response to novel changes that occurred in the region between the late nineteenth and early twentieth century. Martin van Bruinessen and Hamit Bozarsalan are among many scholars that advocate this account of Kurdism. The third school of thought is a Marxist account of Kurdism; Amir Hassanpour and Shahrzad Mojab are two

---

³³ Ibid, p. 92.
³⁴ Elias, N. (1970). *What is Sociology?* Hutchinson, London, p. 17.

academics who in the last decades defended this mode of analysis. Finally, there are individual viewpoints by a group of historians and social theorists such as Robert Olson, Janet Klein, and Hakan Ozoğlu. In this chapter, these accounts will be reviewed briefly.

1.5 Modernist theories and Kurdism

Vali states that Kurdism "is unmistakably modern. Its genesis is the relationship of the self and other with the emergent Turkish, Persian and Arab identities in the early decades of the present century."[35] In his essays on the origin of Kurdish nationalism, Vali argues that Kurdism emerged in the early decades of the twentieth century. However, in his article entitled *Kurdish Nationalism in Iran: the Formative Period, 1942-1947* published in 1996-1997, he formulated a quite different dating: "the birth of the *Komelei Jeyanawai Kurdistan* (Society for the revival of Kurdistan) in September 1942 marked the advent of modern nationalist discourse and practice in Iranian Kurdistan."[36] Here, it seems that Vali has contradicted himself regarding the two periods in which Kurdish nationalism emerged. One can hardly accept the years between 1942 and 1945 as the early decades of the twentieth century.

In contrast to Abbas Vali, van Bruinessen has written many books and articles about Kurds and the Kurdish question.[37] From the outset, his account of Kurdish society and his conception of Kurdism have developed in line with Anthony Smith's theory of nationalism and particularly his definition of *ethnie*. van Bruinessen account represents the most popular method used to construct the narrative of Kurdism. The narrative goes like this: during the late nineteenth century, concepts of nation and nationalism came from Europe to the Middle Eastern communities. The first generation of the Kurdish nationalists emerged in big cities such as Istanbul and Cairo. By the early twentieth century, Ottoman intellectuals, who were discontented about the slow pace of change, organised themselves. In 1908, they revolted against the Sultan and planned to establish a republic. This was an affirmation of Turkish nationalism and national identity. Ottoman intellectuals of Kurdish ethnicity cooperated with

---

[35] Ibid, p. 104.
[36] Vali, Abbas (1996-1997). "Kurdish Nationalism in Iran: the Formative Period, 1942-1947", *The Journal of Kurdish studies*, Vol. II, published by Institut Kurde de Paris, p. 1.

[37] Martin van Bruinessen is a well-known European scholars who has contributed significantly to Kurdish studies. He has published widely no Kurdish communities, identity, and religion.

them at the start. However, as they were subjected to various forms of discrimination, their attention moved towards more ethnic politics. Bruinessen argues that the social and economic changes and continual contact with Western culture had encouraged publication of newspapers, magazines, as well as the formation of political organisations. All this paved the way for the emergence of modern Kurdish nationalism.

Bruinessen focuses on the 1925 revolt of Sheikh Said of Piran who led the Kurdish revolt against the new Turkish Republic. However, crucially for Kurdish historiography he considers it in the light of a sociological examination of Kurdish society. In doing so, he sets out a narrative that pays more attention to the Kurdish Emirates of the sixteenth to nineteenth centuries than has been the case with previous scholars.

Bruinessen has focused on the Kurds as an anthropologist and believes that Kurdish nationalism had variable relations with tribal and religious loyalties.[38] He points out that Anthony Smith uses the French term *ethnie* to designate communities who share common myths of origin and descent; an association with a specific territory and some elements of shared culture; with a sense of solidarity amongst most of their members.[39]

Ethnie is distinguished from ethnicity in that it describes those individuals who share awareness and have recognition of a common culture and myth, rather than their actual heritage, lineage or tribal organisation. Nationhood, in comparison with *Ethnie*, tends to represent a higher degree of integration, which is characterised by a mass of public culture, as well as a certain level of economic and political integration.[40]

However, in the past decades expanding his mode of analysis, he has tried to offer a synthesis for such divisions within Kurdish studies. There is no doubt that Bruinessen is rightly an authority within the field of Kurdish studies. However, a section of this study will concentrate on van Bruinessen's interpretation of Kurdish nationalism in Ehmedê Xanî's *Mem u Zin* demonstrating the inadequacy of his theoretical approach.

---

[38] van Bruinessen, Martin (1992). *Agha, Shaikh and State: The Social and Political Structure of Kurdistan*, Zed Books Ltd, London and New York, p.7.

[39] Smith, Anthony D. (1999). *The Ethnic Origins of Nations*, Basil Blackwell, Oxford, pp.13-16.

[40] van Bruinessen, Martin v (2006). *Kurdish Paths to Nation* in edited by Jabar, F. A., & Dawod, H., *The Kurds: Nationalism and Politics*, Saqi Books, London, p. 32. van Bruinessen refers specifically to Anthony D Smith, *The Ethnic Origins of Nations*, Oxford, 1986 and his *The Origins of Nations, Ethnic and Racial Studies* 12, 1989 and his National Identity, London 1991. He locates Smith in the 'Gellner' school of nationalism.

1.6 Marxist theories of nationalism: Class and Kurdish nationalism

The Marxist school of thought has been present in the politics and theory of the Kurdish nationalist movement from the third decade of the past century, and has left a major impact on the development of Kurdish national movement. It had continued to hold sway well beyond the circumstances of its emergence in Southern Kurdistan politics in the 1930s. However, since the 1980s, the scene has thoroughly changed. There has been major economic, political and social upheaval, and with the collapse of the Soviet Union and the Soviet-type societies of Eastern Europe, an ideological crisis emerged within Marxist theory and politics. Although in Kurdistan, like everywhere else, the heyday of Marxism is over, in many respects, scholars are still trying to come to terms with its legacy. Despite this major shift, Amir Hassanpour and Shahrzad Mojab are among the few scholars and intellectuals that are still trying to articulate their account of Kurdism within the concept of historical materialism.

For the purposes of this review in this section, Hassanpour's account will be examined. Hassanpour analyses Kurdish society in pre-capitalist and capitalist stages of its development. He maintains that as a result of decline of the rural areas and the growth of urbanisation in 1950s, tribal and feudal loyalties loosened and a new middle class emerged in Kurdistan. This new social class generated an anti-feudal, and to a limited extent a modernist, tendency. According to Hassanpour for a long period a dual society, feudal (traditionalist) and bourgeoisie (modernist) continued to co-exist as a reality in Kurdistan. The politics, projects and practices of these two trends generated a different conception of nation building process.

Hassanpour defines the Kurdish question in line with the Marxist theory of national oppression. On one hand, he has always advocated a qualified right of national self-determination for all oppressed nations, including the Kurdish nation. On the other hand, he views nationalism as a masking ideology, and under bourgeois leadership has the dangerous potential to forge a class alliance in pursuit of the propertied classes' interests. In the end, considering the underdeveloped stage of capitalism in Kurdistan, he concludes that for the Kurds national consciousness is an unavoidable historic phase that they must pass through on the way to internationalism and socialism.

Along with this Marxist account of Kurdism, he maintains that the Kurdish nationalist movement has been the moving force in standardization of Kurdish language and modernization of cultural life. The writings of Hassanpour are of great value in identifying a 'Kurdish National Awakening in the seventeenth century", and defining it as a 'Feudal Nationalism'.[41] He suggests "The idea of nation and nationalism, an apparent anachronism in this part of the world in the seventeenth century, did... develop in the particular circumstances of Kurdistan at this time. This national feeling...was voiced by both individuals and the masses of the people."[42] Hassanpour's idea is that the poetry of Xanî can be considered an historical element of Kurdism saying that he "was at least three hundred years ahead of most of his countrymen."[43] Hassanpour, anticipating some criticism of his idea has also pointed out that Kurdish *beyts* (folk ballads) also contained "the idea of national attachment."[44]

1.7 Historical narratives

In this section, the works of scholars who have provided historical narratives of Kurdish national movement, including historians Wadie Jwaideh and Robert Olson, will be examined, and studies by Hakan Ozoğlu, Janet Klein, and Denise Natali referenced. They all regard what Natali terms the 'Late Imperial Period' as being the most crucial time for Kurdism. The foundation for all this modern work is a 1960 thesis, only recently published as a book in 2006, by Wadie Jwaideh.[45]

Jwaideh was not the first person to write about Kurdish nationalism but his work draws together an impressive array of nineteenth century memoirs, government reports and scattered articles by renowned Kurdologists. In doing so, he successfully draws attention to Kurds' long history and quest for national autonomy being deeply rooted in the past

In his study, Jwaideh looked at two main Kurdish principalities: Soran and Botan. Examining them in the later period of the nineteenth century, he concluded that "A strong sense of

---

[41] Hassanpour, Amir (1992). Op. cit, p. 55.

[42] Ibid, pp. 55-6.

[43] Ibid,

[44] Ibid, p. 56. I mention Hassanpour in particular, but his views are shared by Shahrzad Mojab (1996). See her Nationalism and Feminism: The Case of Kurdistan, Bulletin Institut Simone De Beauvoir, Women and Nationalism (16), 1996. p. 67.

[45] The reasons for the long delay are variously given. We get the clearest picture from a review, written by one of his former pupils. "Jwadideh was an Iraqi nationalist, and I do not think that he wanted to be characterized as someone who was promoting Kurdish nationalism. This...he makes clear in his study, had possibilities of gaining strong autonomy and/or independence in the right circumstances—an autonomy and/or independence that would lead to the disintegration of the state of Iraq" Robert Olson of Jwaideh, *International Journal of Middle Eastern Studies*, Volume. 39, No 4, 2007, p.677.

nationality has existed among the Kurds for a very long time."[46] The most important thing for Kurds was to maintain their identity among the dominant nations and the states that encompassed them. This 'sense of being' became the foundation of the Kurdish nationalism in the period he examines. Jwaideh took the lead in tracing the beginnings of Kurdish nationalism to Sheikh Ubeydullah who, in 1880, wanted a united Kurdish nation and, as such, an independent Kurdistan.[47]

Sheikh Ubeydullah belief was that Kurds had the foundation for a Kurdish state, built on the similarities of the Kurdish people in racial, cultural, and linguistic terms, but these similarities were crushed by the systematic suppression of the Kurdish people by Turks and Persians, and finally, the fear of Armenians taking over the Kurds.[48] In his conclusion, Jwaideh emphasised that "It was certainly a nationalist impulse that was behind Shaykh (*sic*) Ubayd Allah's (*sic*) movement, and the sheikh was undoubtedly motivated by Kurdish nationalist sentiment when he declared in a letter intended for the eyes of the representatives of the British government, 'We Kurds are a people apart.'"[49]

Robert Olson pioneered the use of archival sources in delineating Kurdish national sentiments. His book *The Emergence of Kurdish Nationalism and the Sheikh Said Rebellion* drew on British Air Ministry and Colonial Office files. He postulated that "The Sheikh Said Rebellion...was the culmination of four distinct stages of Kurdish nationalism. He 'delineated' these as:

> "(1) the movement led by Sheikh Ubeydullah of Nehri and his Kurdish League...ending with his death in 1883; (2) the role of the Hamidiye Light Cavalry from its creation in 1891 until the outbreak of World War I; (3) the events of World War I to the Treaty of Sevres..; and (4) the aftermath of World War I and post-war developments through the rebellion of Shaikh Said."[50]

Olson argued, crucially, that there were important differences between; "Ubeydallah's rise to prominence...[his] rule was characterized by nationalist goals and that of Bedir Khan Beg was not......... the most important difference between Sheikh Ubeydallah's nationalist aims

---

⁴⁶ Jwaideh, (2006). Op. cit, p. 290.
⁴⁷ Ibid, p. 80.
⁴⁸ Ibid, p. 81.
⁴⁹ Ibid, pp. 291-2.
⁵⁰ Olson, Robert (1989). Op. cit, p. 1.

and the traditional, autonomy–minded Bedirkhan Beg was his publicly stated goal of establishing an independent Kurdistan."[51]

Olson concluded that Kurdish nationalism could have succeeded at this point, were it not for the interference of the European powers. "At the end of this first stage of Kurdish nationalism, all of the European powers, as emphasized in the Treaty of Berlin, were opposed to Kurdish independence movements... Great Britain and Russia had their own reasons for opposing such movements. Only the Ottoman Empire had good reasons for supporting Kurdish independence movements, but not, of course, an independent Kurdish state."[52] Olson argues, following Jwaideh, that the dissolution of the Emirates earlier in the century had led to a situation where 'there was a shift of power to the shaikhs'; "a power greater than that of the petty feuding chieftains.'[53]

Hakan Ozoğlu, author of *Kurdish Notables and the Ottoman Empire*, seems to be the first to challenge the above scholars' opinions on Bedirkhan and Ubeydullah. If, as Ozoğlu suggests, Bedirkhan was a consenting servant of the Ottoman power structure until his revolt, and the evidence produced for this is compelling, then it is logical to attribute his well-known revolt to dissatisfaction with losing elements of his wealth and status. However, it will be demonstrated that other factors were at play when the fissure occurred. As Ozoğlu points out, Bedirkhan was told, "As long as you serve and stay loyal to the Ottoman state, Mehmet Pasha [his rival] cannot do you harm."[54] Other factors, it will be argued, must have been involved to mitigate against these 'reassurances'. One of these will be the way in which Bedirkhan was able to mobilize the loyalties of his followers.

In the course of his rule, Bedirkhan had maintained a sense of independence and "refused to send tribal contingents when these were requisitioned in the Ottoman-Russian war of 1828-9." As Jwaideh notes, Bedirkhan should have been made more cautious in his actions by "the fate of Muhammad Pasha of Rewanduz." However, he was more than just a provincial functionary. His lineage marked him out as a scion of "one of the oldest ruling families in Kurdistan."[55] He therefore had differing aims and expectations to other administrators. Ozoğlu also believed that Sayyid Ubeydullah's aim was no more ambitious than the

<hr>

[51] Ibid, pp. 1-2.
[52] Ibid, p. 7.
[53] Ibid, p. 4. Jwadaih (2006). Op. cit, p.76.
[54] Ozoğlu, Hakan (2004). Op. cit, p.72 citing from BA Mesail-I Mahimme, 1225 report Sevgen *dogu* doc no XXXI.
[55] Jwaideh, Wadie (2006). Op. cit, p. 62.

establishment of an autonomous state, under his leadership, but within the Ottoman state, similar to the Kurdish principalities which existed before. Therefore, he stressed that the Ubeydullah revolt was "a transtribal" revolt rather than a national one."[56]

Ozoğlu also asserts that, "The political and military activities of Kurdish notables in the pre-World War One period were not nationalist; they reflected the desire of powerful Kurdish lineages to consolidate, expand, or recover their regional influence. Kurdish leaders…were mostly members of Ottoman high bureaucracy and as such an integral part of the Ottoman state". Based upon a fundamental belief that "there is a fundamental pattern amongst the Kurdish revolts in [Turkish] Republican history... the Kurds adopted the idea of self-determination to show their dissatisfaction with the center" since "Most…Kurds want only a better life of more equitable understanding with other ethnic groups in Turkey". Concluding that; "in the minds of some Turkish nationalists, any manifestation of Kurdish identity was and is a major threat to the indivisibility of the Republic of Turkey."[57]

To sum up, these modernist scholars have given us interesting alternative approaches to historical accounts that see the Kurdish national identity as mainly, or entirely, the development of a common ethnic origin. This research has identified some inconsistencies and contradictions in these approaches.

Having reviewed these diverse accounts of Kurdish national identity, it is noted that apart from the last group, the rest in different ways analyse the Kurdish national movement in terms of 'modernist' theory. However, as we have argued, the notion of modernity is contested. There are different interpretations of modernity. On the other hand, it is argued that the affinity between the birth of Kurdish nationalism and modernity is exaggerated.

From a historical perspective we have to take into consideration the fact that modernist theories applied to Kurdistan need to take account of the narrative of Empire and imperialism. It might therefore be expected that these modernist accounts take into account

---

[56] Ozoğlu, Hakan (2004). Op. cit, p. 76.
[57] Ozoğlu, Hakan. (Spring 1994). "Kurdish National Discourse: Comparing and Contrasting the Shaikh Said and the PKK Revolts", *Turkish Studies Association Bulletin*, Vol. 18, No. 1, p.91. Ozoğlu, Hakan (2001). "Nationalism and Kurdish Notables", *Middle East Studies*, No. 33 , p.383: Winds of Change: The Kurdish Workers' Party and Turkish Nationhood; idem; Vol. 17, No.2, Fall 1993, pp. 112-3. References also appear in the Olson / Ozoğlu correspondence. Ozoğlu's interpretation of Kurdish Nationalism and his subsequent work must be appraised in the light of these comments. *Kurdish Notables and the Ottoman State*, State University of New York, Albany, 2004. p.3. Ozoğlu is a writer whose book has attracted much, albeit qualified, praise from scholars of Kurdish Nationalism. See Hassanpour, H-Turk (2007), especially important are the comments by Denise Natali (Autumn 2004). "Ottoman Kurds and emergent Kurdish nationalism", *Middle East Critique*, Volume 13, Issue 3 , pp. 383 - 387

the historical circumstances that inhibited or provided the way for modern society in this region. As far as Kurdish society is concerned, this requires the study of the impact of Ottoman and Qajar Empires, as well as the impact of the European imperialist project on the development of Kurdish society.

This study will deal with the background and events that led to the development of a Kurdism or national consciousness, during the reform period of the Ottoman Empire, and it will focus on a particular period: 1800-1850. It will explore the thoughts and struggles of three Kurdish leaders, Abdulrahman Pasha of Baban, Muhammad Pasha of Soran and Bedirkhan Pasha of Botan. These three rulers, who came in succession, strove for recognition of the Kurds as a separate people, with all of the attendant political and cultural implications. This study also analyses the role of three emirates in the development of Kurdism: Baban, Soran, and Botan; which came into existence before Ottomans and Safavids entered Kurdistan. This thesis will address how, during the last three emirates, the Kurds affirmed their identity to resist interference from the Ottoman authorities.[58]

In this study, a different approach will be presented, combining both civil and ethnic interpretation of nationalism as inseparable aspects of one process with different degrees of nationalist consciousness and political organisation. In order to have a systematic approach to the complexity of the issues and conditions that precipitated the emergence and development of Kurdism and nationalism in that period, both the political and cultural context of the development of elements, and the phenomena and reality of Kurdish awareness and movement in the three Kurdish Emirates of Soran, Botan and Baban will be discussed.

1.8 The Scope of this Study

This study attempts to examine the aspects, elements and events of the historical development of Kurdism in the three Emirates. Of great interest are the memoirs of those who, passing through the area for diverse reasons, were witnesses to the events as they occurred, or were able to talk to those who had witnessed them. This, of necessity means that in some sense a textual approach needs to be applied. Great reliance is made upon the writings of poets who flourished in the immediate aftermath of the dissolution of the emirates. Some may argue

---

[58] In the first half of the nineteenth century, especially during the reign of Abdulrahman Pasha of Baban, Muhammad Pasha of Soran, and Bedirkhan Pasha of Botan, tried to develop Kurdish identities.

against the use of such material as being ahistorical or subjective. Although there is some difficulty in dating the composition of their works precisely, thanks to the efforts of many Orientalists the dates of most of the major works are well-established.

The Baban poets responded to the dominance of the South Kurdish language, Sorani. Salim (1805–1869) was one of the great poets and was one of the founders of the Baban School of poetry in the history of Kurdish literature. Alongside his two close friends and relatives Nalî (1800–1873) and Kurdî (1812-1850), he emerged in Silêmanî under the Baban Emirate. These three men created outstanding poetry voiced with an innovative poetic language. Salim is renowned amongst the Kurds as he is reputed to have created Kurdish patriotism and Kurdish resistance poetry in the first half of the nineteenth century. In his work, he stood up against the Ottomans who brought down the Baban Emirate. Salim looked upon the Turks as the enemy of the Kurds and considered them an uncivilised people.[59]

Regarding any allegation of subjectivity or partiality in such writers, this is precisely the quality sought in their work; their own sense of Kurdishness. To offset such a partial approach, the relatively abundant memoirs of travellers throughout the area have been employed. They add a perspective of observation and detail. These will be supplemented further by the use of internal East India Company and British Foreign Office letters, reports and memoranda. These have the value of being written by people for whom the events were fairly recent and were often written with the intention of understanding passing events.

The most prominent British traveller in Kurdistan was Claudius James Rich who was a resident for the East India Company in Baghdad and Kurdistan. He travelled widely through Kurdistan and had a close friendship with the Baban princes. During his visit, he collected much information about political life there and the Kurdish attitude towards the Ottoman officials. Through Rich, we understand that the Kurdish pashas had the intention of serving their own emirate, but the Ottoman officials did not allow them to do this. It was therefore, a constant clash of interests. Rich's memoirs have made a valuable contribution to at least two modern studies of the Kurds.[60]

---

[59] For further information about Salim see: Elaedin, Sejadi, *Mêjui Edebi Kurdi*, The history of Kurdish literature, Am'arif press, Baghdad, 1953 and 1972, pp. 228-246. Hilmi, Rafiq (1956). *Shi'ru Edebyati Kurdi*, A-Shabab Press, Baghdad, pp. 53-83. Professor Marouf Xeznedar (2003). *The history of Kurdish literature*, Vol. 3, Arass press and publisher, Arbil, pp. 117-163.

[60] Rich, Claudius James (1836). *Narrative of A Residence in Koordistan, and on the Site of Ancient Nineveh*, two volumes, James Duncan, London. There are many studies used Rich such as Wadie Jwaideh, (2006). and Martin van Bruinessen, (1992). http://www.oxforddnb.com/view/article/23483; His papers are preserved in the IOL at MSS Eur. A 12–19, B 44–49, C 38, D 232–235, G

1.9 The Focus of this Discussion

During the first half of the nineteenth century, a few Kurdish scholars and poets had started using Sorani Kurdish as a language for literature to promote Kurdish self-awareness. Later, the development of literature in the Sorani language provided a focus for Kurdish Nationalism, and the effects of this on the development of Kurdish identity and its impact on Kurdish Nationalism will be analysed in detail.

This research sets out to examine the early establishment of Kurdish thought and its emergence amongst Kurdish scholars and poets in the first half of the nineteenth century which flourished in three Kurdish emirates Soran, Botan and Baban. The period could be termed as the "early Kurdish enlightenment or genesis of Kurdism". It will be demonstrated that a 'Kurdish sense of identity' can be seen in the thoughts and activities of Kurdish mirs, scholars and poets. The study also looks briefly at some socio-historical factors connected with the history of the geographical space where Kurds have traditionally lived. In the past they were part of the Ottoman and Persian Empires. They are divided between Turkey, Iran, Iraq and Syria. According to Natali, the differing forms of Kurdish Nationalism were a function of the traditional social structures and of the political spaces that became dominant in each state.[61]

It must be borne in mind that no single nationalist camp has existed, because of differences between tribes, which, being dominated by the more important factors of survival and competition for resources and land, often exhibited inherent competitive behaviour. The main aim of the leaders of the emirates was to maintain the position of their emirates, so when it suited them they would co-operate with the empires, and if an opportunity presented itself, when the balance of forces were in their favour, they would show defiance against the state.[62]

In the process of working on this research, diverse perspectives on the subject of the nature of Kurdism are discussed. However, this study initially has a more modest task; to look at the history of three major Kurdish principalities and their demise in the first half of the

---

34–35]

[61] Natali, Denise, (2005). Op. cit, p. xvii.
[62] Ibid, p. 1.

nineteenth century. A period when three Kurdish emirates; Soran, Botan and Baban, worked to sustain a sense of Kurdish identity and struggled to safeguard their self-rule. This also entails the analysis of the background, context, issues and events that led to the development of Kurdish ideas during the Reform, or Tanzimat, of the Ottoman Empire, when the national movements of the diverse peoples within the empire emerged.[63]

1.10 Précis of Issues discussed in each chapter

Aside from the introductory chapter and the conclusion, this thesis contains five chapters. The introductory chapter addresses pertinent theories of nationalism, concentrating mainly on the modernist approaches to Kurdism as expressed in the works of some major authorities on Kurdish nationalism.

Chapter two, *Kurdish Tribes and their Emirates; the Socio-Political Structure*, addresses three main issues: 1) the basic social organization of the Kurds, the 'tribe' and clan structure, and the position of the leaders and their relations with the Kurdish emirates in the first half of the nineteenth century. 2) A general picture of the structure of the emirate will be provided, and its significance as the largest Kurdish administration in Kurdish history will be discussed and lastly the historical overview of the Kurdish emirates will be provided. Furthermore, this chapter addresses the state of affairs of the Kurds between the Ottoman and Persian domination in the sixteenth century, tracing the powerful role the Kurds played in the conflict between the Ottoman and Safavid Empires. While allied to the Ottomans, the Kurdish Mirs kept their autonomy and survived despite wars and the many treaties signed between the two powers.

Chapter three, *The role of Kurdish literature in identity formation before the 19th century*, responds to two significant and related topics in the study of Kurdishness and culture, that of the Kurdish language, and its literature. The Kurdish language has been instrumental in the survival of the Kurdish people's culture and identity. The language became synonymous with Kurdish nation. Kurdish literature has also embraced aspects of Kurdish identity and thought,

---

[63] Indeed, Dawn, C. Ernest (1973). suggests that nationalist thought in Turkey can be traced to this period. "Interest in nationality as a political principle was rekindled among the Moslem peoples by contact with the West. At the turn of the nineteenth century, a few Turks and Egyptian Arabs who had resided in Europe began to become aware of the European ideas of the fatherland and nation. By the middle of the new century, terms for these and reloated concepts existed in both Turkish and Arabic" From Ottomanism to Arabism, Essays on the Origins of Arab Nationalism, University of Illinois Press, London, p. 123.

and has been propagated amongst Kurds; in particular *Mam u Zin* has been legendary in its influence. This, a classic Kurdish epic[64] by Ehmedê Xanî, began to develop and serve as a vehicle for opposition to the two dominant Muslim powers. Xanî has been perceived as the forerunner of the advancement of nationalism among the Kurds. Furthermore, the *medrese* and its role in promoting education and Kurdism will be discussed too.

Chapter four, *The Soran Emirate and its contribution to Kurdism*, discusses the Soran Emirate, in particular the period of Muhammad Pasha (1813-1836). Muhammad Pasha endeavoured to establish a powerful emirate and re-unite the Kurds. Initially, Muhammad Pasha influenced internal affairs, before extending his influence to both sides of Kurdistan. Nevertheless, the Nizami-Cedid army, the new Ottoman force, was sent to destroy the Soran Emirate. Even with assistance from the Persians the Ottoman bid to dismantle Soran was lengthy. The international powers, Great Britain and Russia in particular, played an instrumental role in overthrowing Soran since both powers were in favour of the Ottoman Empire and were not prepared to allow any other power to emerge in the region for fear that they could become a threat to their interests.

The poet Haji Qadir Koyi (1817-1897) played a great role in the development of Kurdism and Kurdish nationalism. Although he is reputed to have written most of his work after he left Kurdistan in 1853, he experienced the destruction of all three Emirates in his formative years. It would be impossible for his mature work not to be informed by what he saw. His work will be treated, albeit critically, as the expression of an eyewitness to these events. This poet and some others such as *Mela* Muhammad ibnu Adam and Haji *Mela* Abdullah Jalizada will also be addressed.

Chapter five, *The Botan Emirate and the Development of Kurdism in the time of Bedirkhan* discuss the role of the Botan Emirate under Bedirkhan Pasha (1821-1847). Bedirkhan wanted to build a strong Kurdish administration and accordingly he concentrated on uniting the Kurds, especially the tribes. Bedirkhan established order and justice among his people, and security and peace were also implemented. The American and European missionaries who had been present in Kurdistan since the beginning of the 1830s penetrated deeply into Kurdish affairs, and American missionaries used religion as a means to undermine Kurdish authority for their own political agenda. This became a key point for European powers to

---

[64] *Mam u Zin* was written by Ehmedê Xanî, who through love story expressed Kurdish national identity and his philosophical ideas as well.

assert pressure on the Ottoman Turks and to attack the Botan Emirate and, ultimately, induce its destruction.

Chapter six, *The Development of Kurdism in the Baban Emirate 1800-1850*, charts and analyses the development of the Baban emirate, and how it enhanced the emirate's position between the powerful Ottoman and Persian states. Later, the Baban emirate attempted to extend its influence but the two powers intervened. Once again, it is demonstrated how an emirate resisted oppression in order to maintain semi-independence. This chapter also discusses the power struggle between Baban, and the Persian and Turkish states, which endured over a lengthy period of time.

In Baban, Mawlana Khalid Naqishbandî (1779-1826), *Mela* Khidir (Nalî) (1800-1873) and Abdulrahman Beg (Salim) (1805-1869), two famous Kurdish scholars and poets in the first half of the nineteenth century, will also be argued, as each served as an inspiration to the Kurdish people. They contributed substantially towards the establishment of a standard Kurdish language in Southern Kurdistan, and were the first to write in the Sorani Dialect, which remains the written language in South and East Kurdistan. The above three poets had close links with the Baban ruling family, which influenced their writing, and produced beautiful poems in support of the Baban Kurdish ruler, also composing equally beautiful poems about the collapse of the Baban Emirate.

Finally, in conclusion, elements of the assembled evidence are drawn together and it is argued that since the eleventh century, Kurds established their own local rule and distanced themselves from the dominant groups around them. They maintained their tribal structures and these helped the Kurdish emirates to sustain their authority over the Kurdish people. It will be shown that Kurdish poets played a great role in developing Kurdish consciousness. In the seventeenth century, Ehmedê Xanî in his *Mem u Zin* thought about the establishment of a Kurdish state. He suggested that a Kurdish King should mint a Kurdish currency and promote Kurdish culture for the purpose of Kurdish unity. With Ehmedê Xanî, Kurdish oral tradition also helped to develop Kurdishness.

During the first half of the nineteenth century, Kurdish political authorities and Kurdish writers created a strong basis for the emergence of Kurdism. This can be clearly recognized in the Soran, Botan and Baban emirates, during the reigns of Abdulrahman Pasha of Baban,

Muhammad Pasha of Soran and Bedirkhan Pasha of Botan. The basis was thus laid in this period for Kurdism to emerge, in a recognisably modern form, at a later stage in Kurdish history.

1.11 A note on sources

This thesis uses four main primary sources throughout the study: Kurdish, Arabic, and Persian sources and the British official records. The Kurdish sources include manuscripts, memoirs and poetical works which are relevant to the period under discussion. The Arabic sources include those which deal with Kurdish history, and Kurdish society. There are a few manuscripts which were originally written in Ottoman Turkish, then translated into Kurdish or Arabic. The Persian sources include Iranian Foreign documents that illustrate the Persian official attitude regarding the Kurdish emirates and their aim towards them.

The British records contain documents, correspondence, and reports from East India officials, The Foreign Office, Indian Office, and War Office. Of great significance are memoirs from British and American missionaries and their agents and British travellers who visited the area for one reason or another. The manuscripts of the Indian Office concerning the emirates have never been used before. There were thousands of manuscript letters and enclosures covering the Kurdish emirates before, during and after the first half the nineteenth century. These documents have been accessed through the British Library, the library of the School of Oriental and African Studies, Senate House-London and the British National Archives in Kew Gardens, London. This work deals with the British documents as external historical texts. It should be noted that some British sources reflect the official or personal attitudes and desires of the diplomats, agents and travellers.

This study also uses contemporary Kurdish, Arabic, Persian and English sources. Extensive use of secondary sources, mainly in Kurdish, English, Arabic and Persian languages has been made. In 2005, when this research commenced, it was difficult as a Kurd to gain permission from Turkish officials to access Ottoman materials in Turkey. As a result, this study draws heavily on documents about the Ottoman Empire held in a range of British archives, including the British Library and National Archive. Access to Ottoman archives in Turkey these days has become much easier and it would be interesting to consult these as an extension of this research.

Chapter Two

Kurdish Tribes and their Emirates; the Socio-Political Structure

2.1 Introduction

In the introductory chapter, theories of Kurdism drawn from the literature on philosophical theory and Kurdish Studies were presented and discussed. To develop a general understanding of Kurdism, this chapter examines in brief the historical background, socio-economic and political systems of the Kurdish dynasties and their emirates. The establishment of the rule of the Ottoman and Persian empires in Kurdistan and how their borders were established in Kurdistan, with reference to the Zahab treaty between the two powers is discussed along with an analysis of the Idris-Selim (the Kurds and the Ottoman) agreement and its impact on the Kurds. Understanding these conditions will enable a better understanding of the Kurdish situation and the features of Kurdish self-awareness in the nineteenth century. Following this, the socio-political structure in Kurdish tribal systems and governance in the Kurdish emirates is examined in detail. The influence of Kurdish tribes and their relationships with the emirates, and the political role of *mir* provides a focus for the discussion. Finally, the emergence of the Kurdish emirates in general before the nineteenth century and their brief history, with special reference to Soran, Botan and Baban is explored.

2.2 Kurdish Dynasties and their States before the Ottomans and Safavids

Before Arab Muslims appeared in Mesopotamia in 637, there were already a significant number of Kurdish people living in the Sasanian Empire. Thus, during the expedition years from 639 and 644 of Arabs against the Sasanian state, Kurds gave their powerful assistance to the Sasanian state.[65] When it became apparent that the Sasanian state was going to be defeated, the Kurdish leaders gradually started to convert to Islam. In the time of the two Islamic Caliphates, Umayyad 661-750 and Abbasid 750-1258, the relationship between Kurds and the Caliphates was not always positive. Kurds rebelled many times against the Umayyads, for instance in 840, 846, 866 and 869 – 883 when some Kurdish tribes supported the Zinj rebellion against the Abbasids.

---

[65] McDowall, David (2000). *A Modern History of the Kurds*, I. B. Tauris, London New York, p. 21.

Between the middle of the tenth century and the end of the twelfth century, a few Kurdish dynasties gained ascendancy. Minorsky stresses, that: "During the first five centuries of the Hijra [eleventh to fifteenth centuries] the Kurds frequently played a considerable part in events and often took the initiative in them."[66] Through subsequent centuries, many Kurdish dynastic states emerged and governed significant parts of Kurdistan. As a result of the Arabs trying to increase their influence during the Umayyad Caliphate by using Arabic at court and starting to Arabise the state, it was made difficult for non-Arab Muslims to gain official positions. In response, the Kurds tried to assert their autonomy and it is in that context that the Kurds attempted to create local self-rule.

Examples of these states include the Hasnawi state, established in 941 by Hasan Barzagani: ruling over Sharazur, Dinawar, Hamadan, Nahawand and Samhgan until 1067.[67] The Dushtak was established by Husein Dushtak in 967, and lasted until 1096. It controlled a large area and had diplomatic relations with other regional states. It was also the first Kurdish government to send representatives to Byzantine, Egypt and Baghdad.[68] The most famous Kurdish dynasty was that of the Ayyubids, of southern Kurdistan-Erbil-Shekhan; from which emerged Salaheddin, born in 1137.[69]

The end of the Abbasid era in 1258 presented a few Kurdish dynasties with political and social opportunities to re-establish their authority. These local entities varied in size and political power according to the geo-political climate of the area in which they were established.[70] The Mongol occupation of Western Asia greatly altered the political history and geography of the region, and Kurdistan in particular.[71] After the Mongols eliminated the Abbasid Caliphate in 1258, a major change in the political map of the area was the establishment of the province of Kurdistan. Hamd-Allah Mustawfi was the first historian to

---

[66] Minorsky, V. (1986). *The Origins of the Kurds, The Encyclopaedia of Islam*, New Edition, Volume V, Published by E. J. Brill, Leiden, p. 1134. Professor Minorsky's opinions were taken seriously by Kurdologists such as Tofik Wahby. See his; *The Origins of the Kurds and their Language*, London, 1964, p. 2. Professor Marouf Xeznedar wrote in his introduction to Minorsky's book "The Kurds", (translated from Russian to Arabic), that Minorsky's ideas were serious and deserve to be appreciated as he was an important scholar and a great 'thinker among thinkers'. who devoted his life in studying and understanding [many] nations including the Kurds. Dr Marouf Xeznedar, from his introduction to "The Kurds" of Minorsky, al-Nujum Press, Baghdad, 1968, p.10.
[67] Zaki, Muhammad Amin (1937). Kholasayaki Ta'rikhi Kurd u Kurdistan, Kurdish text, The brief history of Kurd and Kurdistan, Part II, AL-Arabiya Press, Baghdad, pp. 94-114. Huzni, H. (1929). Awreki Pashwa, Kurdish text, A Glance to the Past, Part II, published by Zari Kirmanji, p. 4.
[68] Huzni, Op. cit, Peshkawtin, p. 28-9.
[69] Zaki, Op. cit, p. 118.
[70] Kennedy, Hugh (1980). The Prophet and the Age of Caliphate: The Islamic Near East from the Sixth to the Eleventh Centuries, Longman, London & New York, p. 251.
[71] These events are usefully summarised by Donald Quataert, The Ottoman Empire, 1700-1922. Cambridge University Press, Cambridge, pp 13-19.

mention Kurdistan in his book, *Nuzhat-al-Kulub*, classifying it as a separate government under the Seljuks.[72]

The Mongol province of Kurdistan did not embrace all lands held by the Kurds; the remainder was divided between five provinces: Jazirah, Armenia, Adharbiyja, Irak Arab and Jabal or Irak Ajam. The province of Kurdistan comprised Alani, Alishtar and Bahar, Khuftiyan, Darband Taj Khatun and Darband Zangi, Darbil, Dinawar, Sultanabad Chamchamal, Sharezur, Kirmanshah, Kirind and Khushan, Kanguvar, Mayidasht, Harsin and Vastam. The capital of Kurdistan was Bahar, and the whole province flourished under Sulaiman Shah.[73] Until the end of fifteenth century, Kurdistan was under different dynasties of Mongol rule. Between 1258 and 1501, the fall of the Abbasids in Baghdad and the emergence of the Safavid Empire, Kurds have rarely been mentioned in the historical record. Thereafter, Kurds gained strong ground in the wars between the two powers of Ottoman and Persia, maintaining self-rule until 1851, when the Ottoman Turks brought down the Baban Emirate, the last Kurdish emirate.

The death of Tamburlain (Timur Lang) in 1404 resulted in the downfall of his empire. In Azerbaijan and Kurdistan, two Turkish tribe confederations, namely Qaraqoyunlu and Aqqoyunlu, were getting stronger. These two confederations gained independence and the areas from northeast of Lake Van to Azerbaijan became the territory of Qaraqoyunlu. Qara Yousif of the Qaraqoyunlu fled from Timur and returned to Kurdistan where he demanded refuge with Shamusddin, the *mir* of Bitlis. Qara Yousif gave his daughter to the *mir* who, in response, gave Qara Yousif part of his emirate and assisted him to defeat Timur and re-establish his influence.[74] Later, around 1450, most Kurdish emirates including Sirt and Hasankeyf had been under the rule of the Qaraqoyunlu.[75] In other parts of Kurdistan around Amid, Mardin, Kharput and Erzincan, the Kurdish *mirs* became subjects of the state of Aqqoyunlu. By 1470, Uzun Hasan of Aqqoyunlu (d. 1497) took Jazira, Bitlis and the Hakkai emirates. Most of Kurdistan became Uzun Hasan's territory. After defeating the last Timur in Iran, there was no one more powerful than Uzun Hasan. He made Tabriz the capital of

---

[72] Mustawfi, Hamd-Allah (1903) *Mesopotamia and Persia under the Mongols; in the Fourteenth Century* A. D., Asiatic Society Monographs, Vol. V, by G. Le Strange, Published by the Royal Asiatic Society, London, p. 55.

[73] Ibid, p.55-6.

[74] Bitlisi, Sharafkhan (1953). *Sharafnama*, Arabic text, Translated from Persian by Mullah Jamil Rojbayani, al-Najah Press, Baghdad, p. 127. Minorsky, V. (1986). Op.cit, p. 457. Van Bruinessen, Martin (1992). *Agha, Shaikh and State*, Zed Books Ltd, London and New York, p.137

[75] Van Bruinessen, Martin (1992). Ibid.

Aqqoyunlu.[76] During this period, the leaders of Aqqoyunlu used tough policies against Kurds and replaced Kurdish princes with Aqqoyunlu governors. This created serious difficulties in relations between Aqqoyunlu and Kurdish chiefs and their princes. Therefore, when the news of Ismael Safavid reached Kurdistan, Kurds in Jezire, Sirt, Hasankeyf and other areas attacked Aqqoyunlu and pushed them out from most of Kurdistan.[77] The weakness of the dominant powers over Kurdistan enabled the Kurds to rise up, resisting outside rule wherever they could.

2.3 The beginning of the Ottoman and Safavid Empires in Kurdistan

The rule of Aqqoyunlu lasted until the emergence of the Safavids when Tabriz was taken by Shah Ismael in 1501 and became Safavid's capital. The geographical position of Kurdistan strengthened the political structure for Kurdistan between the Ottoman and Persian empires. Both states were in conflict over many issues such as religion and the sects of Shi'ism and Sunnism and over the land that lay between them. Each state tried hard to dominate Kurdish tribes and their princes. Therefore, Kurdistan became the battlefield to solve the conflicts between the two empires. After the establishment of the Safavid Empire, relations between the two empires were at their worst particularly during the Safavid period (1501–1722) where there were official and public disagreements in the Islamic world between Shi'is and Sunnis. The adoption of Shi'ism as the national religion of Persia created a fatal barrier to the Pan-Islamic aspirations of Sultan Selim and other Ottoman Sultans, leading to long ideological wars between the two powers.

Shah Ismael formed a strong army and started attacking the Ottomans, capturing wide areas of the Ottoman Empire including Kurdish regions as far as Marash. The Shah sent strong forces of Qizilbash to fight against Kurds in Bitlis, Hakkari and Botan.[78] These new conditions had a negative impact on the Kurds in general and can be considered an important turning point in Kurdish history. To implement his policy, Ismael relied on the Turkoman Qizilbash tribes, and chose them instead of Kurdish governors in Kurdistan. This policy created wider public and official hate and enmity between Kurds and Shah Ismael. Consequently, "Kurdish tribes everywhere united"[79]. Kurdish chiefs sent letters and

---

[76] Ibid. Minorsky, V. (1986). Op. cit, p. 457.
[77] Bitlisi, Sharafkhan (1364). *Sharafnama*, Persian text, Muhammad Abbasi, Published by Elmi Tejran, pp. 284, 334.
[78] Ibid, p. 532.
[79] Van Bruinessen, Martin (1992). Op. cit, p. 141.

messengers to Sultan Bayezid (1481-1512) and Sultan Selim (1512-1520), and called upon the Sultans to attack the Safavid,[80] offering Kurdish assistance in this regard.

Sultan Selim had strong military power. He had already established a powerful Ottoman Empire in Eastern Europe and consequently could not accept the threat of the Safavids. The Sultan turned his forces towards the east and started to attack Ismael, bringing him to the Battle of Chaldiran in 1514, where Ismael and his army were badly defeated and the Safavid capital Tabriz was captured. Idris Bilisi, the Kurdish diplomat, scholar and historian was appointed by Selim as his advisor for the Kurdish affairs, and played an important diplomatic role between the Ottoman and the Kurds. Idris managed to contact twenty-five Kurdish princes including Soran, Amedi, Jezire, Hasankef, Siirt, Khizan and Bitlis to turn in favour of the Ottomans and drive the Safavid governors out of the Kurdish area.[81]

The Battle of Chaldiran affected Kurdish territory tremendously. Thereafter, for more than four centuries, Kurdish territories became the ground for violence and fighting between the Ottomans and Persians. Later, when Selim returned with his army and left no force in Kurdistan, Ismael seized the opportunity to take back what he had lost. Ismael besieged Diyarbekir for a year, but could not enter the city. Therefore, the Kurdish princes in Diyarbekir sent a letter through Idris Bitlisi. They urged Selim for help and stated that: "please help us, we are sincerely with you. Our land is near to Persian land and in some places next to each other. For years those "infidels" have been destroying our houses and fighting against us for fourteen years, without your assistance, we cannot maintain our safety against those oppressors…"[82]

In short, Idris Bitlisi organized the administration in Kurdish regions, and also built peace, security and friendship among Kurdish princes. However, he did not manage to establish a united Kurdish government, as the Kurdish princes wished to be independent in their principalities.[83] It is apparent that Kurdish leaders and princes refused Safavid domination for a number of reasons, wishing to maintain local rule and independence from outside powers where the Ottomans left them in their places to govern themselves. Most Kurds were

---

[80] Ibid, 537.

[81] Bayat, Dr. Fazil (2007). *Al-dawla al-Othmaniya fi al-majal al-Arabi, Arabic text, The Ottoman state in the Arab World*, Published by The centre of the Arab study, Beirut, p. 247. This was taken from Khwaja Saedaddin Afandi, Taj Al-Tawarikh, Turkish text, The Crown of History.

[82] Ibid, p. 249. For the completed letter Akgunduz, Osmanli Kanunnameleri ve Hukuki Tahilleri, Vol. 3, 1991, pp. 206-7.

[83] Ibid, p. 252.

Sunnis and wished to refuse Shi'i rule. Furthermore, the Safavid Shahs' harsh policies against Kurds, leading to the massacre of Kurds by Safavid forces, also prompted Kurdish resistance to Safavid rule.

The Battle of Chaldiran brought many centuries of war and conflicts between the rival Ottoman and Safavid Empires. Sultan Sulaiman the Magnificent (1520-1566) continued his father's policy towards the Safavid Empire, attacking Persia several times. He did not make peace until late into his reign, when in 1554, Tahmasp Shah I (1524-1576) of Persia sent his special envoy with many gifts to Sultan Sulaiman asking for peace. The offer was accepted. Later in 1555, the Amasya Agreement, also known as 'the blessing agreement', was drawn up. Accordingly, eastern Azerbaijan, Kurdistan and Mesopotamia became part of the Ottoman Empire.[84] This was the first agreement between the two empires. The Ottomans recognized the Safavid Empire and they divided Kurdistan and sections of Arab land between themselves. They also promised that there would be no further hostilities, and pledged not to shelter opponents of the other's regimes.[85] Sultan Sulaiman claimed that he made a wall of the Kurds, using Kurds as human shields to protect the eastern border of the empire.[86] He asked for names of the Kurdish princes to be sent to the Porte to be appointed as rulers of their emirates and their tribes.[87] This is another indication that the Ottoman Empire desired that the Kurdish heads and princes should have rights to rule their own territories and be accorded powers to establish their administrations. It can be observed that the Ottomans always tried to attract Kurdish people and their leaders to keep on the side of the Ottomans against the Safavids. To do so, the Ottoman Empire accorded Kurdish princes local powers and roles according to their strength and importance.

The Safavid Empire was in a difficult position when Shah Abbas-i Kabir (the Great) came to power on 2 December 1587. His first task was to reorganize Imperial affairs. In time, these problems were resolved and foreign relations were re-established. Abbas tried several times to persuade the Indians and Russians to back him against the Ottomans, but without success. There was a renewed attack by the Ottomans and they captured districts which were handed

---

[84] Mahdavi, Abd al-Riza Hushang (1349). *Ta'rikhi ravabiti khriji Iran*, Persian text, *A History of Iran's Foreign Relations*, Supahir press, Tehran, p. 20.

[85] Parsadust, Dr Manuchahir (1367). *Rishahai Taarikhi Ikhtilafati Jangi Iraq u Iran*, Persian text, The Roots of the Conflicts between Iraq and Iran, part 3, Suhami and Co. Publisher, Tehran, p. 26-7.

[86] Ahmad, Dr Kamal Mazhar, (1983). *Mezu*, Kurdish text, The History: A Brief Study About Science of History and the Kurd and History, Dar Afaq Arabiya publisher, Baghdad, p.130.

[87] Bayat, Dr. Fazil (2007). Op. cit, p. 359.

to the control of Daulat Yar Khan, the chief of the Kurdish tribe of Siya Mansur.[88] The safety of the eastern empire was dependent upon the defenses provided by this frontier government and consequently the power of Daulat Yar Khan was augmented.

Daulat Yar Khan, relying on the natural strength of his country, took this opportunity to declare his independence. The Kurds maintained their rule until Shah Abbas "the Great" raised a new army and subdued them.[89] In despair, Daulat Yar Khan accepted the Istanbul Peace Agreement on 21st March 1590. Accordingly, Luristan, Sharezur and all other occupied territories of Kurdistan became part of the Ottoman Empire.[90] The reason for the offer of this truce by the Ottomans was a need for Shah Abbas to command the Persian army against an insurrection in Khurasan.[91]

The peace only lasted thirteen years; rivalry and sectarian divisions between Ottomans and Safavids continued. In 1610, the Ottomans attacked and occupied the country as far as Tabriz. The Persians asked for peace, and a new agreement was reached in 1611. This recognized the old border, which went back to Chaldiran, with an extra condition that the Persians must not assist Helo Khan, then the *Mir* of Sharezur and Erdelan.[92] The war between the Ottomans and Persians continued until the Erzurum Treaty of 1843-44, the last agreement before the ending all Kurdish emirates by the middle of the nineteenth century.

2.4 The Boundaries between the Ottoman and Persian Empires

The Battle of Chaldiran between the Ottoman and Persian states was ended by the victory of the former on Kurdish soil. However, the two sides did not sign any agreement at this time. In 1638, after a siege lasting some weeks, Sultan Murad IV recaptured Baghdad with the assistance of Kurdish princes and chiefs. In the massacre that ensued, almost the entire Persian garrison and 30,000 of the inhabitants were said to have perished.[93] Later, Shah Safiyadeen led the Safavid army into Qesri Shireen, but realizing that he could not confront the superior Ottoman forces, sent an envoy to Baghdad to negotiate with Sultan Murad IV (1629–1642) requesting peace.

---

[88] Rawlinson, H. C. (1841). Op.cit, p. 58.
[89] Ibid.
[90] Zaki, Muhammad Amin (1931). Op. cit, p. 176. Mahdavi, (1349). Op. cit, p. 32-33.
[91] Mahdavi, (1349). Op. cit, p. 29.
[92] Zaki, Muhammad Amin (1931). Op. cit, p. 187.
[93] IOR L/PS/20/C190, Mesopotamia, (1919). Handbooks Prepared Under the Direction of the Foreign Office, No. 92, London, p. 21.

Discussions were held and on 17th May 1639, Mustafa Pasha, the Ottoman Grand Vazir and the Shah's representative, signed a peace treaty.[94] Borders were established between the two empires with conditions dictated by the Ottoman Sultan. The boundary passed through the heart of Kurdistan, from Akhisq at the north to Basra at the south, going through Van and Sharazur, Qesri Shireen, Basra and western Kurdistan.

This peace treaty defined the Ottoman and the Persian borders east of the Zagros Mountains.[95] The agreement took so little notice of the Kurds that some of their tribes, such as the Jaff, were separated either side of the border.[96] The border drawn in 1639 has been maintained up to modern times, defining the newly established nation states. As the Kurdish question has not been resolved according to Kurdish wishes, this therefore still remains problematic. Break-out of war between these two countries often arises from the Kurdish border question.[97]

Many castles and fortresses were destroyed in Kurdistan due to their position between the two powers: "The fortresses of Kotour and Maukew, on the frontier of Van, and the fortress of Maghausberd, towards Kars and Van, [which] will be demolished by the two parties, and so long as the Shah will not have molested the fortresses of Akhiskha, ..., Van, Sharezur."[98] The result of this was the destruction of fundamental symbols of Kurdish autonomy and the heritage of the country. In 1639, Bitlis remained independent, with Hakkari and Amêdi, also under Kurdish princes. However, in 1660 or thereabouts, the Kurdish dynasty again acknowledged Turkish suzerainty.[99]

The two protagonists expressed the hope that the treaty would last until the end of the world, concluding: "This happy peace will last and be maintained until the day of resurrection, and whoever shall alter it after having heard it, verily this sin shall be upon those who have altered it."[100] Despite these honorable aspirations, hostilities were constantly restarted whenever either side felt powerful enough to gain an advantage.

---

[94] IOR L/PS/10/266 Turco-Persian Frontier: A Treaty of Peace between Turkey and Persia, signed at Zahab on the 17th May in the year 1639, Translation of Copy of Treaty preserved in Imperial Library at Vienna, No. 1, p. 204-6.

[95] Ibid.

[96] Soane, E. B. (1910). *Report on the Sulaimania District of Kurdistan*, Superintendent Government Printing, Calcutta, p. 29.

[97] McLachlan, Keith (1994). The boundaries of modern Iran, published by UCL, London, pp. 47-56.

[98] IOR L/PS/10/266 Turco-Persian Fronier, Op. cit, p. 204b.

[99] Soane, E. B. (1910). Op.cit, p. 29.

[100] Curzon, George N. (1892). *Persia and Persian Question*, Vol. I, Longmans, Green, and CO., London, pp. 204-4.

Shah Abbas (1585–1628), tried to lure Kurdish loyalty away from the Ottoman Turks. He appointed Prince Sharafadeen, the famous Kurdish historian, to write, in Persian, a history of the Kurds and their genealogies. He wished to prove that the Kurds had ancient associations with Persia and the East. Shah Abbas managed to take advantage of a Kurdish alliance against the Uzbek army. Yet the moment he subdued the Uzbeks, his hostility shifted to the Kurds. The Kurdish *mir* of Erdelan, who as a reward for his services against the Uzbeks had demanded recognition of his sovereignty by Persia, was seized and executed in 1613, by the Persian Shah.[101]

In the eighteenth century, at the end of the Afghan supremacy, the Russian agreements with Tahmasp Mirza gave Persia the power to rid itself of the Afghans whilst allowing the Ottomans a free hand, when they took possession of Kurdistan, Nakhchiwan, Tabriz, Khoi and Ganja in 1725–7.[102] At the same time, Hasan Pasha of Baghdad led the Ottoman Turks in the invasion of Persia, when they captured Kirmanshah, stopping for the winter, intending to progress to Hamadan in the spring. Upon his death in early 1724, his strategy was continued by his son, Ahmad Pasha, who became Pasha of Baghdad and commander of the Ottoman army there and later took Hamadan.[103] With this move, a huge swathe of Western Persia, including Kirmanshah and Zahab, became Ottoman territory.

After crushing some internal revolts, Nadir turned his attention to the capture of Kirmanshah. Instead of then marching straight to Baghdad, he made for Kirkuk, in the hope that Ahmad Pasha would come out from Baghdad to meet him.[104] In March 1733, Nadir surrounded Baghdad and during its siege large numbers died from famine and disease. He later occupied Samarra, Hilla, Karbala and Najaf amongst other places.[105] The plight of Baghdad was so disastrous that Ahmad Pasha sent envoys to Nadir to arrange the terms of his surrender.[106] This situation forced the Ottoman Porte to send a large army consisting of some 80,000 men under ex-Grand Vazir Topal Osman to the relief of Ahmad Pasha at Baghdad. After a long confrontation between the armies and huge losses on both sides, Nadir was defeated. The "Persian soldiers were in a sorry plight, many being on foot and almost naked."[107]

---

[101] Safrastian, Arshak (1948). Op. cit, p. 42-43.
[102] Soane, E. B. (1910). Op.cit, p. 29.
[103] Lockhant, L. (1938). *Nadir Shah: A critical Study Based Mainly Upon Contemporary Sources*, Luzac & CO., London, pp. 12-3.
[104] Ibid, p.66.
[105] Ibid, p. 67.
[106] Ibid, pp. 67-8.
[107] Ibid, p. 71.

After a wait of two months, Nadir mounted a counterattack and managed to capture the fortress of Surdash near Silêmanî. Then, at the end of 1736, a treaty was agreed between Nadir Shah and Sultan Ahmad delimiting the frontier after many victories over the Ottoman Turks. In 1746, after Nadir's unsuccessful raids against the Ottoman territories, a second and more important treaty was signed between Nadir Shah and Sultan Muhammad. Under its terms, Azerbaijan and the province of Iraq became Turkish territories; Turkey also regained Zahab which was organized as a Turkish province, and the current town of Zahab was built by the ruling Pasha, a chief of the Bajalan Kurds.[108]

2.5 The Ottoman-Kurdish Agreement

There were two main factors behind the Ottoman-Kurdish Agreement and Ottoman Empire's need for the Kurds. First, the Ottomans wanted Kurdish Sunnis to be against the Safavids and Qizilbash Shi'is who wanted to establish their strong influence in central and eastern Anatolia particularly among Turkmen tribes. Kurds were in this regard kingmakers between the Ottoman and Persian Safavids. Second, the Ottomans agreed to grant the Kurds autonomy to keep the balance between the Ottoman *walis* [governors] and the Kurdish *mirs* and to use them against each other. Thus, the Ottoman *walis* in the centres such as Baghdad, Mosul, Erzurum and Diyarbekir exploited the disagreement between the emirates and conflicts amongst emirs ruling dynasties for their interests and for the benefit of the empire. By weakening emirates and their emirs, the Ottomans maintained power. The mountainous geography and Ottoman interests prevented the growth of powerful Kurdish emirates. The Ottoman *walis* tried to put obstacles in the way of the Kurdish *Emir*s ambitions to build up strong political and military power. This will be discussed in chapters four, five and six of this thesis.

The feudal structures of the Ottomans encumbered the political and administrative systems of the empire. Ottoman policy was to consider Kurds as a semi-independent bulwark against Persia.[109] Therefore, in 1514, Idris Bitlisi convinced Sultan Selim to give him power and to appoint him as his organizer of Kurdish affairs.[110] An agreement was made between the Kurdish princes and Bitlisi who represented Sultan Selim I with regard to Kurdish issues.

---

[108] Soane, E. B. (1910). Op.cit, p. 30.

[109] Armenia and Kurdistan (1920). Op. cit, p. 17. Van Bruinessen, Martin (1992). Op. cit, p. 136.

[110] Bitlisi, Sharafkhan (1953). Op. cit, p. 431. McDowall, David (2000). A Modern History of the Kurds, I. B. Tauris Publishers, London New York, p. 28.

Idris Bitlisi managed to control Kurdistan for the Ottomans. Without his efforts, it would have been impossible for the Ottomans to maintain control over Kurdistan.

Sharafkhan Bitlisi argues that Idris Bitlisi claimed that Kurdish princes called upon the favour of the Sultan to retain the hereditary principle for Kurdish rulers and in return agreed to recognize Ottoman authority.[111] Idris Bitlisi worked in favour of both the Kurds and the Ottoman Empire, managing to bring peace them. He saved Kurdish local-rule and the hereditary Kurdish princes continued to govern their affairs. After some negotiation, Sultan Selim I agreed to such terms and issued a decree for maintaining the freedom and independence of the Kurdish Emirates. When a head prince died or the Emirate had no head figure, either the authority was to be passed to his son or the people should adopt local custom to fill the position. Then it would be blessed by the sultan's deed. The Kurds should give assistance to the Turks during war and the Turks should help the Kurds against aggressors. Finally, the Kurds should incorporate *zakat* (charity) and contribute towards central government.[112]

This agreement was later mutually renewed with Sultan Sulaiman. This avoided the destruction of the Kurds and Kurdistan and saved the Ottomans from fighting them. With the dispensation of some financial assistance, the Ottomans managed to secure their eastern borders relatively cheaply.

Evliya Çelebi appreciated the role of Idris in promoting hereditary Kurdish autonomy and emphasized that as Kurdish local rulers such as Egil Kurdish Government's *Beg* (governor) was not an Ottoman *Beg*, he could not be removed by the central power. If he died whilst in office, without a son to succeed him, then other members of his family would be allowed to succeed him.[113]

Furthermore, contemporary Arab scholar Dr Sayyar al-Jamil argues that this Ottoman-Kurdish Agreement became a fundamental document for Ottoman dealings with the Kurdish Emirates and their leaders.[114] The agreement reflected the Kurdish sense of independence and

---

[111] Ibid.

[112] Zaki, Muhammad Amin (1931). *Kholaseyeki Taerikhi Kurd u Kurdistan*, Kurdish text, *A brief history of Kurd and Kurdistan*, Dar-al-Salam Press, Baghdad, p. 166. Sharafkhan, (1953). Op. cit, notes in pp. 436-7.

[113] Celebi, Evliya (1979). Op. cit, 28.

[114] Al-Jamil, Dr. Saiyar A. (1991). *al-Othmaniyah wa Takwin al- Arab al-Hadith 1516-1916*, Arabic text, The Ottomans and the establishment of the New Arabs 1516-1916, Dar-alKuttab liltabaawa al- nashir, Mosul, p. 343.

became the basis for political negotiations between them and the Ottoman Empire. Also, it was the first *agreement* between the empire and any of its subjects. The attitude towards independence exhibited by the Kurds towards the Ottoman Empire is exemplified by a remark in a British Report on Mesopotamia in 1922 that "the Kurds, who have never been thoroughly obedient to the Ottoman repression, were, in the reign of Sultan Abdulhamid brought under partial control."[115] In other words, for about three and a half centuries, Kurdish princes continually ruled their people according to the Ottoman-Kurdish Agreement.

Shakir al-Khasbak suggested that Bitlisi's plan has however resulted in the occupation of Kurdistan by the Ottomans.[116] In reality, the Idris Bitlisi aim was twofold: to make peace between Kurds and the Ottoman Empire on the one hand, and to maintain the Kurdish emirate on the other. In this way, Bitlisi secured Kurdish self-rule which marked an official recognition era of the Kurdish emirates by the Ottoman Empire.

2.6 The Impact of the Ottoman-Kurdish Agreement on the Kurds

The Idris-Selim agreement was an important event in Kurdish political history. Sharafkhan stated that according the agreement, the Kurdish princes supplied the Ottoman Sultans with troops whenever they were needed; in return, they retained their sovereignty.[117] Muhammad Amin Zaki stressed that the administration which Bitlisi established in Kurdistan reflected the circumstances he found there. He divided each *Wilayat* (province) into a *Sinjaq* (semi-province). As a sign of its independence, a Kurdish prince governed each *sinjaq* and each province was provided with a flag and a drum as a sign of official recognition by Sultan Selim. It was not possible to run Kurdistan efficiently without such an administration.[118]

Kurdistan was situated strategically on the eastern frontier of the Ottoman Empire, facing Persia, its traditional enemy. Therefore the Ottomans believed they should have a special deal with the Kurds. Both Gibb and Bowen argue that keeping the population content was the only way they would accept the rule of the Ottomans.[119] The Ottomans, unlike their practices in other parts of the empire, refrained from the imposition of Turkish rulers on the Kurds. Most

---

[115] The War Office (hereafter TWO) IOR L/PS/20/202/1 *Military Report on Mesopotamia (Iraq)*, (1922). (Northern Jazirah) Area. 1, Compiled by The General Staff, British Forces in Iraq, 1st Edition, London, p. 3.

[116] Khasbak, Dr Shakir (1959). *al-Kurd wa al-Masala al-Kurdiya*, Arabic text, *Kurd and the Kurdish Question*, al-Rabita Press, Baghdad, p. 24-5.

[117] Bitlisi, Sharafkhan (1953). Op. cit, pp. 431-433.

[118] Zaki, Muhammad Amin (1931). Op. cit, pp. 168-9, Celebi, Evliya, (1979). Op. cit, p. 35.

[119] Gibb, H. A. R., Bowen, H. (1950). *Islamic Society and the West*, Vil. I, Issued under the auspices of the Royal Institute of International Affairs, Oxford University Press, London New York Toronto.

parts of Kurdistan retained a form of semi-independence in each province. The main result of the situation was that the Kurds remained under the Kurdish princes and leaders.[120]

The authorities of the Ottoman Empire knew the importance of the Kurdish element in their conflict with the Safavids, but tried to gain dominance. Al-Damaloji stressed that the Ottomans were intolerant towards the Kurds and broke their promises to them when the Kurdish territory was divided into small principalities. Al-Damaloji has argued, the Kurdish position was stronger than they realised, and they could have eventually gained more power.[121]

Nuri Darsimi accuses Bitlisi of being a secret agent for Sultan Selim and his administration in the Kurdish region. He believes the agreement contributed to the loss of Kurdish autonomy and the exposure of Kurdistan to warfare from both the Ottomans and Persians.[122] Thomas Bois agrees and believed that Bitlisi brought a misfortune to his people.[123]

Rashid Yasami, an Iranian Kurdish historian has stated that the joining of Kurdish princes with Sultan Selim, together with Bitlisi's efforts in the battle of Chaldiran weakened the army of Shah Ismael. Yasami suggests that the Kurds did not profit from the Sultan's promises that they should keep their independence when it was decided to divide Kurdistan, and that both empires ruled the Kurds aggressively and later destroyed the Kurdish Emirates.[124]

However, not all scholars agree. It has also been argued convincingly that the Ottomans gained great benefit from the Idris-Selim agreement, using the Kurds to destroy uprisings and popular movements against the Ottoman Sultans from other territories of the empire. Meanwhile, the Kurds maintained the security of the Eastern Ottoman borders from the Persian Empire and played a crucial role in the occupation of Baghdad on behalf of the Ottomans after the death of Shah Ismael Safavid and in this way the Kurds maintained their semi-autonomy.[125]

---

[120] Creasy, Sir Edward, S. (1878). *History of the Ottoman Turks: From the Beginning of their Empire to the Present Time*, London, p. 447.

[121] Al-Damaloji, Sadiq (1952). *Amarat Badinan aw Amarat al-Ammadiya*, Arabic text, The Badinan Emirate or al-Amedi Emirate, al-Ittihad al-Jadid Press, Mosul, p. 18.

[122] Darsimi, Dr M. Nuri (1952). *Darsim fi Taarikh Kurdistan*, Arabic text, Darsim in the History of Kurdistan, al-Ani Press, Aleppo, p. 193. Zaki, Muhammad Amin, (1931). Op. cit, p. 175.

[123] Bois, Thomas (1973). *Lamha an al-Akrad*, Arabic text, A General View about the Kurds, translated from the French by Muhammad Sharif Ohtman, al-Nuaman Press, al-Najaf, p. 15.

[124] Yasimi, Rashid (1369). Kurd ve Peyvestaki Nejadi 'U, Persian text, Kurds and its ethnic relation, fourth edition, Bunyadi Afshar Press, Tehran, p. 204.

[125] Zaki, Muhammad Amin (1931). Op. cit, p. 170.

According to the agreement with the Ottoman Empire, the recognition of the Kurdish Emirates was necessary for both the Kurds and the Ottomans, as the two sides had legitimate rights to be together. At that time, the Kurds provided more help to the Ottoman state. Whilst it was within the interests of the Ottoman Empire, they retained the Kurdish Emirates. The agreement provided the basis for a united community of Kurds. The vast territories of the Ottoman Empire and the mixed administration of the empire drew from both the Byzantine Empire and the Islamic system. The Ottoman Empire implemented a provincial system rather than trying to build a centralized state policy. It seems that many Kurds considered themselves as Ottoman subjects or citizens under the Ottoman-Kurdish agreement, but saw themselves as distinct from the other Ottomans. However, when Kurdish assistance was no longer needed in the mid-nineteenth century, the Kurds were brought under the direct rule of the central government.[126] It seems that Kurdish Emirates could not maintain their self-rule independently without the Idris-Selim agreement.

Before the Ottomans arrived in the Kurdish area, the Kurds had an organizational structure to administer their society. [127] It could be said that it was the same structure, which became the foundation for the Kurdish Emirates through the Ottoman Empire from 1514 until 1850, which carried the seeds of national ambition. Kurdish leaders fought imperial states to preserve their rule over Kurds and attempted to put a larger portion of Kurdish land under their influence. The Emirates continued to expand their territories which were inhabited by Kurds, Nestorians, Chaldeans, Catholics and Jews.[128] Although there was occasionally friction between them, the Emirate administration attempted to maintain law and order in the wider territory.

Various accounts from the sixteenth and seventeenth centuries are cited by HFB Lynch in his 1901 travel memoir, noting the autonomy and power possessed by its ruler "a Kurd in only nominal allegiance to the Shah of Persia."[129] Kurdish princes were strong and had political ambitions to keep their own powers; the Turks, meanwhile, had no influence over them until

[126] Al-Durra, Mahmud (1966). *Al-Qaziya al-Kurdiya*, Arabic text, The Kurdish Question, Dar al-Taliaa, second edition, Beirut, p. 46.
[127] Bitlisi, Sharafkhan (1953). *Sharafnama*, Arabic text, translated from Persian by Mulla Jamil Bandi Rozbayani, al-Najah Press, Baghdad, look for Kurdish emirates such as Erdelan, p. 106, Cizire, p. 147, Soran, p. 273, Baban, p. 289, Mukryan, p. 299.
[128] Kinneir, John Macdonald, (). Op.cit, p. 456.
[129] Lynch, H. F. B. (1901). *Armenia; Travels and Studies*, London, p.148.

the end of the first half of the nineteenth century.[130] Large cities in Kurdistan played a prominent role in establishing the Emirates. Diyarbakir, Bitlis and Amedi became economic and cultural centres, and later the Emirates were named after their respective capitals.[131] On the other hand, during the first half of nineteenth century, the Kurdish Emirates produced agricultural surpluses and were exporting many products.

2.7 The Ottoman administration in Kurdistan

After the Battle of Chaldiran, the Ottomans wished to divide the administration of Kurdistan into small territorial units. The accession to power of the Ottomans in Eastern Anatolia, confluent with attempts by their rivals, the Safavids, to control the region, prevented the Kurds from having a powerful emirate within the Ottoman administration. According to Evliya Çelebi, a Turkish traveler who journeyed through Kurdistan in the seventeenth century, there were two large Kurdish Vilayats in the mid- sixteenth-century, namely Diyarbekir and Van. The former contained nineteen small provinces, known as *sanjaks* and five independent Kurdish *hukumet* (governments).[132] Added to these there were another thirteen *sanjaks* run by Ottoman administrators.

In Evliya Çelebi's estimation, Van contained thirty-seven *sanjaks,* twenty of which were hereditary held by the families of Kurdish princes. The Ottoman Sultans had a right to appoint the governors of these *sanjaks*, but only on condition that they chose the rulers from amongst the Kurdish ruling families. Thus, Ottoman authority remained very restricted. Of the remaining territories, some were large Kurdish Emirates, such as Mahmudi, Bitlis, Hakkari and Baradost: over these regions the Ottoman Sultan had no right of appointment. As noted by Çelebi, this meant the Emirates could establish independent governments.[133]

---

[130] Khalfin, Dr. N. A (1969). *Al-Siraa ala Kurdistan*, (Arabic text), Conflict over Kurdistan, translated from Russian by Dr. Ahmad Othman Abubakr, al-Shaab Press,, Baghdad, p. 14.

[131] Bitlisi, Sharafkhan (1972). *Sharafnama*, Kurdish text, The Kurdish History, translated from Persian by Hejar Mukryani, p.17.

[132] Çelebi, Evliya (1979). *Kurd la mêjui drawsekanida, Siyahetnamey Evliya Çelebi*, Kurdish text, Translated from Turkish by Sa'd Nakam, Published by Kurdish Academy, Baghdad, p. 12. Longrigg, Stephen Hemsley, (1925). *Four Centuries of Modern Iraq*, The Clarendon Press, Oxford, p.20. Van Bruinessen, Martin (1992). Op. cit, p 158.

[133] Çelebi, Evliya (1979). Op. cit, pp..200; 208-9 who refers to only 13 of the remaining 17] See also Van Bruinessen and Boeschoten, (1988). (Eds) pp 121, 123

2.8 Kurdish Tribal Society

Through close examination of the structure of Kurdish society, one finds the inhabitants of Kurdistan to be of many different Kurdish tribes and non-tribes. Until the end of the nineteenth century, Kurdish tribes were commonly nomadic, searching for new pastures for their cattle, or semi-nomadic, living a pastoral lifestyle, breeding animals, selling wool and leather and turning these materials into tents. Non-tribal groups usually lived in villages as settled farmers and peasants, surviving on their agricultural produce.[134] Kurdish tribes played a major role in Kurdish society and the establishing of the Kurdish emirates. The geographical size of Kurdistan, its agriculture, wide range of mountains, rich soil, plentiful water and four seasons around the year are all factors enabling tribes of all sizes to make their home in Kurdistan. From the beginning of the twentieth century, most Kurds have tended to live in big cities or have settled in villages; few continue the nomadic tradition of travelling with animals to valleys, hill-tops and mountains.

2.9 Tribes under the Empires

The dominant powers over Kurdistan used Kurdish tribes for their interests. Accordingly, during the Safavid Empire (1501–1722) many Kurdish tribes were deported outside Kurdistan, some settling in remote corners of the Zagros.[135] After the First World War, nomadic tribes were reduced to a very small percentage of the population.[136] The livelihood of the sedentary mountaineer Kurds was gained through their success as "industrious agriculturalists, … [who] … cultivated every available piece of land in the vicinity of their villages, showing great capacity in diverting and damming streams, draining and ditching for the purpose of irrigating the terraced fields in the vicinity of their villages; these fields bear crops of barley, wheat, maize, and excellent tobacco." [137]

The Jaff tribe, for example, dwelled as semi-nomads who could assemble ten to twelve thousand houses or tents. They mainly inhabited the area around Sharezur, and were scattered

---

[134] Al-Azzawy, Abbas (1947). Op.cit, p. 6.

[135] Minorsky, V. (1945). "The Tribes of Western Iran", *The Journal of the Royal Anthropological Institute of Great Britain and Ireland*, Volume 75, Parts I-II, p. 74.

[136] League of Nations (1925). *Question of the Frontier between Turkey and Iraq*, Report submitted to the Council by the Commission instituted by the Council Resolution if September 30th, 1924, Geneva, August 20th, p. 41.

[137] Sykes, Sir Mark (1908). *The Kurdish Tribes of the Ottoman Empire*, Published the Royal Anthropological Institute of Great Britain and Ireland, London, p. 454.

along the border, on both sides of the frontier between the Ottoman Empire and Persia.[138] Often, nomadic Kurds of the highlands crossed the frontier and many of them had relations and parents who had settled in tribes living either side of the border.[139] This factor prompted the Council of the Commission of the League of Nations to include a special clause in the Protocol for the regulation of any argument which might arise as a result of tribal migrations. The nomadic and semi-nomadic tribes had fairly limited political ambitions; the most important undertaking for them was gaining their livelihood. Unskilled in the development of the land, the nomadic tribes preferred to breed horses in the highlands, as well as keeping livestock in great numbers. These tribes were wealthy stock-keepers and had an extensive knowledge of weaving and tent making.[140] The more established tribes had much wider social and economic relations within Kurdish society and also formed associations with outsiders.[141] The political border line of the Ottomans and Persians did not prevent tribesmen renting districts from each other.[142]

Peasantry among the Kurds was equally common; the sedentary Kurds were usually good agriculturalists. From 1845 until 1847, Layard passed through the Kurdistan countryside and described it as hosting the most beautiful and sublime scenery, with patches of land on the declivities of the mountains which were cultivated with extraordinary skill and care.[143] During the Russian and Persian War (1827–1828), occasional migrations took place. Abbas Mirza received the Kara-papa Turkish tribe who came from Georgia and rewarded them the district of Solduz in the south west, as well as the lake of Urumie where the Mukri Kurdish tribe was driven away from one of their historical regions.[144] The remaining Kurdish *ra'yyahs* (the followers of the head of the tribe) were employed by Kara-papas to cultivate the soil.

The Ottomans, as part of their plan for socially engineering the Empire, had plans to change the natural demography of Kurdistan. During the reign of Sultan Selim (1512–1520), the Ottoman government wanted to transfer the Karagetch Turkish tribe to compensate Kurdistan for the loss of some Kurdish tribes whom the Ottomans had forcibly removed and settled in

---

[138] Fraser, J. Baillie (1840). Travels in Koordistan, Mesopotamia, &c including an Account of Parts of those Countries Hitherto Unvisited by Europeans. With Sketches of the Character and Manners of the Koordish and Arab Tribes, ard Bentley, London, p. 167.
[139] League of Nations (1920). Op.cit, p. 40.
[140] Kurdistan and the Kurds, (1919). The War Office (hereafter TWO), London, p. 16.
[141] Southgate, The Rev. Horatio (1840). Narrative of a Tour Through Armenia, Kurdistan, Persia, and Mesopotamia with Observations on the Condition of Muhammadanism and Christianity in those Countries, Vol. I, Tilt and Bogue, London, p. 286.
[142] Ibid, 32.
[143] Layard, Austen Henry (1867). *Nineveh and its Remains, A Narrative of an Expedition to Assyria during the Years 1845, 1846 & 1847*, John Murray, London, p. 139.
[144] Rawlinson, H. C. (1841). Op. cit, p. 13.

Western Anatolia. However, this policy did not work completely; Kurds continued to identify as Kurds maintaining their own language and culture, whilst people from Turkish tribes began to identify as Kurds. Sir Mark Sykes stated that:

> "soon lost their language and became to all intents and purposes a Kurdish tribe. Further, owing to the fact that for some years after their re-settlement they were protected and favoured by the Ottoman Government, many families of local nomadic Kurds joined their encampment and so helped not only to increase their numbers but to complete the transformation of the Turcoman clan into a Kurdish tribe." [145]

Even though Kurdish tribes accepted the reality of their division amongst several states, they shared a common "Kurdish" feeling in their hearts with other tribes. To a modernist theoretician of nationalism this may seem a contradiction, as they perceive the phenomena to consist of an expression of exclusivity. Yet the realities of 'Kurdishness' have taught Kurds to develop their national identity along lines incorporating 'differences' within its framework.

2.10 The Kurdish tribal organization

The appellation 'tribe' has often been used by European commentators to describe 'other' non-western societies. This term was applied to the organisation of Kurdish society from its first appearance in European literature. As Bois wrote in the Encyclopaedia of Islam "A fundamental element of Kurdish society is without dispute, the tribe."[146] Indeed, Kurdish tribes were of interest to European politicians and officials of the nineteenth century and early twentieth century who studied them as part of their states' political interest.[147] In the modern academic world, a number of books have been published on this subject.[148]

---

[145] Sykes, Sir Mark (1915). Op. cit, p. 472.

[146] Bois, Th (1986). *The Encyclopaedia of Islam, Kurdish Society*, New Edition, edited by Bosworth, C. E., Donzel, E. van, Lewis, B., and Pellat, CH., Volume V, E. J. Brill, Lieden, p 471.

[147] For example, see H. C. Rawlinson, Notes on a Journey from Tabriz, through Persian Kurdistan, to the Ruins of Takhti-Soleiman, and from thence by Zenjan and Tarom, to Gilan, in October and November 1838, The Journey of the Royal Geographical Society of London, Volume Tenth, 1841. Mark Sykes (1908). "The Kurdish Tribes of the Ottoman Empire", *Royal Anthropological Institute of Great Britain and Ireland, London.* , E. B. (1910). *Report on the Sulaimania District of Kurdistan*, Superintendent Government Printing, Calcutta. E. W. C. Noel (1919). *Notes on Kurdish Tribes*, Government Press, Baghdad.

[148] For example, see the pioneering work appears to be Leach, E. R. (1940). *Social and Economic Organisation of the Rowanduz Kurds*, LSE Monographs on Social Anthropology, No 5, London. Barth, Fredrik, (1953) *Principles of Social Organization in Southern Kurdistan*,

The Kurdish tribe (*ashirat* in Kurdish and Arabic, or *Xêl* in Kurdish) is understood in this study as a clan, rather than simply an economic unit. A tribe may vary in size and organisation. It was once the largest unit in Kurdish society and played a social, economic and political role within it. *Xêl* depends on the bloodlines of united groups related to each other by ancestry. According to Shakir Khasbak, "the Kurdish tribes are united around land. They constitute groups of people with shared ancestry ….a Kurdish tribe can be divided into two groups of different family lineage, one group being the leaders of the tribe and the others simply group members."[149] In other words, a Kurdish tribe is a social organization, but also has a political body, and may be considered a territorial and economic unit. Thus, a tribe is a socio-political unit which has territorial and economic roots. Tribes are based upon descent and kinship, real or putative.[150]

Abbas Al-Azzawy an Iraqi Arab scholar, who studied Kurdish society and Kurdish tribes in detail, believed that Kurdish tribes generally gathered around districts or villages and became attached to the land throughout the generations.[151] For example, the tribes of Bilbas, Dizaiyi and Talabani united around land. Van Bruinessen has stated that, "the Kurdish tribe is a socio-political and generally also territorial (and therefore economic) unit based on descent and kinship, real or putative, with a characteristic internal structure. It is naturally divided into a number of sub-tribes, each in turn again divided into smaller units: clans, lineages, etc."[152] However, van Bruinessen has observed the Kurds were more concerned with establishing political affiliation over and above lineage through a common ancestor and that political allegiance to to a particular lineage is in fact more important than kinship.[153]

It should be noted that Kurds themselves use different terminology to describe their organisation. It may therefore be useful to give a brief overview of how society was organised and the different terminology used. In Sorani terminology, a "clan" (*tire or tayefe*) is smaller than *Ashirat-Xêl*. Clan members were related to each other by ancestry. *Tira* are sub-divided into groups of *berebabs* (lineages), one of the most basic of Kurdish tribal structures. In Botan villages, people use different terminology. In both small and large

Boktrykkeri, Oslo. Van Bruinessen, Martin (1992) *Agha, Shaikh and State*, Zed Books Ltd, London. Yalcin-Heckman, L. (1991) "Tribe and Kinship among the Kurds, Frankfurt", *European University Studie*, Series XIX, Bd. 27.

[149] Khasbak, Dr Shakir (1972). *Al-Akrad*, Arabic text, *The Kurds*, Shafiq Press, Baghdad, p. 346.

[150] Van Bruinessen, Martin (1992). Op. cit, p. 51.

[151] Al-Azzawy, Abbas (1947). *The Tribes of Iraq, Kurdish Tribes*, Part II, Al-Maarif Press, Baghdad, p. 13.

[152] Van Bruinessen, Martin (1992). Op. cit, p. 51.

[153] Ibid.

agricultural villages, people are divided into a number of units called *bavik* (from *bav*: father in English). Lineages are usually unbreakable units; as van Bruinessen has observed, "lineages by a sometimes large number of unrelated adherents; each *bavik* belongs to one of the two clans (Mahmudkan and Etmankan), and each possesses a specific, spatially separate, part of the village land."[154] Fredric Barth observes that lineages are joined together by economic and clan ties.[155] In most of Kurdistan, whether in Soran or in northern Kurdistan, the lineage (*berebab-bavik*) was led by an older man, informally chosen and given authority by other lineage men because of his influence and reputation. This was a large family bound together through kinship. Some individuals held a share in the land and not everybody originated from the same male bloodline. *Berebabs* are related to each other through a narrower common ancestry. Many Kurdish tribes consisted of large numbers of families. One of the largest tribes was the Rewandi, which in the first half of the nineteenth century was estimated to include almost 12,000 families under the Soran Emirate.[156]

2.11 The *Xan* -Agha

The Kurdish terminology for a social unit and the head of that social unit is not always the same. According to regions and dialects, names might differ. For example the "*Xan*" or "Agha", differs from "*Mir*". Each tribe was controlled by a *Xan* (chief) or *Agha* (leader). As tribal systems were localised, different parts of Kurdistan produced differing social systems. For example, in the Meriwan and Hewraman districts of Eastern Kurdistan, "Iranian Kurdistan", *Tayefe* is used for *Ashirat* (tribe) such as *Tayefei* Hayyarbagi, *Tayefei* Fatihalibagi, and *Tayefei* Barambagi. Their chief is termed *Xan*, a hereditary position.

The *Xan*'s main duty was to represent his *tayefe* (tribe) with dignity, running the internal affairs of the *tayefe*, as well as being responsible for any formal dealings with other *tayefes*. He received help from members of his *tayefe* to run the "Guest House" where notables of *tayefe* and other visiting guests were accommodated. None of the above mentioned areas differentiated in their nomenclature for their leader. All were called *Xan*, irrespective of

---

[154] Ibid, p. 57.
[155] Barth, Fredric (1953). Op. cit, p. 38.
[156] Rawlinson, H. C. (1841). "Notes on a Journey from Tabriz, through Persian Kurdistan, to the Ruins of Takhti-Soleiman, and from thence by Zebjan and Tarom to Gilan, in October and November, 1838, with a Memoir on the Site of the Atropatenian Ecbatana", *The Journal of the Royal Geographical Society of London*, Volume Tenth, p. 25.

whether their *tayefe* is large or small. In Eastern Kurdistan *tayefe* is the only known tribal system.[157]

In the Soran areas of Southern Kurdistan, the head of a tribe is called *Agha* as with the Mirawdeli. Two generations ago, the leader of Jaff ashirat used to be termed Pasha, as with Hama Pasha, father of the late Mahmud Pasha. The title was conferred by the Ottoman Turks, after Mahmud Pasha the chieftain of Jaff was termed Beg due to the collapse of the Ottoman Empire. In both the above mentioned *ashirats*, leadership is hereditary and patriarchal; it descends from a father to his eldest son. This was the case with the Jaff leader from Begzade, an unusual organization known as *pishtmale* (around the house). The Jaff leader had a powerful influence over Begzade and different *tires*. Therefore, the leader or Beg of the Jaff *ashirat* needed to be descended from the Begzade family. There were three branches of Begzade among the Jaff, namely Waladbagi, Barambagi and Muradbagi; "the political head may be drawn from any of these."[158] From the end of the nineteenth and beginning of the twentieth centuries, Mahmud Pasha was the leader of the Jaff. The head of the smaller part of this *ashirat* is called *tira* and led by the Rais. His position is similarly hereditary and patriarchal and confers traditional rights over quite specific pastures and camping sites.[159]

Among the Hamawand tribe, the leaders are called *Agha*. There is no "senior" leader, and each branch possesses its own *Agha*. In this case, Kurdish terminology does not make a distinction between leaders of tribe, clan or lineage. All of them are known as Agha with some exceptions; in some parts of northern Kurdistan, the head of lineage is called *mezin* or *magul* not Agha.[160] This may be a leader who "is either similarly hereditary", or, "if there is no suitable son of the old *Agha*, a new *Agha* is elected by the villagers. These *Aghas* will generally have the position and means to support a group of retainers…They thus have a vaguely institutionalized mechanism to enforce their authority".[161]

2.12 Influence of an Agha through his *Diwaxan*

On the whole, Kurds are hospitable people, as they welcome foreign travellers and local guests alike. In Kurdish villages, most people have a special room or separate building for

---

[157] I am indebted to Sheikh Latif Shiekhulislam for this information.
[158] Barth, Fredrik (1953). Op. cit, p. 41.
[159] Ibid, p. 37.
[160] Ibid, p. 80.
[161] Ibid, p. 47.

visitors called *Diwaxan* or *Miwanxana*-Guest House]. Apart from sheltering guests, *Diwaxan* have other functions. They serve as places for exchanging knowledge, making important decisions and reconciling differences. The guest rooms in Kurdish villages retain significance for every household. Yalcin-Heckmann has observed villages in the Hakkari area and has stated, "the main guest-cum-living room's social importance for the household members and the village social relations, is reflected through the objects contained in it."[162]

Levels of comfort provided demonstrate the status of the connections, wealth and generosity of the household. Through presiding over guests, the Agha will receive information from the outside world before anyone else. He relies on the support of his near relations to run the internal affairs of the tribe. In Kurdistan, among every tribe and village, there were notable families who played social, economic and political roles in tribal and village affairs. During the early centuries of the Ottoman Empire, local notables called *ayan* had some degree of power within the Ottoman administration, in the central and provincial government. The notable or *ayan* in the Ottoman Empire became an important political force especially through the Russo-Ottoman War of 1768-74 when the Ottoman government needed *ayan* for financial funds and recruits for the military; in return they were recognised as representatives of both the people and the government.[163] In Kurdistan in general, the notables of tribes and villages established a form of advisory council to look into all serious issues that arise within a tribe, but the Agha's decision remained the most important one in his tribe or village. However, at the level of the emirate, Aghas always supported the *mir*, both financially and militarily.

2.13 Kurdish emirate system

The Kurdish Emirates maintained their existence for centuries, and during that period they experienced many internal and external crises, playing an important role in establishing Kurdish cultural identity. Three main factors may explain how the Kurdish Emirates survived between the thirteenth and nineteenth centuries. Firstly, the mountainous nature of the Kurdish region, being situated strategically between Persia, Anatolia, Caucasus and Mesopotamia assisted survival. Secondly, the Kurds would not accept direct foreign rule and resisted central authorities throughout the seventh and tenth centuries. Thirdly, Kurdish rulers

---

[162] Yalcin-Heckmann, Lale (1991). *Tribe and Kinship among the Kurds*, Peter Lang, Frankfurt, p. 139.
[163] Ozoğlu, Hakan (2004). Kurdish Notables and the Ottoman State, State University of New York, p. 11.

believed that they had a hereditary political legitimacy which came either from religion or from social and economic roots. In general, the *Mirs'* ability to command the tribes' loyalty was an index of their ability and personality. Therefore, without the *Mirs*, both Ottomans and Persians found no way to govern Kurds.

The Kurdish *mirs* understood their society, and they manipulated the Kurdish community for their own benefit. For example, there were many tribes which were under the government of the Pasha of Silêmanî (Baban), all of whom provided infantry and horses and also gave financial support and paid a yearly tribute.[164] The Kurdish Emirate had a wide range of trade outside of Kurdistan, such as with Tabriz, Erzerum, Hamadan, Baghdad, Mosul, Damascus and Casbin.[165] They organized a regular army, offices, collected taxation, had diplomatic connections with British political agents in Baghdad, Constantinople, and Tehran, and other foreign powers, including Egypt.

The Kurdish Emirates understood that one of the elements of independence was to have their own legal tender. Sharafkhan stated that some Kurdish Emirates had their own currency and laid an administrative taxation on their people; they built castles in the sixteenth century, as Cizire had fourteen castles at the time.[166] In addition, the Kurdish Emirates did not recognize any limitation to their territorial borders and they always tried to extend their powers to other places as much as they could. Later, they extended beyond the borderlines between the Ottoman and Persian Empires. When the two powerful states were weak, the Kurdish Emirates and their Pashas tried to gain an improved independent position, and when the empires were strong, they struggled to maintain their rule accordingly.

The Kurdish Emirate acknowledged the general sovereignty of the central government. However, as V. H. Aksan notes: "as the Russians threatened the entire northern arc [of the Ottoman Empire] after 1768 that concentration of men and resources led to a neglect of relations with the southern tier [...] allowing both Kurds and Arabs to drift ever further away from imperial oversight."[167]

---

[164] Rich, Claudius James, (1836) *Narrative of a Residence in Koordistan, and on the Site of Ancient Nineveh; with journal of A Voyage Doen the Tigris to Bagdad and an Account of a visit to Shirauz and Persepolis*, Edited by his widow, Vol. I, James Duncan, London, pp. 280-1.
[165] Ibid, pp. 305-6.
[166] Bitilisi, Sharafkhan (1953). *Sharafnama*, The Kurdish History, Arabic text, translated from Farisi (Persian) Mullah Jamil Bandi Rozbayani, al-Najaf Press, Baghdad, p. 157-8.
[167] Aksan, V. H. (2007.). Military Reform and its Limits; in Aksan and Goffman (Eds) *The Early Modern Ottomans*, Cambridge, p.119

However, during the Ottoman reforms, little by little, the power of the Emirates and Pashas were ended and replaced almost everywhere by Turkish authority that "destined to understand the mediating role these princes had fulfilled with regards to the local population."[168] In Kurdish society the tribal system still noticeably existed, but the ruling order contained few tribes. Kurdish Emirate administrations maintained law and order in the wider territories. A single dynasty held control, and the Emirates adopted the name of the dynasty: examples include the Baban Emirate originating from the Baban dynasty, the Soran Emirate originating from the Soran ruling family, and the Botan Emirate which related to the Botan house as if they were dynastic ethnic states. In this system, the rulers and the people distinguished themselves from others by links to their ethnic origin. The position of the Kurdish Emirates between two superpowers, and disunity among the Emirates, were two major obstacles blocking progress and which later proved instrumental in their failure.

2.14 The role of the *Mir*s

The personal strength of a leader was very important for empires in the past. Strong leaders were awarded titles designating their status, such as Pasha in the Ottoman Empire and Khan in the Persian. The position of *Mir*-Prince in Kurdistan required an individual with a powerful personality. A *mir* is appointed by the centralised power, whilst a tribal leader tended to be found or endorsed by local kinship networks. Attributes such as courage, kindness and hospitality were elements that designated a strong *Mir*. A *Mir* was a head of Kurdish emirate, with powerful authority who commanded the emirate forces and had to be obeyed by all his people.[169] Strong personality and ambition were important characteristics of successful *Mirs*. Charismatic *Mirs* in Kurdish emirates tried to extend their emirate's territory, improve social life, build better administrations, strengthen armies and promote education.

Mirs governed much broader territories than tribal leaders; the latter tended to have influence over a much smaller group of people, bound to them by blood relationships in some form or another. In the seventeenth century, when Evliya visited Kurdistan, he observed that the head of a particular tribe stayed in the court of the *mir* "as guarantors of their tribes' obedience." Sometimes, a son or brother of the tribal leader had to be sent to the *mir*'s residence where they had to stay in the service of the *mir* and could be regarded as well-treated hostages and

---

[168] McDowall, David (2000). A Modern History of the Kurds, Revised Edition, I. B. Tauris, London, p. 47.
[169] For more details see: Van Bruinessen, Martin (1992). Op. cit, pp. 74-5.

in this way the *mir* maintained control over their tribes.[170] For example, the Jaff tribe, one of the strongest and biggest Kurdish tribes, provided the Pasha of Silêmanî with one thousand good horsemen in times of need.[171] Rostam Agha was a powerful man and the chief of the Zengena tribe; he was proud to be a servant of *Mir* Silêman Pasha of Baban.[172]

During the period of Evliya's visit, *Mirs* collected revenues from animals and from tailors, weavers and tanners as well as an annual tax upon all flocks in Bitlis.[173] The ability of the *mir* was an important factor for the success of the Kurdish Emirate; therefore, whenever a powerful *mir* appeared, the Emirate flourished, strengthening itself and seizing more Kurdish territories. This will be shown in chapters four, five and six in the discussion about Muhammad Pasha of Soran, Bedirkhan Pasha of Botan and Abdulrahman Pasha of Baban.

2.15 The Kurdish Emirates before the nineteenth century

The early structures of the Ottoman State were somewhat flexible; as one historian has put it, "the Ottoman state builders manipulated, often with success, a constantly shifting matrix of alliances and tensions with other socio-political forces. This was a process of carefully selected exclusions as well as inclusions, improvisations as well as continuities."[174]

The title of Emir was first used simply to define a leader. The first Kurdish dynasty to rule territories outside of Kurdistan were the Shadaddids who administered Ganja from 951 to 1075 A thirteenth century chronicle records how these lands were "ruled by an amir … [who] … was independent in his affairs."[175]

After conquest of Kurdistan by the Ottoman Empire in 1514, Kurdish territories were divided "into twenty-four governments, of which five were to be completely autonomous under Kurdish chieftains, and a further eight likewise under native families, but with the right of supervision reserved to Ottoman officials, the other eleven…becoming Ottoman provinces of

---

[170] Van Bruinessen, Martin (1992). Op. cit, pp. 164-5.
[171] Fraser, Baillie (1840). Volume I, Op. cit, p. 167.
[172] Ibid, p. 179.
[173] Ibid, pp. 166-7.
[174] Kafadar, C. (1995). *Between Two Worlds*, University of California, California, p.121.
[175] Minorsky, V. (1953). *New Light on the Shadaddids of Ganja*, London, p.7. The dynasty is briefly discussed by Jwaideh, Wadie, (2006). Op. cit, pp, 14-15.

the normal kind".[176] Eleven out of twenty four Kurdish territories passed under direct
Ottoman rule. As Strohmeier sourly observes,

> "several semi-independent, quasi dynastic Kurdish principalities were
> established…so-called emirates … alongside tribal confederations [which were]
> awarded privileges such as the right to coin money …[having] … dispensation from
> the obligation to pay tributes and recruit soldiers for the Ottoman forces. In return for
> virtual independence they were expected to recognize Ottoman sovereignty, keep
> order and patrol the border with Persia".[177]

Shields also notes that "After the initial conquests […] the Ottoman government
acknowledged the important services that mountain rulers could provide to the empire." Until
the beginning

> "of the nineteenth century, the population remained under the control of local
> grandees […] Acknowledging the enormous expense that subjugating and directly
> administering the local population would have entailed … [they] … directed the emirs
> of the mountains to maintain law and order, remit taxes and provide troops to defend
> the borders against the enemy at hand".[178]

Bruinessen observes,

> "the first tax register of Diyarbekir, made in 1518, does not mention any of the
> Kurdish chieftains except Çemişgezek (where temporally there was centrally
> appointed *sancaqbegi*) and unimportant Cermik …In a frontier zone […] political (and
> military) allegiance is more important than the regular payment of taxes."[179]

The three above observations suggest that there were Kurdish dynasties in charge of the
Kurdish internal affairs.

The term 'Emirate' designated the scope and range of their power. In time, the 'Emirate'
became the main political and social administration established in the region of Kurdistan to
rule over the people there. The Emirate had different administrative foundations and

---

[176] Parry et al (1976). *A History of the Ottoman Empire*, Cambridge, p.72

[177] Strohmeir, M. (2002). "Crucial Images in the Presentation of A Kurdish National Identity", *SEPSMEA*, Vol. 86, Leiden, p.10

[178] Shields, S. D. (2000). *Mosul Before Iraq*, New York, p.52. She gives no source for the assertion, citing only Van Bruinessen, pp.177-80 which deals mainly with the rise of Bedr Khan. Her remarks on taxation are therefore questionable.

[179] Van Bruinessen, Martin and Boeschoten, Hendrik eds (1988). *Evliya Celebi in Diyarbekir*, E. J. Brill, Leiden, p.17.

departments to rule its external affairs. Officially, it was not fully independent, but from time to time did exercise its rule autonomously.[180]

The tribal system was the foundation of the Emirate, with a strong leader who tended to possess more vision, leadership and ambition than his fellows and who made an effort to establish stronger management beyond his tribe. Some Kurdish tribal leaders played an important role in the establishment of some sort of wider and higher level local administrations to assist in their rule of Kurds. In the sixteenth century, when the Ottoman Empire defeated the Iranian Safavids, the Ottoman extended its power to the principality and officially appointed the hereditary ruling dynasty to administer it.[181]

2.16 The Soran Emirate before 1800

The Soran Emirate existed before the domination of the Ottomans over Kurdistan in 1514.[182] The first recorded reference to Soran comes from Sharafnama. No firm date for its establishment is offered. Sharafkhan gives the following origin-myth that the Soran Emirate was established by Isa son of Kalos. He was a shepherd and reportedly very kind; he shared all he earned amongst his friends and villagers who became very close to him. His friends in the village began to call him *mir* or prince. Later, people from nearby villages began to follow Isa. He decided to extend his influence and attacked Rewan Castle. Around the castle were a lot of *sor* (red stones). Isa and his followers took over the castle and established local rule and it the name *Soran* (from *sor* or red stone) was given to his government.[183] After Isa's death, later generations of his family governed the Soran Emirate. As the result of the battle of Chaldiran in 1514 between the Ottoman and Safavid empires, Said Beg of Soran was able to take more territories between Erbil and Kirkuk.[184] In 1534, when Sulaiman the Magnificent returned from Baghdad, *Mir* Ezzaddin Sher was the ruler of Soran. He was hostile to the Sultan's servants. As punishment, the Mir of Soran was killed by the Sultan, and his emirate was given to Husein Beg of Dasina 'a Yezidi'. The first Sorani dynasty therefore lost their stewardship of the area. Later *Mir* Saifaddin, the son of the deceased *mir*

[180] Van Bruinessen, Martin (2002). "Kurds, states and tribes", in Faleh A. Jabar and Hosham Dawod (eds.), *Tribes and power: nationalism and ethnicity in the Middle East*, London, published by Saqi, pp. 165-183.
[181] Ibid, p. 122.
[182] Bitlisi, Sharaf Khan (1973). Sharafnama, *The Kurdish History*, Kurdish text, translated from Persian by Hejar Mukryani,, pp. 485-7.
[183] Ibid, pp. 486-7.
[184] Minorsky, V. (1986). Op.cit, p. 457. Bayat, Dr. Vazil (2007). Op. cit, p. 255.

Hussein Beg, defeated Hussein Beg of Dasina and then regained control of the Soran Emirate.[185]

When the news of Hussein Beg of Dasina's defeat reached Istanbul, he was called to visit Istanbul and was later killed by the Sultan. *Mir* Saifaddin was convinced by Yusuf of Baradost to go to Istanbul to regain his entire emirate and be recognised by the Sultan. Instead, he was killed.[186] Anarchy spread in the Soran Emirate, and the Soran *mir* did not regain rule until the end of the reign of Sultan Sulaiman the Magnificent.

The Soran emirate was ruled by *mirs* from the ancient and well-known tribe of Rewandi. The Rewandi ruled Soran for centuries, until the first half of the nineteenth century, and maintained their independence both against Persia and the Ottoman. For this reason, the Soran mirs were regarded by the Kurds with great respect.[187] The Soran Emirate's function was to administer more widely forts in Kurdistan. For 500 years the fort of Rewanduz was the bastion of the Soran, in their mountains.[188] The Soran Emirate and its contribution to Kurdism will be discussed in further detail in Chapter 4.

2.17 The Botan Emirate before 1800

It is not clear when the Botan Emirate began, but certainly it existed in the sixteenth century. According to *Sharafnama* Sileman Khalid was the chieftain of Botan and that he had three sons, *Mir* Abdulaziz, *Mir* Abdal and *Mir* Badir. After the death of Silêman, his eldest son Abdulaziz became the ruler and he appointed each of his brothers as governors of the various districts of the emirate. Henceforth, three Botan dynasties were established, the first established in the name of Azizi or Azizan where Cizire became the capital. The second was Abdali and the third was Badri. Whilst Sharafkhan does not mention when the Botan Emirate was established, he notes that the eighth mir Ezzaddin Abdal in 1394 went to Tamerlane in Mardin and accepted his rule.[189] This incident may indicate that the Botan might have been established as far back as the the beginning of the fourteenth century. Muhammad Amin Zaki states that it was established after the Zangi government had collapsed, which according to

---

[185] Bitlisi, Sharaf Khan (1973). Op. cit, p. 493.
[186] Ibid, pp. 494-5
[187] Rawlinson, H. C. (1841). Op. cit, pp. 24-5.
[188] Ibid.
[189] Ibid, p. 151.

him could have occurred in 1247.[190] Anwar Al-Maei, another Kurdish historian, believed that the Botan Emirate was established in 1161 by Abdulaziz, after internal conflict within its ruling family weakened the Zangi state.[191]

The Azizan dynasty was descended originally from a Kurdish tribal chieftain.[192] In the sixteenth-century, the three sons of the late *mir* divided the Botan Emirate territories among themselves. After a period of confrontation, the *mir* of Cizire became the strongest of the three sons, dominating the other two.[193] Kamaran Bedirkhan believed that the origin of the Bedirkhan people can be traced to an Arizan village near Jezire. The word Arizan mutated into Azizan. Kamaran Bedirkhan believed that relations existed between the Botan dynasty and first Islamic generation.[194] The capital city of Botan was Jezire. Jezire had always been the centre of the Botan Emirate; there were many mosques, *medreses*, churches, public baths, and palaces.[195]

Many significant historical events occurred within the Botan Emirate. *Mirs* of Botan participated in wars, siding with the Ottoman Empire against Tabriz and Baghdad in 1534, and with Sultan Murad III (1574-1595) in his war against Georgia and Shirwan.[196] In 1603-4 again, the Botan Emirate under *Mir* Sharif took part with the Ottomans in their campaign against the Janissary commander in Baghdad.[197] This emirate witnessed the building of many *medreses* in the time of *Mir* Shaeaf such as *medrese* Sor where Melayê Cizîrî (1567–1640) taught.[198]

When in 1820 Claudius James Rich visited Kurdistan, Botan was weak and had no great influence; the capital Cizire was described as being "in a very ruinous condition."[199] Yet later in 1821, when Badir Khan took control, the Botan Emirate had gained such power that both the Ottoman Empire and foreign powers were obliged to take its new status and influence into account (see chapter 5 for details).

---

[190] Zaki, Muhammad Amin (1937). Op. cit, p. 146.
[191] Al-Maei, Anwar (1999). *Al-Akrad fi Bahdinan*, Arabic text, Kurds of Badinan, second edition, Khabat press, Duhok- Southern Kurdistan, p.p. 112-3.
[192] Ibid, p. 112.
[193] Van Bruinessen, Martin (1992). Op cit. p. 177.
[194] Bedirkhan, Kamaran (1949). "The Arzizan or princes of Bhotan", *Journal of the Royal Asiatic Society*, Volume xxxvi, London, p. 249
[195] Bedirkhan, Jeladet (1998). "Al-Hayat Al-jamieiyh fi Kurdistan", Arabic text, "Social life in Kurdistan", translated by Hajar Ibrahim, Matin Magazine, No. 75, April 1998, Duhok, pp. 97-8.
[196] Hururi, Salah (2000). *Imarat Botan*, Arabic text, *The Botan Emirate*, Khabat Press, Duhok, p. 27.
[197] Ibid, p. 28.
[198] Ibid, p. 29.
[199] Rich, Claudius James (1836). Op. cit, Volume I, p. 157.

2.18 The Baban Emirate before 1800

The Baban principality played a major role in many areas of Kurdish society. Sharafkhan emphasized that it was a significant Kurdish province of the sixteenth century. Eighty years after the *Sharafnama*, the Kurdish scholar Saiyd Abdulsamad Saiyd Salih Tudary wrote a Persian text known as *Nur al-Anwar* in which he twice mentions the Baban emirate. Tudary had access to a document which dated back to 670H-1276AD in which he found the name of Prince Khalid Ahmad Babani.[200] This is an indication that the Baban emirate existed 320 years before Sharafkhan finished the *Sharafnama* and suggests it was established at least fifteen years prior to the establishment of the Ottoman Empire. Other evidence exists which bears witness to the early existence of Baban. Hussein Huzni Mukryani wrote that some Baban Princes visited Dushtik state in 967.[201]

Mir Budagh was the founder of the Baban dynasty, calling his territory Baba or Baban,[202] a term that was shortened from his grandfather's name, Baba Qubad. Hussein Huzni stressed that Mir Budagh was the real founder of the Baban dynasty.[203] He extended his domain beyond its original boundaries.

Mir Budagh established a council of notables as a consultative body. He organized an army and when he had sufficient strength he took Lajan, Kona Lajan from Zarza and Soran. Later he took Shino from Soran and Bane.[204] He also controlled Kirkuk.[205] When he took Sharbajer from his cousins, he divided his administration into sub-provinces and installed someone close to him to reign in his stead. He also created a flag and a drum, and coined money as symbols of his sovereignty.[206] After a while, he renewed Maran castle.[207] When Mir Budax, the *Mir* of Baban, died, as he had no son, his nephew, Budagh Rostam, took his place. The latter also lacked a son; therefore on his death, the servants became responsible for the emirate.[208]

---

[200] Tudary, Saiyd Abdulsamad Salih, Nur al-Anwar, translated from Persian to Kurdish by Muhammad Mela Karim, who selected a few chapters and published them under the name of Chamkeki Mêzui Hewraman u Meriwan, A Part of the History of Hewraman and eariwan, Salman al-Aazami Press, Baghdad, 1970, p. 14-15.

[201] Huzni, Hussein (1927). Op. cit, p. 7

[202] Huzni, Hussein (1931). *Awrêki Pashwe*, Kurdish text, A Look to the Back, Vol. 3, Part. 1, Published by Zari Kurmanji, Rewanduz, p. 30.

[203] Ibid.

[204] Ibid, pp. 31-2.

[205] Ibid, p.519.

[206] Ibid, p. 33.

[207] Ibid, pp. 33-35.

[208] Sharafkhan, Op. cit, p.521.

In the third decade of the sixteenth century, as a result of internal and external conflicts among the rulers, Baban shrank. It controlled only a tiny district of Merge by Khidr grandson of Baba Silêman, who ruled very weakly; after his death the second era of the Baban Emirate ended.[209] There was thus a hiatus for five or six decades. The new age of the Baban started with Feqê Ahmad of Dareshmane who united Merge and Pishder under his leadership in 1664. The Ottoman Sultan granted him these two districts to rule.[210] It would appear that Feqê Ahmad was unwilling to take his family to Mir Budagh, as Mukryani believed that Feqê Ahmad was from the Baban dynasty;[211] by this Faqê Ahmad had laid the first stone of the governorship, and he bequeathed the family name Baban.

Feqê Ahmad had two sons, Khan Budax and Silêman Baba (1074-1089 H/ 1663-1675 C.E.). The latter had a good reputation during his father's reign. In 1076 C.E., he led an army and took Sine from Erdelan and Sauj Bulaq from Mukryan. He placed his sons and brother as his representatives in every district.[212] He added Qeredagh, Bazyan and Sharezur to his domains, and also transferred his capital to Qeĺa Çolan in 1080 H./ 1669-70 C. E..[213] As Longrigg has acknowledged, by the second half of the seventeenth century, *Mir* Silêman was an important individual in Sharezur.[214]

After Feqê Ahmad's death, Khan Budagh, who was very ambitious, extended his authority to Ako, Bilbas, Alan and Mawet,[215] and transferred his central administration to Mawet in 1664–5.[216] In 1080 H/ 1667 C.E., when the Ottoman-Russian war started, the Sultan requested help from Mir Silêman of Baban, who went to his assistance. When the victories won by the Kurds were related to the Ottoman Sultan, he sent *Mir* Silêman a traditional robe to signify his gratitude and addressed him as Pasha.[217]

The failure and break-up of the Erdelan emirates gave *Mir* Silêman the opportunity to fulfill his desire to extend his power. In 1103 H / 1691-2 C.E., he attacked Erdelan and took Meriwan, Awroman and Seqiz. He installed Zorab Sultan as the Governor of Seqiz and

---

[209] Zaki, Muhammad Amin (1939). Ta'rokhi Silêmanî u Wlati, Kurdish text, The History of Silêmanî and its Surroundings, al-Najah Press, Baghdad, pp. 45-6.
[210] Qaftan, Tofiq 1969). *Mêzui Hukumdarani Baban*, Kurdish text, The History of the Baban Rulers, Sulaiman al-A'zami Press, Baghdad, p. 12-3.
[211] Huzni, Hussein (1931). Op. cit, part. 4, p. 83
[212] Huzni, Hussein (1931). Op. cit, part. 5, p. 87.
[213] Nazim Beg, Hussein 2001). *Ta'rikh al-Amarat al-Babaniyh*, Arabic text, The History of the Baban Emirate, translated from Turkish by Shukur Mustafa and Muhammad Mullah Abdulkarim, Mukiriani Press, Hawler, p. 65.
[214] Longrigg, Stephen Hemsley (1925). *Four Centuries Of Modern Iraq*, The Clarendon Press, Oxford, p. 80.
[215] Qaftan, Tofiq (1969). Op. cit, p. 16. Nazim Beg, Hussein, (2001). Op. cit, p. 61.
[216] Nazim Beg, Hussein (2001). Op. cit, p. 64-5.
[217] Huzni, Hussein (1931). Op. cit, part. 5, p. 86.

caused Ibrahim Beg Mir-Iskandar to be executed.[218] This was a political mistake as the Persian court was enraged; representatives were sent to Baghdad to complain about *Mir* Silêman and to call for him to be overruled.

The following year, Khan Ahmad Khan raised an army against the Baban Pasha. Simultaneously, Shah Sulaiman Sefavi (1666–1694) sent an army, said to be 40,000 strong with the same purpose, when *Mir* Silêman was heavily defeated.[219] Some records mention that the defeat of *Mir* Silêman was caused by a joint force of Persians and Turks. The expeditions of the Ottomans against the *mir* were due no doubt to suspicion of his growing power and consequent lack of respect for his Ottoman neighbours. Therefore, the Pasha of Baghdad took with him the Pashas of Diyarbakir and Aleppo to thwart the Kurdish Pasha's desire.[220]

The Baban Pasha realized that, with these two rival powers united against him, he would face serious trouble. Therefore, when the Ottoman forces reached the Bazyan plain, he contacted the commander and enquired why they proposed to attack. The commander asked him to surrender; the Mir contemplated whether to fight or surrender, as he did not want to be humiliated. Later, he received a second letter from the Turkish commander, again demanding surrender. In the light of his own and Kurdish interests, *Mir* Silêman decided to place his brother Taimur Beg in charge of the Baban emirate and surrendered. He was exiled to Istanbul where he died in 1698.[221]

Taimur Khan Beg ruled for seventeen years at peace with his neighbours. He was succeeded by Bakr Beg. Taimur Khan, because of some disagreement amongst his family, had allowed some years of inflexible Ottoman control by the Pasha of Sharezur. This control ended with the rise of Bakr Beg.[222]

Under Bakr Beg, the Baban authority was located between the Sirwan (Diyala) river to the south and the lesser Zab to the north. It included all areas between the Kifri-Altun Kupri roads, from the west and the Ottoman and Persian boundaries.[223] Bakr Beg maintained the

---

[218] Rabino, H. L. (1911). Compiled by, *Confidential Report on Kurdistan*, Simila, Printed at the Government Monotype Press, p. 78
[219] Rabino, H. L. (1911). p. 78. Longrigg, Stephen Hemsley, (1925). Op. cit, p. 80.
[220] Longrigg, Stephen Hemsley (1925). p. 80-1. Nazim Beg, Hussein, (2001). Op. cit, p. 69.
[221] Nazim Beg, Hussein (2001). Ibid, p. 75.
[222] Longrigg, Stephen Hemsley (1925). Op. cit, p. 81.
[223] Ibid.

ruling authorities, making an accord with Erdelan. He was interested in agriculture and irrigation, both of which progressed well. There were signs already of a developing culture.[224] He dispensed justice among his subjects, offering them an equitable government.

His intention to attack Kirkuk caused his relations with the Ottomans to deteriorate and in 1714 the decision was taken to remove him.[225] Hasan Pasha of Baghdad marched against Baban. The latter fought very hard and many sacrificed their lives for the sake of their country. Later in 1715, Bakr Beg was killed by the Pasha of Baghdad.[226] Hasan Pasha on his own initiative appointed a Mutasallim (the governor of a sub-province) for Qeĺa Çolan and attached it to Sharezur. [227] During this time, The sons of Taimur Khan Beg and Bakr Beg were infants. As minors they could not take power in Baban. The Mutasallim was not a capable man, and unable to maintain unity and peace in the territory. Ahmad Khan (of Zengene) backed by Persia, interfered in the Baban territories, occupying Qeredax, Sengaw, Bazyan and Sharezur.[228] This situation lasted for six years until Khana Beg challenged it.

His first act was to call together the notables of Baban for a meeting; there he outlined the situation prevailing in the Baban emirate. He described two options to the assembly; either to surrender in humiliation or to rise up against Ahmad Khan Zengene. The majority who were present agreed with his proposal to fight for their rights and people; they declared that a nation that enjoyed its liberty could not accept occupation.[229]

Khana Beg ordered his forces to attack Ahmad Khan Zengene; after several battles, he recovered the territories that Zengene had previously occupied. In due course, Khana Beg showed wider designs against Persia.[230] During 1720, a rebellion took place throughout Persian Kurdistan and Luristan. In the same year Malik Mahmud Sistani the Governor of Tun, in northeast Persia, flouted the Shah's authority. Malik Mahmud was a determined man who claimed descent from the Safavids and belonged to the Kayani family of Sistan.[231]

---

[224] Ibid.
[225] Zaki, Muhammad Amin (1939). Ta'rokhi Silêmanî u Wlati, Kurdish text, The History of Silêmanî and its Surroundings, al-Najah Press, Baghdad, p. 59.
[226] Ibid.
[227] Ibid, p.60.
[228] Nazim Beg, Hussein (2001). Op. cit, p. 78.
[229] Nazim Beg, Hussein (2001). Op cit, p. 80-1.
[230] Ibid, p. 85
[231] Lockhart, L. (1938). *Nadir Shah*, Luzac & Co., London, p. 6.

Khana Beg took advantage of this situation by marching on Erdelan, reaching the frontier of Mariwan and then advancing up to Sina. Ali Guli Khan of Erdelan dared not oppose him and fled to Isfahan where he was forced to surrender to Khana Pasha who soon after declared himself Wali of Erdelan.[232]

Khana Pasha wished to establish a powerful state, and further extend his territories from Kirkuk to Hamadan. He developed Sina, building beautiful mosques with tall minarets and schools. In 1724, he appointed his son Ali Khan as a governor of Sina and returned to Baban. Ali Khan was an educated man and spent much time with writers and poets. When Nadir Shah took over in Persia, Ali Khan fled after six years of rule.[233]

2.19 Conclusion

In this chapter, a number of claims have been made. The relationship between Kurds and Umayyad and Abbasid was not great, Kurds did not have any role in their local-rule. During the two Islamic Caliphates, Kurds rebelled several times against both Umayyad and Abbasid. Later, in the eleventh to the fifteenth centuries, gradually, Kurds managed to establish their own governments, for example Hasnawi and Dushtak. Between the collapse of Abbasid in Baghdad in 1258 and the appearance of Safavids in 1501 the major event for the Kurds was that for the first time in history, Kurdistan appeared as one of the provincial governments within the Mongol Empire. It is clear that historical events from the time of the Mongol Empire to the end of the Ottoman Empire deeply affected Kurds and Kurdistan and are important to examine in order to understand Ottoman and Kurdish history. During the time of the two Turkoman states of Qara Quyunlu the Shi'i and Aq Quyunlu the Sunni, part of Kurdistan was under the former but the larger part of Kurdistan under the latter. At the beginning of the sixteenth-century, the Turkoman states played a pivotal role in the conflicts between the rival empires of the Ottoman Sunnis and the Safavids Shiis.

In 1501, when the Safavid Empire was established, strong Shii sectarianism became a turning point in the history of Muslims. From the outset, the mostly Sunnis Kurds became a target of the Safavids and suffered under their rule. Thus, with the help of Idris Bitlisi, a high ranking Ottoman official and a Kurd himself, the Kurds and the Ottomans made an agreement

---

[232] Rabino, H. L. (1911). Op. cit, p. 80.
[233] Ibid, p. 81.

together. Accordingly Kurds managed to regain their hereditary rule and to keep their autonomy, due to a concurrence between the interests of Kurdish princes and the Ottoman Empire. In return, the Kurds had to support the empire financially and militarily. This lasted until the *Tanzimat* (the Ottoman reforms in the second quarter of the nineteenth-century), which imposed a system of centralization by force where necessary, especially over control of local finances, on all non-Turk ethnic groups. From this point, Kurds struggled to retain their autonomy over their affairs.

Therefore, in the first half of the nineteenth century, when the very existence of the Kurdish emirates was questioned, with the only outcome being either survival or collapse, the Kurdish emirates resisted strongly against the centralizing authority whose main aim was to bring Kurdish autonomous under control as the Ottomans wished. The resolutions of numerous conflicts have only yielded agreements to manipulate the borders in the interests of those controlling them; Kurdish aspirations suffered many times from these blights.

In the conflicts between Ottomans and Safavids, the issue was about the expansion of those two empires at the expense of the Kurds. Neither empire could endure such psychological stress from the heavy pressure caused by regular conflicts between them. These continual disputes sapped the strength of both the powerful and the powerless in both states. The Kurds were caught in the middle and became the victims.

The Battle of Chaldiran and the emergence of two powerful warring states in the region changed the direction of the Kurdish question. Both states, at enmity with each other, remained aggressive towards the Kurds: this situation was further exacerbated when Russia and Britain extended their interests in the area. Under even these adverse circumstances, the Kurds kept their distinctive identity, and maintaining a desire to re-establish and preserve their self-rule.

The Kurdish tribal system reflects the social and economic organization of Kurdish society. Through tribal organization and Kurdish emirates, Kurds have been united together in the face of the dominant powers. Both, tribes and Kurdish emirates felt attached to their land and defended it as far as they could. Furthermore, through the emirates, they tried very hard to maintain their local rule, the rule of Kurdish emirates which existed before the Ottomans and Safavids fought against each other in 1501.

Kurdish Emirate administrations maintained law and order in the wider territories: examples include the Baban Emirate originating from the Baban dynasty, the Soran Emirate originating from the Soran ruling family, and the Botan Emirate related to the Botan house or Azizan family. In this system, the rulers and the people distinguished themselves from others by links to their ethnic origin and to their territorial land. The position of the Kurdish Emirates between two superpowers, and the disunity among the Emirates, have both been major obstacles to the progress of the Kurdish Emirates and contributed later to their failure.

Chapter Three

The role of Kurdish literature in identity formation before the 19th century

3.1 Aims and main themes

The Kurdish language has been instrumental in maintaining the survival of the Kurdish people's culture and their identity. The Kurdish language has become synonymous with the Kurdish people. This chapter outlines the themes and elements of Kurdish identity carried in oral traditions especially in the historical epic *Dimdim*, symbolic of Kurdish resistance against a dominant power. This chapter deals with two significant and related topics in the study of Kurdishness and culture in the period before the nineteenth century, that of the Kurdish language, and its literature. The role of Kurdish religious and social organisations in influencing the development of Kurdish consciousness and identity is addressed in this chapter. Paramount amongst these is the mosque, and its attendant seats of learning, the *medrese* (school), and its role in bringing Kurdish students together to meet and to study. *Medrese* has been discussed as an important centre for the development of Kurdish culture and literature for collective Kurdish self-awareness. These were a major factor in the transmission of Kurdish traditions and folklore. The use of the Kurdish language in the *medrese* helped establish the Soranî dialect as the primary tongue of 'Kurdism' in the Baban and Soran emirates before their demise. Discussion focuses upon the awakening of Kurdish self-consciouness in Bitlisi's *Sharafnama* and *Mem u Zin* of Xanî with reference to other classical poets before and after Xanî such as Melayê Cizîrî (1567–1640) and Khana-i Qubadi (1704–1778).

Kurdish literature has also embraced aspects of Kurdish awareness and thought, and has been propagated amongst Kurds; in particular *Mam u Zin* has been legendary in its influence. This, a classic Kurdish epic[234] by Ehmedê Xanî, began to develop and serve as a vehicle for opposition to the two dominant Muslim powers; the Ottoman and Persian Empires. Xanî has been perceived as the forerunner of the advancement of self-conciousness among the Kurds.

In the first chapter, Kurdism was broadly defined as 'a self-consciousness and awareness of being a Kurd, and part of a wider group of other Kurds' stressing their contra-distinction with

---

[234] *Mam u Zin* was written by Ehmedê Xanî, who through love story expressed Kurdish national identity and his philosophical ideas as well.

other peoples. The use of the Kurdish language to express ethnic and cultural elements of this distinctiveness, along with the consciousness of national solidarity and aspirations of freedom through self-rule was discussed.

This chapter focuses on Kurdism through the eyes of Kurdish scholars and poets. In this regard, Kurdism and Kurdish unity will be discussed from diverse angles. The promotion of Kurdish culture and use of Kurdish language, particularly in the context of pre-nineteenth century classical literature and folklore, Kurdish suppression at the hands of the dominant powers and the expression of Kurdish feeling in the early time of Kurdish proto-nationalism will be discussed. The chapter also outlines the themes and elements of Kurdish identity carried in oral traditions especially in the historical epic *Dimdim*, and moves on to focus on the discussion of Kurdish identity in Bitlisi's *Sharafnama* and *Mem u Zin* of Xanî with reference to other classical poets before and after Xanî such as Melayê Cizîrî (1567–1640) and Khana-i Qubadi (1704–1778).

The role of Kurdish religious and social organisations in influencing the development of Kurdish consciousness and identity will be addressed. Paramount amongst these is the mosque, and its attendant seats of learning, the *medreses*. These were a major factor in the transmission of Kurdish traditions and folklore. The use of the Kurdish language in these was a major factor in establishing the Soranî dialect as the primary tongue of 'Kurdism' in the Baban and Soran emirates before their demise.

From the beginning of the nineteenth century, Middle Kurdish [Soranî] became a written language. Ever since, the Kurdish language played a major role in distinguishing Kurds from their neighbours.[235] This type of written Kurdish was started from Silêmanî by the most famous scholar and religious leader Mawlana Khalid who used Silêmanî as the sub-dialect of the Baban Emirate capital, and then other Kurdish poets and scholars in other parts of Kurdistan, such as in the Soran Emirate and Iranian Kurdistan, followed him.

There were several reasons for the emergence of Soranî dialect as a written language. One reason was that Kurdish dialects were used to explain Arabic texts in Kurdish mosques by

---

[235] Blau, Joyce and Suleiman, Yasir (1996). *Language and ethnic identity in Kurdistan: An historical overview*, in *Language and Identity in the Middle East and North Africa*, edited by Yasir Suleiman, Curzon, London, p. 154.

Kurdish *ulama* (scholars).[236] Another reason was the appearance of the creative intellectuals who played a crucial role for using Kurdish language and promoting it to become a collective identity and power for their case; the third reason was that the Kurdish *mirs* of Baban Emirate promoted the use of Kurdish especially Abdulrahman Pasha (1789-1813).[237]

Silêmanî is part of a collection of sub-dialects, such as Mukri and Sineyi, which together form the dialect currently labelled Soranî (Middle Kurmanjî) which is applied generally as the name of the dialect assembly[238] which is one of the most important Kurdish dialects. Soranî has been a written language for scholars and poets since the beginning of the first half of the nineteenth century and it has been a major linguistic vehicle for Kurdism. The main areas of Soranî-speaking Kurdish populations are the regions of Kirkuk, Germyan, Silêmanî, Erbil, Rewanduz in Iraqi Kurdistan, Sine, Mehabad and Bokan in Iranian Kurdistan and other areas.[239] It is important to point out that Kurdish identity was transmitted through two important channels – the *medrese* and mosque tradition, which consisted of centres of Kurdish learning and the birthplace of written Kurdish literature, and through the institutions of performance of the rich and varied Kurdish folkloric literature, transmitted orally.

At the time that Kurdish writing began to flourish, the socio-political influence of the states that divided Kurdistan, along with its geographical position, was problematic for the Kurds, as it prevented them from being able to maintain their local rule. This follows Smith's *Frontier ethnie* hypothesis, which discusses how geopolitical or strategic-economic boundaries can affect a territory containing peoples with common origins or ethnicity. An example that Smith mentions is the impact of both the Ottoman and Persian Empires on the Kurds:

> "In the process of conflict, self-images and stereotypes of neighbours and enemies are generated, which become crystallized in legends and symbols... these legends and symbols later form the stuff of ethnic chronicles and epics, which in the modern era

---

[236] Hewramani, Heme Karim (2008). *Mêjui perwerde u xwêndin le hujrekani Kurdistanda*, Kurdish text, History of education and study in Kurdistan medreses, Hewlêr, p. 2.

[237] Blau, Joyce (1996). Kurdish Written Literature, in Philip Kreyenbroek and Christine Allison, edited by, *Kurdish Culture and Identity*, Zed Books Ltd, London and New Jersey, P. 22.

[238] Hassanpour, Amir (1992). *Nationalism and language in Kurdistan 1918-1985*, Mellen Research University Press, San Francisco, p. 19.

[239] Ibid, p. 21.

then provide sources for the paintings, poetry and music that form the peculiar cultural heritage of each nation." [240]

Thus, for Kurds, being a frontier ethnie enhanced associated myths and legends and helped produce a heightened collective Kurdish identify becoming a key catalyst for their nationalism. Therefore, a constant factor affecting all these is of course the impact of the regional powers on such developments. The frontier between the two powers was more or less stabilised by a settlement imposed by Sultan Murad IV and Shah Safi ad-Din, in 1639.[241] This was despite the centralisation policies of both empires which enabled the survival of the following principalities: Mukryan and Erdelan (in Persia); Botan, Hakari, Badinan, Soran and Baban (in the Ottoman Empire) – the last two of which were ceded to Iraq after the First World War. [242]

3.2 Importance of the Oral Tradition

Oral tradition helps in the maintenance of Kurdishness, in the sense that oral culture is shared across generations. As Christine Allison observes, the role of oral tradition becomes more necessary and political where in the context of despotic or authoritarian states other means of written communications are suppressed. Therefore "Oral tradition, along with other aspects of folklore, is an important element in discourses of nationalism and identity all over the modern Middle East; Kurdistan is not an exception in this respect." [243] Though Allison makes this remark in the context of modern Middle Eastern politics, for the Kurds, due to enduring conditions of political oppression, oral tradition has historically been a powerful element of identity, self-consciousness and self-expression in the relation of the other. It has been argued that oral literature offers one of the richest sources for studying social, cultural and spiritual aspects of life in Kurdistan.[244]

Although *Dimdim* as a tradition has different forms and genres, in terms of its content and description of events, it has the elements of an epic. In this sense Kurdish *beyts* (as the long

---

[240] Smith, Anthony D. (1999). *The Ethnic Origins of Nations*, Basil Blackwell, Oxford, p. 84.

[241] Edmonds, C. J. (1971). "Kurdish Nationalism", *Journal of Contemporary History*, Vol. 6, No. 1, p. 87.

[242] Ibid.

[243] Allison, Christine (2001). *The Yezidi Oral Tradition in Iraqi Kurdistan*, Curzon Press, London, p. 6.

[244] Rasul, Dr Izzaddin Mustafa (1979). *Lêkolinewey Edebî folklory Kurdî*, Kurdish text, *A Study in the Kurdish Folkloric Literature*, Silêmanî University Press, Silêmanî, pp. 8-9.

narrative poems are known in many areas)[245] share important characteristics of the epics of other nations. They 'tell a story of some national or local significance. The authors tend to be anonymous, with its composition located in the mists of time. The characters are usually 'heroes' and 'warriors'" and they "[incorporate] myth, legend, folk tale and history [that tend to] embody the history and aspirations of a nation in a lofty or grandiose manner."[246] Important examples of widespread and influential oral traditions in *Dimdim* will be discussed in the next section.

3.3 Kurdish Identity in *Dimdim*

Oral traditions including *Dimdim* are about specific Kurdish groups rather than Kurds in general. *Dimdim* reflects a spirit of resistance to outside government, a common theme in oral tradition. To the Kurds, the *Dimdim* is a very important work. Along with Xanî's *Mem û Zîn*, and the *Newroz* narrative, it is often mentioned as a traditional text representing a defining element in Kurdish history and identity in relation to the other. We know also from its first collection by Jaba in 1860 that the poem had some significance then as a part of Kurdish 'folklore'. This stretches the provenance of the poem, in oral tradition back to the nineteenth century.[247]

The fact that to this day that *Dimdim* has maintained its position as a key part of the oral tradition, demonstrates the Kurds' admiration of its core messages. In consequence, it has proven to be an inspiration to many Kurds who have now incorporated its themes into modern literature. Poems are still being written, along with adaptations and variations of short stories, novels and poems that use the same narrative base for new Kurdish literature.[248] *Dimdim* was and remains an important element in the growth of national feeling amongst the Kurds as a symbol to promote their sense of collective heritage.

---

[245] Hassanpour defines beyt in the <u>Encyclopaedia Iranica</u> as: a genre of Kurdish folk art similar to Azerbaijani Turkish *dastanor helaya* .. *Beyt* is an orally transmitted story which is either entirely sung or is a combination of sung verse and spoken prose. It is distinguished from Kurdish lyrical folk songs *(hayran, qatar and lawk)* by its essentially narrative character and, generally, its length. *Beyt* is also generally distinguished from the Kurdish narrative genre *hekayet or cirok* (story) by its sung verse form. In contrast to its Azeri counterpart, singing is unaccompanied by instruments. Hassanpour, Amir (1990). Encyclopaedia Iranica, Volume IV, Routledge & Kegan Paul, London, p. 12. Chyet, Michael L. (1991). *And A Thornbush Sprang Up Between Them": Studies On "Mem u Zin"*, A Kurdish Romance, Volume One, U.M.I Dissertation Information Service, Michigan, p. 79.

[246] Cuddon, J. A. (1992). *A Dictionary of Literary Term and Literary Theory*, Blackwell, Oxford, p. 284.

[247] Huseny, Abdulhamid (1981). Abduhamid Huseny collected a version of *Dimdim* in 1972 in Mehabad from beytbêj (ballad singer) Ahmad Karim Milxwar Pirot Dimdim. According to Ahmad, he was taught this variant by his father, who had learnt it from his own father. We can see from this transference of the poem over several generations His Grand father was known as '*Dimdim*' to his neighbours, through his renowned performances of this piece, p. 3.

[248] Mustafa Salih Kareem (1960). wrote a short story entitled: *Shehidani Qeʰai Dim-Dim*, Martyrs of *Qeʰai Dimdim*, Zin press, Silêmanî. Ereb Shemo (1975). wrote a novel about the same story, titled, *Qeʰai Dim-Dim*, Published by Kurdish Academy, Baghdad.

3.4 Historical Background in reference to the *Dimdim*

Historically, the *Dimdim* was about the struggle of Amir Khan, a powerful Kurdish chieftain of *Baradost* who lived near the Lake of *Urmiya* in Persian Kurdistan. He actively opposed Persian rule under Shah Abbas II (1585–1628) who tried to build a strong central government and bring back all ethnic regional governments under his control. Therefore, he imposed Shi'sm on Sunnis including the Kurdish local authority in the South East of Persian Kurdistan in the districts around *Dimdim, such as* Targawar, Margawar, Baradost and Shino.[249] Shah Abbas also imposed heavy taxes on those who did not readily convert to Shi'ism, which caused the Kurds to rebel against the Shah. In order to quell this uprising, the Persians collected the most powerful of their forces from Asfahan, Tabriz, Khorasan and other places to fight against the Kurds.[250]

Amir Khan rebuilt the *Dimdim Qeĺa* in 1609,[251] an unconquerable fortress which was situated in the *Targawar* region which had been destroyed during the first campaign of Muslim Arabs when they came to spread their religious message and identity.[252] Amir Khan also established a strong army in order to help strengthen and consolidate his local power. He believed that Shah Abbas could not be trusted, and suspected one day in the future it would be necessary for him to defend the emirate.[253] To Pirbudaq Khan, the governor of Tabriz, it seemed the *Baradhost* Kurds were becoming too strong. The Shah distrusted the motives of Amir Khan, causing him to protest against the rebuilding of the *Dimdim*. However, Khan refused Shah's demand, by saying, "If he is a Shah, I am a Khan."[254], implying that if he was a Persian Shah, then Amir Khan was a Kurdish Khan.

3.5 Sources for *Dimdim Variations* of *Dimdim*

The *Dimdim Qeĺa beyt* will be discussed here; particularly its role in promoting Kurdish identity. *Dimdim* is a story that has been repeatedly collected from oral sources in Kurdistan.

[249] Jalilov, Ordixani (1967). Koordskii geriocheskii epos "Zlatorookii Xan" (Dimdim), Nauka sssr, Moscwa, p. 10.
[250] Ibid, p. 12.
[251] Hassanpour, Amir (1996). Encyclopaedia Iranica, Volume VII, Mazda Publishers, California, p. 404.
[252] Tawahudi, Kalimullah (1364). Op. cit, p. 41.
[253] Qaftan, Salih (1969). *Mêjui Netewey Kurd*, Kurdish text, History of the Kurdish People, Salman A'zami Press, Baghdad, p. 350.
[254] Mann, Oskar (1975 *Tuhfayi Mudhaffariyyah in the Kurdish Mukri Dialect*, Introduced, Collated and set into Kurdish letters by Hêmin Mukryani, Kurdish Academy Press, Baghdad, p. 207. Huseni, Abdulhamidm, (1981). Op. cit, p. 16.

An early version was published in Kurmanjî by Jaba in 1860.[255] The first Soranî version was published by Oskar Mann in 1905.[256] Kurdoev also published *Dimdim* in a collection of folklore texts in the Soviet Kurdish dialect and published in 1962 C. E..[257] There are various other versions. I refer to Ordixan Jelil's text, for identifying elements of Kurdism in the story.

Regardless of differences between many texts the *Dimdin,* for the Kurdish people it remains a national epic that describes Kurdish resistance and struggle in the face of Persian oppressors. Both the Kurdoev and Jelils' texts of *Dimdim* epic clearly show that the Kurds were opposed to external rulers, and fought to maintain their self-autonomy. This is in evidence at end of the epic: the context places the reader in response to the last attack of Shah Abbas against Qeĺa*i Dimdim,* when Amir Khan proudly says:

Xelqê me nayê rayê,	Our people, would not take the enemy's path
Hîviya dijmin e ji meydanê,	Hoping to fight against the enemy,
Mîna şêra ew sêr dikê,	Stand as lions,
Herr tim mîna dijim alt dikê,	That always destroy enemies,
Me ne xofê eskerê te,	We are not afraid of your soldiers,
Me ne xofê xanê T'ewreze,	We are not scared of the Tabriz ruler,
Kele ranake ji himbeze.	Our braves will not retreat.
Me ne tirs xanê Çînmeçîne,	We are not frightened by the ruler of China,
Qirnake xelqê me,	Who cannot eradicate our people,
Me ne xofê xanê T'imeçîne,	We are not worried by the Timur Khan,
Bela neke xelqê me ji çiyae,	He will not be able to separate our people from our mountains,
Gû nav mezhebê te kin	Fuck your school of thought
Tacê te qebûl nakim,	I am not accepting your crown,

[255] Huseny, Abdulhamid (2537 Kurdi). Manzumay Hamasi Dimdim, The Revolutionary Epic of Dimdim, Persian text, MA Dissertation, has not published yet, Shiraz, p. 4.

[256] Mann, Oskar (1975). Op. cit. Rasul, Dr Izzadeen Mustafa (1979). *Lêkolinewei Edebi folklori Kurdi*, Kurdish text, A Study in the Kurdish folkloric literature, Silêmanî University Press, Silêmanî, p. 53.

[257] Kurdoev, Kanat Kalashevich (1976). *Komaele teksti folklori Kurdi*, Kurdish text, A collection of folklore texts in the Soviet Kurdish dialect, Edited, introduced it put into Kurdish Soranî by Shukur Mustafa and Enwer Qadir Muhemmed, published by Kurdish Academy Press, Baghdad.

Kurdistanê bê nav nakim.[258]   I will never bring a bad name to Kurdistan.

(Jalilove, Ordixani Jalil, p :110)

In the above verses, originally collected by Jaba in 1860 C. E. and written down in 1967 C. E., we understand that the identity of Amir Khan and his people were Kurdish identity. In all versions of *Dimdim* the common subject is heroic resistance to the Shah and ultimate failure and glorious death. The hero's identity varies but the major point is Amir Khan is always Kurdish and the Shah is always Persian. So it shows a discourse of Kurdishness and resistance.

In the 1976 Kurdoev text, Amir Khan was building a strong fortress as a preparation for his independence from Shah Abbas (of Persia).[259] His interpretation coincides with the historical view of Eskander Beg Turkmani who was with Shah Abbas during the siege of *Dimdim*. Eskandar and said that Amir Khan wanted to preserve the rule of his principality, in the face of both Ottoman and Safavid Empires.[260] This is evidenced by a verse when Shah asks the Kurdish Khan to accept his rule or he would be killed:

Qebûl bike tu vî tacî,   You, either recognize this crown,
Qebûl nekî te dikujim.[261]   Or refuse it and I will kill you.

In reply, the Kurdish Khan says:

Tajê te ser serê te be,   Keep your crown for yourself,
Kuştina mera weha be,   Let us be killed
Kurdistan bê nav nebe.[262]   Kurdistan would not have a bad name.

The *Dimdim* narrates many heroic sides of a story about Kurds defending the fortress and their regions against the Persians. The garrison of the *Qela* is a symbol of courage in opposing Persian rule. Some versions also demonstrate how Kurdish women also took part in the struggle. They are depicted as fighting the Persians alongside their men, once all the latter

---

[258] Jalilov, Ordixani Jail (1967). Op. cit, p. 110.
[259] Kurdoev, Kanat Kalashevich (1976). Op. cit, pp. 195-6.
[260] Hassanpour, Amir (1996). Op. cit, p. 404.
[261] Kurdoev, Kanat Kalashevich (1976). Op. p. 202.
[262] Ibid.

had been killed, their wives and other women would not submit themselves to the Persians. For instance, in the following text by Abdulhamid Huseni, it says:

Paşî Xan Evdal û Kake Xanî Lepzêrîne	After the death of Khan Abdal and Kake Khan of Lepzêrîne,
Nakewine des hucûmekey derpêşîne[263]	We will not surrender to the attacks of blue-trousered ones. [the Persians].

Dimdim has functioned as an inspirational paradigm for future generations, rather than being accurate in terms of historical detail. What it seeks to convey is 'feeling' and therefore we can see it as affirmation of what makes Kurds 'determined' to be Kurdish, a key element in the conveyance of 'Kurdism'

To summarise, in different parts of Kurdistan, alternative versions of the *Dimdim* epic may be found. Each version acts as symbol of the Kurd's struggle and resistance against the dominant powers. The *Dimdim* poetic story also reflected the Kurdish desire for self-governance and at the same time provided a strong element to identify the Kurds from others. *Dimdim* reflected Kurdish heroism against the Persian king and became part of the culture of resistance and patriotism.

3.6 Language, consciousness and identity: the religious context

In the sixteenth century, literacy was in the hands of the elite who were Islamic scholars and students of religion. Kurds prior to the nineteenth century were, as we shall see later, aware of their differences with Turks, Persians and Arabs; so to some extent they developed their own identity through their awareness of these distinctions in particular their way of life and their language. At the beginning of that century, Kurdish written language took a large step forward, when its development strengthened alliances to be formed between the Kurdish literary elite in different parts of Kurdistan.

As in any other part of the Islamic world, although the most important function of a mosque

---

[263] Huseny, Abdulhamidm (1981). Op. cit, p. 38.

was worship, other functions included teaching, the reading of the Quran, interpreting Quranic texts and learning reading and writing. Therefore mosques and *medreses* (schools) were closely associated. Spreading mosques and *medrese* in Kurdistan were a clear indication that Kurds were interested in education and learning. Wherever there was a small village of even a few houses, there was a mosque and a *medrese*.[264] Kurdish mosques produced hundreds of Kurdish scholars (*Ulama*), who contributed great services to Islamic knowledge and Kurdish language and literature. Kurdish *Ulama* had a great reputation in Kurdistan, the Ottoman and Persian empires and even beyond. Individual scholars grouped in Kurdistan under names such as the *"Sharezuriyekan"*, *"Penjwiniyekan"*, *"Sineiyekan"*, *"Betushiyekan"*, *"Berzinjiyekan"*, and other individuals, were among Kurdish *Ulama* who contributed to Islamic knowledge, learning and religion in many parts in the Islamic world such as Mecca, Medina, Cairo, Damascus, Istanbul and Indonesia.[265]

There were many famous *medreses* scattered throughout Kurdistan. Most of the larger *medreses* tended to be sponsored by the established Kurdish dynasties and local people. *Medrese* in Kurdistan produced *melas* for religious affairs, and played a key role in bringing about national awareness among Kurds in different parts of Kurdistan. Their main aim was to educate future religious leaders, rather than vying for future political leadership.[266] As *medreses* were a primary source for education in Kurdistan[267], they also offered an opportunity for *feqês* (Kurdish students) and *melas* to meet during their travels throughout Kurdistan, and even as far as Baghdad, Istanbul, Egypt, and India. These journeys facilitated social, educational and permanent movement throughout both parts of Ottoman and Persian Kurdistan.

The importance of the *medrese* as a medium for education amongst Kurds has been discussed by Zinar.[268] I will cite specific examples in Baban at a later point in this work. One product of the medrese was Mawlana Khalid who travelled for his studies in many famous *medreses* and cities in Kurdistan, such as Qeredax, Silêmanî, Baĺekayeti, Xurmaĺ and Sine. He also

---

[264] Al-Qizilji, Muhammad (1938). *Al-Ta'rif bi masajid al-Sulaimaniya wa madarisiha al-diniya*, Arabic text, Introduction to Mosques of Silêmanî and its religious schools, Al-Najah Press, Baghdad, p. 4.

[265] For More details see Al-Qizilji, Muhammad, ibid. Al-Khal, Muhammad (1961). *Al-Sheikh Ma'ruf Al-Nodihi Al-Barzinji*, Arabic text, Al-Tamaddun Press, Baghdad. Mulla Abdulkarim Al-Mudarris, (1983). *Ulama'na fi khidmat al-'lim wadin*, Arabic text, Our ulama in the service of knowledge and religion, Dar al-Hurriya Press, Baghdad. Bruinessen, Martin van (2000). Religion in Kurdistan, in *Mullas, Sufis and Heretics: The Role of Religion in Kurdish Society*, The Isis Press, Istanbul.

[266] van Bruinessen, Martin (1998). The Kurds and Islam, in *Islam Des Kurds*, Publication de l'ERISM, Paris, p. 24.

[267] Ibid p.40.

[268] Zinar, Zeynelabidin (1998). *Medrese Education in Northern Kurdistan, Islam des Kurdes, Les Annales de l'autre Islam No 5, INALCO-ERISM*, Paris. pp 39-58 translated by Martin van Bruinessen.

travelled to the city of Delhi[269] and it was in India that he received the *ijaze* from Shaikh Abdullah.[270] The Kurdish poet Mewlewî (1806-1882) too studied in various established *medreses* in Erdelan and Baban such as those of Nodşe, Sine, Bane, Silêmanî, Heĺebje, Tewêĺe and Jwanřo.[271]

His career emphasises the importance of the Kurdish *medrese* as a centre for the development of Kurdish culture and literature for a collective Kurdish identity. The majority of the Kurdish *melas-ulama* were religious elite who, in addition to teaching the Islamic knowledge also made a major contribution to the development of Kurdish language and literature. From the beginning of the sixteenth century up to the middle of the twentieth century, all Kurdish scholars, poets and Kurdish chieftains, princes and leaders of political movement were educated in *medrese* and had *medrese* background.[272]

3.7 The Emergence of Kurdish literature as a vehicle for 'Kurdism'

It was after the Battle of Chaldiran (in 1514) when the first instances of the use of Kurdish language in written poetry appeared, with the first poets emerging in Botan at the end of sixteenth century; including the pioneers Ali Harirî (1530–1600), Feqê Teyran (1563–1641) and Melayê Cizîrî (1567–1640). They were influenced by Persian poetic traditions and classical norms, but they used the Kurdish language to incorporate the elements of Islamic classical poetry, which was developed by the Arabs and Persians. This was especially the case when they identified their feelings of Kurdish 'togetherness', when, as Xeznedar says, "…they stressed that they were Kurds and they used the Kurdish language to write their poems."[273]

The custom of writing in Kurdish in other Ottoman-controlled areas of Kurdistan was nurtured in *mosques* and *medreses*. Evliya Çelebi, the Ottoman traveller and state official, who visited several Kurdish emirates in the middle of the seventeenth century, wrote about

---

[269] Muderris, Mela Abdulkarim (1979). *Yadi Merdan*, Kurdish text, Remembering the great men, Mawlana Khalidi Naqishbandî, Published by Kurdish Academy, Baghdad, pp. 12-4. Waziri, Amir (1386). *Naqishbandi dar Kurdistan*, Persian text, Naqishbandî in Kurdistan, Kurdistan book binding, Sine, Iran, pp. 180-1 & p. 189.

[270] van Bruinessen, Martin (1992). *Agha, Shaikh and State: The Social and Political Structures of Kurdistan*, Zed Books Ltd, London, p. 223.

[271] Sejadi, Ela'edin (1971). *Mêjui Edebi Kurdi*, Kurdish text, The history of Kurdish literature, second addition, Ma'arif Prees, Baghdad, pp. 277-8.

[272] Mela Kerim, Muhemmed (1998). Mewlewî: A Great Poet and Alim of Southern Kurdistan; in *Islam des Kurdes*, publication de l'ERISM, Paris, pp. 59-106.

[273] Xeznedar, Prof. M. (2002). *Mêjui Edebi Kurdî*, Kurdish text, The History of Kurdish Literature: 14 -18th Centuries, Second Volume, Aras Publishers House, Erbil-Kurdistan, p. 344.

the existence of books in the Kurdish language in the *medreses*.[274]

3.8 The Importance of *Medrese* in Promoting Kurdish Identity

In Kurdistan, the institution of the *medrese* played an important role particularly in the development and use of the Kurdish language and promoting of Kurdish identity. Since establishment of *medreses* in Kurdistan in the eleventh or twelfth centuries, many famous *medreses* such as Sitrabas in Diyarbakir, Medreseya Sor of Cizre, *medrese* of Bayezid, and the *medrese* of Shamdinan. Bitlis, provided education in Kurdish language to hundreds of thousands of students or *feqês*.[275] Evliya Çelebi witnessed flourishing culture and religious life in many Kurdish cities such as Bitlis, Cizire and Amadiye and saw *melas* writing poetry in Kurdish.[276] In other words, existing *medreses* in the main Kurdish cities mentioned above provided education in Kurdish and using their language became a tool to promote Kurdish self-awareness.

Mela Muhammadi Qizilji was a very influential Kurdish scholar. In his book entitled *al-Ta'rif bi masajid al-Sulaimaniya wa madarisiha al-diniya*, (Introduction to Silêmanî mosques and its religious schools) he wrote about the mobile *medreses* found in Kurdistan in the eighteenth century which followed the movements of the Kurdish tribes.[277] He also stated that there were many famous mobile *medreses* in the eighteenth century in numerous cities such as Qeĺa Çolan, Kirkuk, Erbil, Sine and Meriwan.[278]

The journeys of the *feqês* facilitated social, religious and educational interaction throughout Kurdistan. For example, in Silêmanî, there were *feqês* who came from all around Kurdistan including cities such as Mehabad, Sine, Seqiz, and Bane, were under Persian rule. They had colleagues from Rewanduz, Koye, Kerkuk and Erbil. Mewlewi, who travelled to Meriwan, Sine, Bane, Silêmanî, Helebje and Jwanřo.[279] Hajî Qadiri Koyî travelled to Xoşnaw, Erbil, Serdeşt, Mehabad, Shino and Silêmanî.[280] This helped the rise of Kurdish identity; by mobilising the students they could adopt sentiments of belonging to one people. Mawlana

---

[274] Bruinessen, Martin van (1998). Op. cit, p. 24.
[275] Zinar, Zeynelabidin (1998). Op. cit, p. 40. Zinar exaggerated the numbers of feqês.
[276] Bruinessen, Martin van (1998).Op. cit, p. 24.
[277] Al-Qizilji, Muhammad (1938). Op. cit, pp. 6-7.
[278] Ibid, p. 27.
[279] Sejadi, Ela'din (1971). *Mêjui Edebi Kurdî*, Kurdish text, The History of the Kurdish Literature, second edition, Ma'arif Press, Baghdad, pp. 277-8.
[280] Ibid, p. 342,

Khalid and the poet Mustafa Begi Kurdî (1809-1849) used *Kurdî* as their surname or nickname.[281]

3.9 Promotion of Kurdish Language and Literature

Although there were no Kurdish education centres as such in Kurdistan; the *medreses* were places where Kurdish was freely used to explain Quranic verses. It is, I feel, significant that, at a later period, these institutions were shut in Turkey for both secularist (repression of religion) and nationalist (assimilation of non-Turks) purposes. For Kurds, as Zinar suggests, this was aimed at; "primarily assimilating the Kurds, cutting them off from their past...making [them] forget their own past" Thus, albeit retrospectively, emphasising the important role these institutions played in the cultural transmission of 'Kurdishness'.[282] There is no doubt that up until the middle of the twentieth century, Kurdish intelligentsia all across Kurdistan were educated, or partly educated, in *medreses*: as a result, Kurdish writing and literature began to emerge from mosques and *medreses*.

3.10 Written Literature

During the sixteenth and seventeeth centuries, two magnificent pieces of literature written by Kurdish scholars emerged, namely ***Sharafnama* and *Mem û Zîn*.** Both became important for later generations and played a role in promoting Kurdish self-consciousness. These will now be discussed.

3.11 *Sharafnama* and *Mem û Zîn*

There are two texts that represent the great historical shift to a new way of representing and introducing Kurdish identity among the educated and political circles of Kurdish society. They include clear ideas and definitions of Kurdism. The first text is *Sharafnama*, a history book written in Persian by the famous Kurdish statesman and historian Sharafaddin or Sharafkhan (1543-1603/4). The second is *Mem u Zin*, by Xani, a key protagonist in developing Kurdish literature in introducing nationalist and patriotic themes. Kurdish

---

[281] Ibid, p. 327.
[282] Zinar, Zeynelabidin (1998). Op. cit, p.41.

literature, whilst a distinctive style and genre of its own, further developed oriental cultural heritage.

3.12 Kurdish Historical identity in *Sharafnama*

To put the work of *Sharafnama* into context, we may consider two earlier historical books written by Kurdish writers. Firstly, Ahmad bin Yosif al-Azraq al-Farqi's "Ta'rikh al-Farqi-history of al-Farqi", finished in 1176 is the first historical book written by a Kurdish historian.[283] This provided a history of the Kurdish Marwanid state in the tenth and eleventh centuries.[284] Secondly, Ma'mun bin Bega Beg's book entitled "Muzakarat Bega Beg" [memories of Bega Beg], finished in 1574, was originally written as a petition by Bega Beg the *mir* of Erdelan to Sultan Murad III. This book gave details of the beginning of the conflicts between the Ottoman and Safavid empires and their interference in Kurdish affairs. Furthermore, it discussed the emirates of Sharezur, Kelhor and Erdelan, the bloody events that took place between the two empires, and their impact on the later Kurdish history.[285] *Sharafnama* was the third book written about Kurds. Kurdish historical identity will now be discussed.

Before the sixteenth century Bitlis Kurds had managed to establish their own emirate. This reality existed centuries before the Ottoman and Safavid Empires came to being. In 1200 C. E., the leader of a large Rojekî confederation of Bitlis was recognized and appointed as a governor of Bitlis.[286] After a while, Bitlis conquered vast territories from all around and became so famous and powerful that no power could enter the area without their consultation.

Sharafkhani Bitlisi (1534–1603/4) was a Kurdish *mir* of the Bitlis Emirate and renowned for writing the first inclusive history of the Kurds, entitled: *Sharafnama*. It was completed on 30 Dhul-hijja 1005-28 D. H.-August 1596 C. E..[287] It was originally written in the dominant scholarly language of the time, Persian. At the time of its writing, there were over forty

---

[283] Ahmad bin Yosif al-Azraq al-Farqi (1959). *Ta'rikh al-Farqi*-history of al-Farqi which was finished in 1176.[283] Arabic text, introduced and noted by Dr Badawi Abdullatif Awaz, Cairo.

[284] Kocer, Segvan Muhammad Seid (2010). *Ta'rikh Miyafariqin wa Amad*, Arabic text, The History of Miyafariqin and Amad, MA dissertation, published by Kurdish Academy, Erbil, p. 13.

[285] Ma'mun bin Bega Beg (1980). *Muzakarat Bega Beg* who finished in 1574, translated from Turkish to Arabic by Muhammad Jamil al-Rojbayani and Shukur Mustafa, Baghdad.

[286] Van Brunessen, Agha, Shaikh and State, p. 163.

[287] Haig, LT. Colonel Sir Wolseley (1932). *Comparative Tables of Muhammadan and Christian Dates*, Luzac & Co., London, p. 21.

Kurdish chiefdoms in existence.[288] They achieved limited success in gaining social and political influence.

Sharafkhani Bitlisi could be described as a pioneer in documenting Kurdish identity. His efforts could this be described as a work of general history, as his focus was more on preserving knowledge of the history of Kurdish dynasty along the lines of the independence they attained aiming to preserve the lessons of history for posterity.[289] Yet he acted critically, as on occasions he complained that rather than uniting in the common good of the people as a whole, the emirates tended to act in their self-interest; as he preferred a more centralised approach in the running of their affairs.[290]

Sharafkhan gave up his position of political authority to devote himself entirely to the writing of the history of his people. Sharafkhan spent about thirty-five years in the Safavid court, such a long time did not make him forget his Kurdishness, and he always kept his ties with his original tribe in Bitlis. In 1578 he fled from the Safavid Empire and returned with 400 men to Bitlis.[291] He became a ruler of Bitlis, after short period when he was 53 years old he stepped down and devoted the remainder of his life to writing about Kurdish history.[292]

Even so, Sharafkhan managed to make an enduring impression on Kurdish sentiment throughout subsequent generations. According to the author, having a strong sense of being a Kurd had prompted him to write about Kurdish history in terms of their governments, principalities and their princes; in order to prevent them from being forgotten and enable the heritage to be kept for future generations.[293] He says, "I have written *Sharafnama* to prevent Kurdistan dynasties from being forgotten."[294] In these terms it could be seen as very important work, in documenting Kurdish history up to its completion, in 1596. For the purposes of this study, this will be examined briefly in conveyance of Kurdish identity and how Sharafkhan expressed his Kurdish identity therein.

---

[288] Hassanpour, Amir (2003). "The Making of Kurdish Identity". In Vali, Abbas, edited by, *Essays on Kurdish Origins of Kurdish Nationalism*, Mazda Publishers. p. 113.

[289] Ibid, pp. 111, 113.

[290] Ibid.

[291] Mezher, Dr Kemal (1983). *Mêeju*, History, Kurdish text, Dar al- 'Afaq al-Arabiya Press, Baghdad, p. 106.

[292] Ibid.

[293] Bitlisi, Sharafkhan (1953). *Sharafnama*, Arabic text, The History of the Kurdish states and their emirates, translated from Persian by Mulla Jamil Bandi Rojbayani, al-Najaf Press, Baghdad, p. 9. Persian was the dominant scholarly language of the region, comparable to the position of Latin in Europe or Mandarin in China.

[294] Sharafkhan says in Persian موسوم "بشرفنامة" زمتااحوال خلو دهای عظيم للسان كرديتان در حجاب ستر ولكتمان هند. Abbasi, Muhammad (1343). Edited by, *Sharafnama*, Persian text, Elmi Publisher, Tehran, p. 9.

3.13 Kurds in *Sharafnama*

Certain elements in *Sharafnama,* may shed light on the way Kurds highlight their sense of Kurdism. In reading Sharafkhan's pioneering work about Kurdish history, by association, one may be able to feel how the author had pride in his Kurdish identity. In the introduction, he states that his sense of being a Kurd had prompted him to record Kurdish roles in history and for the lessons that might be learnt from Kurdish experiences.[295] Although at the time he wrote in a non-Kurdish tongue, Persian, his contribution ensured that Kurdish sentiment found expression. This feeling of being a Kurd was a very important element in the preservation of Kurdish culture and feelings that was later drawn upon. In time, Kurdish became a written language.

In *Sharafnama,* Sharafkhan wrote in detail about each and every Kurdish *wilat* – government, *hukkam-* plural of *hakim* - governors, and *salatin-* plural of sultan.[296] He was careful not to exclude any principalities; he mentioned some of them as *saltanate* – sultanate which were independent, while others were not. He started with Diyarbakir, the Kurdish independent *saltanate,*[297] and finished with Bitlis.[298] Sharafkhan aimed to find connections among Kurds; he wrote about all Kurdish people and their emirates within both sides of the Ottoman and Persian empires, he also included Kurdish populations from Diyarbekir to Luristan as one ethnic group while he was aware of the differences of Kurdish dialects, which he believed could feature as four distinct groupings: Kurmanjî, Lur, Kalhor and Goran.[299]

Sharafkhan's thoughts were not limited to one region of the Kurds, when he uses *tawa'ifi Akrad,*[300] he clearly meant all Kurdish tribes, all Kurdish dialects, all Kurdish areas, all Kurdish *mazhabs* (sects) and all districts in Kurdistan. For Sharafkhan, political power was a very important element for having a central administration. He says:

"vilayet z sultan cho khali shavad

---

[295] Bitlisi, Sharafkhan, (1973). *Sharafnama*, The History of The Kurds, Translated from Persian to Kurdish by Hejar, published by Kurdish Academy Press, Baghdad, p. 12. Bidlisi, Shrafkhan (1343). *Sharafnama*, Ta'rikhi mofasali Kurdistan, Persian text, edited and noted by Muhammad Abbasi, Elmi Press, p. 9.
[296] Bidlisi, Shrafkhan (1343). Ibid, p. 11.
[297] Ibid, p. 10
[298] Ibid, p. 17.
[299] Ibid, pp. 23-4.
[300] Ibid, p. 18.

when the position of a sultan or a king is vacant

every head of a village would become a *wali* (governor)

Therefore, for Sharafkhan, the king's position is crucial for the establishment of a powerful government. Furthermore, in his opinion, a strong king could unify Kurdish tribes in one administration. Without a king, every village head would wish to rule his village as he wished.

3.14 Kurdistan in *Sharafnama*

Sharafkhan was the first Kurdish historian who mentioned the boundary of Kurdistan and used the term Kurdistan to define Kurdish *welat* (homeland), that is homelands. In his view "Kurdistan started from Hurmuz in the south of the Persian Gulf extending to Malatiya and Marash in the north, from the north Faris province, Iraqi 'Ajam, Azerbaijan and small and large Armenia, from the south Iraqi Arab, Mosul and Diyarbakir."[302] In all likelihood he exaggerated; at the time, no other writers went so far in their claims about the boundaries of Kurdistan.

Sharafkhan transformed the idea of Kurdish in a very important qualitative way. Together with establishing a strong ground of Kurdish historiography, he provided a methodological construction of what Kurdism means bringing together as its elements land (geographically identified) language (including variants of dialects) and political power and administration. He also relates all these to one constant element which is the Kurdish character and the ability of Kurds to match other peoples in terms of courage, knowledge and self-administration.

---

[301] Ibid, p. 498.
[302] Ibid, p. 24-5.

3.15 The emergence of Kurdism in Kurdish poetry before Xanî

Before the time of Xanî, one can find a few Kurdish poets who expressed the view of being
Kurds which may have inspired Xanî himself. In the following section, this will be discussed
in detail.

3.16 Melayê Cizîrî (1567–1640)

Cizîrî is the first known poet who pioneered writing poetry in Kurmanjî. He was a highly
educated *Mela* versed in Islamic sciences, Arabic language and Persian literature. What
prompted him to write in Kurdish rather than the more privileged languages of the dominant
powers is an issue which has still not been studied and clarified. However, Melayê Cizîrî was
proud to write in Kurdish. Being proud of both his language and the poetry he produces in it,
Melayê Cizîrî compares his work in beauty to Hafiz and Sa'di from Shiraz who were the
most famous Persian poets. He wrote:

Ger lû'lu'î mensûr ji nezmê tu dixwazî
Were şî irî "Melê" bîn te bi Şîraz çi hacet [303]

If you are looking for poetic pearls,
Come see the poems of *Mela*, you do not need to go to Shiraz

During this early period of Botan emirate, the emergence of Kurdish poetry was a promising
sign for Kurdishness; as it is marked by these verses of Cizîrî which emphasizes the
distinction between Kurdish and Persian and Turkish identities. He even includes an
important geographical identification of this distinction by mentioning the word Kurdistan
and describing himself proudly as the flower of Botan and light of Kurdistan.

Gulî baxî Êremî Bohtan im
Şeb çiraxî şebî Kurdistan im [304]

---

[303] *Dîwanî* Melayê Cizîrî, (1361). Kurdish text, Completed work of Melayê Cizîrî, edited and explained by Hejar, published by Srush,
Tehran, p. 128.
[304] Ibid, p. 534.

I am the blossom of Botan's heavenly garden,

The illuminating light of Kurdistan's night.

In twenty-two long verses, Cizîrî wrote a poem for the *Mir* of Botan, whom he praised, and thanked God for securing his victory over his enemies. In effect he praised the *Mir* for his achievements, not the *Mir* himself. Cizîrî wrote poems in the eulogy of *Mir* of Botan as representative of the Kurdish people:

Ey şahenşahê Muezem! Heq nîgehdarê te bê
Sureyê "înna fetehna" dûr û madarê te bê [305]

    Oh, the greatest king of kings, May God protect you!
    The Qura'nic verse of "Verily we have granted thee a manifest Victory" may it surround you

In another verse Cizîrî praises *Mir* of Botan and his authority. He says:

Ney tenê Tebrîz û Kurdistan liber hukmê te bin
Sed wekî şahî Xurasanêdi ferwarê te bê [306]

Not only Kurdistan and Tabriz also should be part of your realm,
Many like the governor of Khurasan should come under your authority

Cizîrî used the word "Kurdistan", something which had not been done in poetry before. However, in general his poetry covered themes shared by Persian and Arab classical poetry, such as *ishq* (yearning love), wine and religious themes.

Together with two other Kurdish poets Ali Heriri (1530-1600) and Feqê Teyeran (1563-1641), Cizîrî provided a precedent for Ehmedê Xanî to follow. Xanî mentions Cizîrî, Ali Heriri and Feqê Teyeran's names in his prologue.[307] However, it was Xanî who brought about a great change in the context of Kurdish literature, especially in the way in which he expressed his identity in the refraction of these two poets.

---

[305] Ibid, p. 510.
[306] Ibid, p. 511.
[307] Xanî, Ehmedê, (2010). *Mem û Zîn*, Yildirim, Kadri , Avesta, Istanbul, verses 6/17 251- 6/18 252, p. 158.

Kurdish poetry demonstrates a sense of group identity at a very early stage in the development of the Kurds as a nation. Although many of them were well versed in many languages, it was, as we shall see, the language of Kurdish which they chose to express themselves.[308]

3.17 Establishing the project of a Kurdish literature: *Mem û Zîn*, by Ehmedê Xanî (1650–1707): The Kurdish National Epic[309]

Xanî was the first Kurdish thinker, linguist, scholar and poet to advance Kurdism during the second half of the seventeenth century. Perhaps he is the most famous and highly regarded poet by his own people. As Joyce Blau recently has put it, "his *Mem û Zîn* ... [a]long '*mathnawi*' of 2655 distichs, rich in poetic imagery and lyrical scenes, has immortalised Xanî for the Kurds, as Firdawsi was immortalised by the Persians, and Homer by the Greeks."[310]

He played a leading role in creating Kurdish consciousness and made the Kurds believe that they were distinct from the dominant peoples. He also encouraged them to realise their rights in having power and government. Thus, we need to consider him in an appropriate historical context; particularly, in terms of his classic long lasting work "*Mem û Zîn*".[311] Most people who have written about Xanî, such as Hassanpour, Lescot, and Shakely, agree that when he wrote *Mem û Zîn* he had a political purpose.[312] Xanî's purpose, as Chyet (1991:61) suggests, was to create a literary collection in Kurdish to show that Kurds have their own language and literature like the Persians, Turks, and Arabs of the region. According to Chyet (1991:61), Xani believed that the Kurds could be "a great nation in their own right".[313] Even today *Mem*

---

[308] See chapter five for more details.

[309] Some of the known publications and commentaries on the *Mem û Zîn*: Dr. Izzadeen Mustafa Rasul wrote his PhD thesis comprehensively about Ehmedê Xanî, titled Ahmadi *Khani* sha'iran wa mufakiran, Arabic text, Ehmedê Xanî: poem and thinker, al-Hawadth Press, Baghdad, 1979. *Mem û Zîn*, Published by Jin, Aras Press, Halab, 1947. Piremêrd, *Mem û Zîn*, Jin Press, Silêmanî, 1932. Ata Muhammad, *Mem û Zîn*, Kamarani Press, Silêmanî, 1978. *Mem û Zîn*, published by Giwi Mukryani, first edition, Kurdistan press, Hewler, 1954, Second edition same press and same place, 1968. Hejari Mukryani (1960). put *Mem û Zîn* into Soranî, Najah Press, Baghdad. Hejari Mukryani, (1989). edited and annotated, *Mem û Zîn*, Kurdish Institute Press, Paris. Ubaidullah Aiybiyan, (1340 shamsi). *Crika-I Mem û Zîn*, Kurdish text with Persian translation on opposite pages, Shafaq press, Tabri., Muhammad Boz Arsalan, (1968). *Mem û Zîni* Ehmedê Xanî, Hilal Press, Istanbul. Salah Saadalla, (2008). Translated by to English. Yildirim, Kadri , (2010). Translated and analysed by, Ehmedê Xanî , *Mem u Zin*, Avesta, Istanbul, and some other writers. and some other writers.

[310] Blau, J. (2006). *Refinement and Oppression of Kurdish Language* in Jabar and Dawood, *The Kurds: Nationalism and Politics*, London, p.104

[311] Badirkhan, Celadet Ali (July 1953). "An open letter to Mustafa Kemal from a Kurdish Chief", translated by Major F. F., Rynd, *Journal of the Royal Central Asian Society*, Vol. XXII, Part. III, p. 471.

[312] Chyet, Michael L. (1991). "*And A Thornbush Sprang Up Between Them*": Studies On "*Mem u Zin*", A Kurdish Romance, Vol. I, U.M.I Dissertation Information Service, Michigan 1991, p. 61.

[313] Ibid.

û Zîn remains relevant to the Kurdish nationalist cause; also Xanî's influence extends all over Kurdistan and *Mem û Zîn* is read among Kurds and other peoples.

A few Kurdish stories from the oral tradition can also be found as literary works. *Mem û Zîn* is one such oral tradition that can be found in many Kurdish dialects too. There are, for example, Kurmanjî and Soranî versions of the original folk epic *Memi Alan*.[314] *Mem û Zîn* has been the subject of much discussion amongst scholars interested in Kurdish nationalism and identity. The key arguments are those by Ela'din Sejadi, Dr. Izzaddin Mustafa Rasul, Ferhad Shakely, Michael L. Chyet, Martin van Bruinessen, Amir Hassanpour, Abbas Vali and Dr. Kamal Mirawdely. [315]

In general, the concern of the traditional works is love in both its real and metaphorical senses as Xanî himself differentiates them. However, the purpose of Ehmedê Xanî's *Mem û Zîn* is far from telling just a love tale of two lovers. Ehmedê Xanî's version is very different, as it requires a competent level of educational achievement for its comprehension. One needs to have a good understanding of Islamic theology and philosophy, Kurmanjî dialect, Arabic, Farsi, and Turkish languages and the vocabulary, imagery and style of Islamic classical poetry and Kurdish culture and way of life.

For this reason, in the course of this chapter, Kadri Yildirim's[316] text of Ehmedê Xanî's *Mem u Zin* is considered as the most reliable and will be used for quotations. He was well-versed in the Kurmanjî dialect, with a very good background in Islamic knowledge. As a professor at Mardin University for Kurdish Studies, he writes in a language making use of the vocabularies and expressions of the Kurmanjî-Kurdish. His version offers an opportunity to interpret and present the *Mem u Zin*. Above all, the Yildirim version is already in the properly vocalised Latin script of Kurmanjî.

---

[314] Syamand, Esmat Sharif (1957). *Dastani Memi Alan*, Karam Press, Sham. Zaza, Nuraddin, (1958). *Memi Alan*, Damascus. Dr. Ma'ruf Khaznadar, *Nusus al-Folkloriya min Mem û Zîn wa Memi Alan*, Folkloric texts of *Mem û Zîn* and *Memi Alan*, al-Sulaimaniya Magazine, No. 2, Year 2, September 1969. Lescot, Roger, *Textes Kurdes*, Vol. 2, Meme Alan, Institut Francais de Damas, Beyrouth, 1942.

[315] Sejadi, Ela'din (1952). *Meju i Edebi Kurdi*, History of the Kurdish Literature, Ma'rif Press, Baghdad. Rasul, Dr. Izzaddin, Mustafa, (1979). *Ahmadi Khani 1650-1707 Poet and Thinker*, al-Hawadith Press, Baghdad. Shakely, Ferhad, Kurdish Nationalism in *Mem û Zîn* of Ehmed-i Xani, Sweden, 1983. Chyet, Michael L., (1991). *"And A Thornbush Sprang Up Between Them": Studies On "Mem u Zin", A Kurdish Romance*, Two Volumes, U.M.I Dissertation Information Service, Michigan. Bruinessen, Martin van (1992). *Agha, Shaikh and State*, Zed Booksa Ltd, London, Hassanpour, Amir (1992.). *Nationalism and Language in Kurdistan 1918-1985*, Mellen Research University Press, San Francisco, his article The Making of Kurdish Identity , in Vali Essays on *the Origins of Kurdish Nationalism* and another article in *Gzing Magazine*, No. 9, Autumn 1995, Sweden. Vali, Abbas, (2003). edited, *Essays on the Origins of Kurdish Nationalism*, Mazda Publishers, Inc. Mirawdely, Dr. Kemal (2007). *Mem û Zîn: Rendered into Standard Kurdish with a General Study*, Renj Press, Silêmanî.

[316] Yildirim, Kadri (2010). Translation and Conceptual Analysis by, Ehmedê Xanî . *Mem u Zin*, Avesta, Istanbul.

3.18 Background of the Poet

Ehmedê Xanî was one of the prominent Kurdish poets and scholars of the seventeenth century. He had written two scholarly and poetic books [317] besides *Mem û Zîn*, which nationalist Kurds in general regarded as the first book promoting Kurdish nationalism. The importance of *Mem û Zîn* was apparent and it is generally accepted, now, to be the national epic of the Kurdish people. Therefore, scholars who write about Kurdish identity, Kurdism, and Kurdish nationalism cannot avoid *Mem û Zîn*.

Xanî had a royal and scholarly background; his father Elyas was a well-known Islamic scholar, a teacher and a writer. According to the Ottoman archive, Xani's Father Elyas bin Rostam was appointed as a teacher in the *medrese* in Bayezid and later in 1644, he became a writer in Amir Bayezid's court.[318] Xanî's grandfather whose name was Ayaz was also an Islamic scholar and was first in this family to be known as a *mala*-Islamic scholar; his great grandfather *mir* Rostam (died in 1534) was *Mir* of Qeĺai Sor.[319] Xanî was fourteen when he started writing poems, and he was twenty when he became a special secretary for writing for the court of the *mir* of Bayezid.[320] It seems that this position had a positive impact on him as he learned lessons to do with politics and administrative affairs which were reflected in *Mem û Zîn*.

Ehmedê Xanî wrote *Mem û Zîn* during the conflicts between the Ottomans and Persians, observing how this had created turmoil in Kurdistan. In 1691, whilst he was staying in the Kurdish town of Bayezid on the frontier of the Ottoman and Persian empires. Whilst there, he used his presence as an opportunity to promote the Kurdish language by founding a large Kurdish school, in which the principal language was Kurdish.[321] One of his books was *Nûbara Biçûkan* (Childrens' New Fruits) which was the first Kurdish-Arabic dictionary written especially for Kurdish pupils to learn Arabic in *medreses* and it was turned out to be extraordinarily popular and ever since has been used in *medreses* in Kurmanjî-speaking areas.[322] *Nûbara Biçûkan* was written in verses to be memorized easily by Kurdish children.

---

[317] Xanî wrote *Nubari Bickan* and *Eqidei 'iman* as well. These two books were published several times in Turkey without place and date of publishing. The former was also published in Damascus in 1955.

[318] Al-Doski, Tahsin Ibrahim (2005). Jawaher al-ma'ani fi sharih diwan Ehmedi Xani, Arabic text, Pearls of meaning in interpretation of diwani Ehmedê Xanî, Spirez Press, Erbil, p. 18.

[319] Ibid, p. 18.

[320] Ibid, p. 24.

[321] Soane, Ely Bannister (1012). *To Mesopotamia and Kurdistan in Disguise*, John Murray, London, p. 388. Soane made mistake when he indicated 1591 instead of 1691.

[322] Hassanpour, Amir (1992). Nationalism and Language in Kurdistan 1918-1985, Millen Research University Press, San Francisco, p. 89.

In this educational book for children, Xanî put the Kurdish language against other ethnic group's languages in the region such as Arabic, Persian (*Ecem*) and Turkish (*Romî*). He dealt with education as an important element for knowledge and success in life across all generations especially in childhood. Thus he was very concerned that Kurdish children should learn their language as a medium of education and understanding. This is clear from the introduction he starts his dictionary with:

Bîsmî llahî rehmanî rehîm
Mebdê her `ilmikî navê `elîm

Hemd û sena û şukiranî
Jib o wî xaliqê rehmanî

Ku fesahet û beyan daye lîsanî
Lîsan daye însanî

Hindê selewat in hemî
Li resûlê me yî Ummî

Ku bûne peyrewêd wî
Ereb ecem kurmanc û romî

Ji paş hemd û selewatan
Ev çend kelîmene ji luxatan

Vêkxistin Ehmedê Xanî
Navê Nûbara Biçûkan danî

Ne ji bo sahêb rewacan
Belkî ji bo biçûkêd kurmancan

Wekî ji Quranê xelas bin

Lazime li sewadê çavnas bin

Da bi van çend reşbelekan
Li wan tebî `iet melekan

Derê zihnê vebêtin
Her çî dixunin zehmet nebîtin

Umîdî ji tifalan
Ku me `emel betalan[323]

Thanks, praises and compliments
To who is (God) The Creater and The Merciful

Who gave fluency and eloquence to language
And gave language to human beings

Whatever there are praises
All be upon our honest *resul* (messenger)

Who had among his followers
Arab, Persian, Kurdish and Turkish

After thanks and praises
These words of languages

Illuminated by Ehmedê Xanî
Who gave a title of *Nûbara Biçûkan*

It is not for adults
It is for Kurdish childern

---

[323] Le Coq, Albert von (1903). *Kurdische Texte Zweiter Teil*, part. II, gedruckt in der Reichsdruckerei. Anhang Zwei kurdische Handschriften aus Damaskus, Berlin, pp. 1- 2. See also Le Coq, Albert, *Kurdische Texte*, Kurmangi- Erzählungen und –Lieder APA – Philo Press / Amsterdam, pp. 1-2.

When they finish the Qur'an

They should be familiar with literacy

By reading this book (dictionary)

For those who have the nature of angels

The door of their minds be opened

What they read would not be difficult for them

Those children are our future

They are our hope.

It should be mentioned that *Nûbara Biçûkan* was written in 1094 D. H-1683 C. E. when Xanî was 33 years old[324] and he taught it to Kurdish *feqês* in *medrese*. *Nûbara Biçûkan* was the beginning of dictionary- writing in the history of Kurdish literacy.[325] This strong educational background, teaching and experience demonstrated by Xanî in *Nûbara Biçûkan*, were reflected later in more developed ideas of Kurdism in *Mem û Zîn*.

It seems that Xanî possessed a comprehensive knowledge of Kurdish folklore, particularly the *Meme Alan* poetic story (beyt) – from which he drew inspiration in the composition of *Mem û Zîn*. Xanî also demonstrates an awareness of epics in the Arabic and Persian languages – such as *Mejnun u Leyla, Yousif u Zuleikha, Shaikh Sanan, Shirin u Parwiz,* and *Wamiq u Azra*, all of which are referenced in *Mem û Zîn*.

In all likelihood, Xanî must have realised that the use of Kurdish would have a significant impact upon its accessibility by using it would narrow its appeal and potential audience. Considering it was such a seminal work, he must have had a very strong reason for choosing Kurdish over the other languages, in wide use at the time. To this day, Xanî remains widely

---

[324] Ciwan, Mûrad (1997). Ehmedê Xanî, Jiyan, berham *û* bir *û baweriyên wî,*,Kurdish text, Ehmedê Xani, his life, his works and his ideas, DOZ-Basim-Yayin, Ltd, Istanbul, p. 89. Xanî wrote another book known as '*Eqîda Îman Fî Beyan El `eqîde we Eltewhîd" zekerehu Ehmed Elxanî,* (Belief in Faith) it is in verses and explains the principles of Islamic faith and was written to be used in Kurdish medreses. This work was published in Le Coq, Albert von (1903). *Kurdische Texte Zweiter Teil,* part. II, gedruckt in der Reichsdruckerei. Anhang Zwei kurdische Handschriften aus Damaskus, Berlin, pp. 33-47.

[325] As far as it is known, there is no evidence to prove that if there is any other Kurdish dictionary older than *Nûbara Biçûkan*. Ciwan, Mûrad (1997). Ibid, p. 89.

respected, and his version of the *Mem u Zin* is often praised among the Kurdish nation, where it is often circulated in Kurdistan amongst the people in the mosques.

3.19 Major elements of Kurdish identity in *Mem û Zîn*

The most important theme of *Mem u Zin* idea was to overcome the state of disunity among the Kurds by constructing a sense of collective belonging. Xanî therefore encouraged the Kurds to examine the causes of their state disunity and by aiming to establish a Kurdish Kingdom to end this state of affairs. It is therefore unsurprising that Xanî's legacy has had such as an important role and impact in promoting what may be described as the emergence of the first Kurdish nationalist and reformist intellectuals in the late nineteenth century and early twentieth century in the Ottoman Empire. He uses his whole reconstruction of *Mem u Zin* to make the Kurds feel proud of the distinctive characteristics of their Kurdishness. Often questioning the Kurds' apparent loyalty to the Ottoman Empire, he instead suggested that it should be replaced by a drive to royal sovereignty. He was concerned with the fragmentary nature of Kurdish authority; which he thought led to their lack of power, thus creating further difficulties for them. As he wrote in verses 5/14 202 5/16 204:

Ger dê hebûya me padîşahek	If we had a King,
Laîq bidiya xwedî kulahek	Upon whom God had bestowed a crown
Te ʿiyîn bibûya ji bo wî textek	And allocated a throne
Zahîr vedibû ji bo me bextek	Then our fortune would have emerged
Hasil bibûwa ji bo wî tacek	Our king would have his crown
Elbette dibû me ji rewacek[326]	We would have gained value and prestige.

Xanî's concept of power was closely tied with that of a monarchy, the crown being representative of a nation. He thought that the trappings of monarchical power would help the Kurds to gain respect amongst other nations. He believed only if they had sovereignty, they would be recognised as having a place amongst nations and would have *dîn û dewlet* (religion and governance) and then Turks, Arabs and Faris would accepted to be dominated by Kurds.[327] Xanî's conception of a monarchy was, however, one that would work to assist the Kurdish people in order to release them from foreign subjugation. He emphasised that it was

---

[326] Yildirim, Kadri (2010). Op. cit, verses 5/14 202 5/16 204, p. 153.
[327] Ibid, verses 5/44 232- 5/44 233, p. 155.

the responsibility of a Kurdish king to defend Kurds, enabling them to be free from despotic rule and revive their national identity and culture.

Xemxarî dikir li me yetîman
Tînane derê ji dest leîman [328]

He (Kurdish king) would show concern for us orphans and poor,
And release us from the control of villains

In his succeeding lines he does outline some other obligations of a compassionate monarch: the defence of its people, the promotion of sciences, culture, and all trappings of both faith and governance (*dîn û dewlet*). He asserted that their need for a sovereign was essential for any future development and prosperity. That is why in his poems, he often tended to focus on a Kurdish power; so as to provide an effective challenge against rival nations; such as the Turks, Arabs and Persians. He wrote:

Tekmîli dikir me dîn û dewlet
Tehsîli me dikir ilm û hîkmet [329]

We would have completed the establishment of faith and authority (state),
We would have obtained science and wisdom,

In a footnote, Bruinessen suggests the phrase *din u dewlet* as being 'more amorphous' than 'modern usage' of '*dewlet*' as language indicating a 'state'. He suggests that the poet's intention is to "juxtapose [..]," or contrast the concept in the manner of a "similar expression *din u dunya*, spiritual and worldly affairs"[330] As I shall explain later Xanî used the term *dewlet* three times making clear that he meant a sort of Kurdish kingdom.

Xanî believed that eventually the Kurds should establish their own kingdom. He had a positive outlook towards the Kurds and regarded their princes as generous and brave. Xanî understood that to establish a Kurdish authority, the Kurds possessed strong character,

---

[328] Ibid, verse. 5/17 205, p. 153.

[329] Ibid, verse 5/45 233, p. 155. *Kurdistan*, newspaper, No. 4, 21st May, 1314, 3rd June 1898, p. 2.

[330] Bruinessen, Martin van (2003). *Ehmedi Xani's Mem û Zîn and Its Role in the Emergence of Kurdish National Awareness* in A Vali *Essays On The Origins of Kurdish Nationalism*, p. 44.

knowledge, wisdom, generosity, and bravery but what they lacked was a confident, just and compassionate leadership:

Her mîrekî wan bi bezlê Hatem
Her mêrekî wan bi rezmê Rustem [331]

Every one of their princes is like Hatam for generosity,
Every one of their men is like Rostam for bravery

He also emphasized that *dewlet* was needed before knowledge and wisdom could be disseminated and prosperity be achieved.

Xanî focused on the influence and power of a Kurdish king might exercise for the benefit of his people, writing in the poem nine separate couplets, proclaiming his desire for Kurds to have a monarch. He stressed that amongst his people, a king should promote consciousness in order to solve their problems. In his view, a king should provide his subjects with the ability to gain some form of education and should encourage the advancement of the sciences. Moreover, the king should mint a Kurdish currency to enable trade and commerce, as well as providing sustenance for the poor.

Above all he believed that the king should enable the Kurds to stand amongst other nations so that they could be a people free from oppression and have autonomy to run their own affairs. In short he wanted a king to gain the faith of Kurds and provide them with leadership. It is clear that Xanî, in his writings, talked about most of the elements that were needed at the time for existence of a state. A reliable and firm leader was required, one with nationalist sentiments; expressing a desire that unity could be established amongst Kurds. He also acknowledged they might need a powerful international patron to achieve this:

Rabit ji me ji cîhanpenahek   To appear for us in the world a supporter,
Peyda bibitin me padişahek. [332]   To emerge among us a monarch.

---

[331] Yildirim, Kadri (2010). Op. cit, verse 5/31 219, p. 154.

[332] Ibid, verse 5/8 196, p. 152. Xanî, *Kurdistan*, newspaper, No. 8, p. 4.

He declared that it is natural to have an affinity within one's own society; repeatedly condemning the subordination of the Kurds, and lamenting that their leaders should share responsibility for the infliction of foreign subjugation on their people:

Xanî was the first writer to point out the strategic geo-political position of the Kurds between Ottomans and Persians. Xanî considered them to be trapped between the former, as their victims, and the latter as their occupiers. Emphasizing that the conflict between the two empires were not in the interests of the Kurds, he acknowledged that nevertheless they were embroiled in it. Thus, Xanî's poems reflected his ethno-nationalistic sentiments:

Her du terefan qebîlê kurmanc
Bo tîrê qeda kirine amanc
Goya ku li ser heddan kilîd in
Her taîfe seddek in sedîd in
Ev qulzumê Rom û behrê Tacîk
Gava ku dikin xurûc û tehrîk
 Kurmanc dibin bi xwûnê mulettex
Wan jêk ve dikin mîsalê berzex [333]

To both sides Kurdish people
were the targets of their arrows
Seen as keys to the border
Every tribe a dam in the frontier.
When the *qulzumê Rom* (Turks) and *behrê Tacîk* (Persians)
Come out to fight and make a move
Kurds are stained with blood
Being separated from each other by isthmus.

Despite the fact Xanî thought that Kurds were brave, kind, and resilient, he remained critical in his recognition of the disagreements between them. On occasion he expressed sorrow for the Kurds; suggesting that if Kurds were united, together they could have had freedom. [334]

---

[333] Ibid, verses 5/34 222-5/37 225, p. 155. Xanî, Ehmed, *Kurdistan*, newspaper, No. 8, 18th November, 1314, p. 4.
[334] Ibid, verses 5/45 233-5/46 234, pp. 155-156.

Ger dê hebûwa me serfirazek

Sahibkeremek suxennewazek

Neqdê me dibû bi sikke meskûk

Nedma wehe bêrewac û meşkûk [335]

If we had a victorious leader,

With generosity and sympathetic speech

We would have had our minted money

Would no longer remain valueless and dubious

Xalib nedibû li ser me ev Rûm

Nedibûne xerabeyeê di dest bûm[336]

Turks could not to dominate us

Our country would not have been in ruins.

Rasul (1989, p. 95) rightly states that "Xanî defines the essence of Kurdish question in his time by the control of the Ottoman and Persian empires on parts of Kurdistan and their attempts to destroy Kurdish emirates as wars were raging and Kurdish emirates were ruined to appear again." To confront this situation, Xanî stated his belief that if the Kurds had their own monarch and state, then the Turks, Arabs, and Persians would all accept to be the Kurds' servants

Ger dê hebûwa me îtîfaqek

Vêkra bikira me înqiyadek

Rom û ereb û ecem temamî

Hemiya ji me ra dikir xulamî[337]

Had we unity amongst us,

And we all subscribed to one idea

Then all the Turks, Persians and Arabs,

---

[335] Ibid, verse 5/11 199-5/12 200, p. 152. Xanî, *Kurdistan*, newspaper, No. 8, p. 4.

[336] Ibid, verse 5/18 206, p. 153.

[337] Ibid, verse 5/43 231-5/44 232, p. 155.

Would have worked for us like servants.

There are some elements in *Mem û Zîn* illustrating Xanî's thoughts towards the society of his time. He felt that the Kurdish *mirs* shamed themselves by accepting subjugation by Turks and Persians. He does not think that common people share the responsibility for this. Although the terms 'poets and poor people' may have had a different conception from what we have today, it is clear that he uses the names in contrast to the *mirs* and *hakims*: He writes:

Tab'iyetê wan eger çi `iare	Subordination to the occupier is shameful,
Ew `iari li xelqê namidare	It's the shame of notable people
Namûs e li hakim û emîran	Shame upon governors and princes
Tawan çî ye şa`ir û feqîran [338]	What is the crime of poets and poor people?

In the next verse he conceives of the Kurds as one single people; he says:

Da xelqi nebêjitin ku 'Ekrad	That people could not say Kurds
Bê me`irîfet in, bi esl û bunyad	have no education, origin and foundation
Enwa`iê milel xudankitêb in	All peoples have books,
Kurmanci tenê bêhisêb in [339]	Only Kurds are not counted.

Xanî used the word "*milal*" (Arabic for "millet"). *Milal* in the above verse refers to different ethnic peoples. Among all ethnic peoples, only Kurds do not have their own writing or books. In writing in Kurdish, Xanî was able to promote Kurdish identity and Kurdish literary heritage. Later Xanî praises the Kurdish language and describes every word of it as a jewel, and he believes that the Kurdish language is like a precious pearl, a language for identifying Kurdish people. He explains his project:

Safî şemirand vexwari durdî
Manendê durrê lisanê kurdî
Înaye nîzam u întîzamê
Kêşaye cefa ji boy `amê. [340]

---

[338] Ibid, 5/21 209-5/22 210, p. 153.
[339] Ibid, verse 6/6 240-6/7 241, pp. 157-8.

He took what is pure, drank the sediments

Like a pearl, he brought the Kurdish language

Into organisation and order.

He suffered for the sake of the general public.

He wrote in Kurdish, so that people could not say that Kurds have no awareness, and have no origin and foundation.[341] Therefore, Xanî considered Kurdish language to be a pillar of Kurdism.

3.20 Xanî's Use of *Mem û Zîn* to express Kurdish ~~National~~ Sentiment

A key issue is the use Xanî made of *Mem û Zîn* as a vehicle for his Kurdish sentiments.[342] It is apparent that he used it to appeal to Kurdish consciousness, in a hope that Kurdish sentiments would be aroused. Yet exactly what this meant to Xanî now is unclear; although often such references are present in his poem: *Mem û Zîn*. Xanî directly announces that he is a Kurd from mountains and he writes from his Kurdish soul. He express his commitment to Kurds and clarifies his position among his people, therefore, he is calling on them to accept his work and says:

Kurmanc im u, kûhî û kenarî
Van çend khabared Kurdewarî
Îmda bikirin bi husnê eltaf
Îsxa bikin ew bi sem'ê însaf[343]

I am Kurdish, coming from the foot of mountains

These tales from Kurdewari [Kurdish tradition]

Stamp them with your kind-heartedness

Listen to them with ears of fairness

---

[340] Ibid, verse 6/4 238-6/5 239, p. 157.
[341] Ibid, verse 6/6 240, p. 157. Da xelqi nebêjin ku "Erad   Bê me'rîfet in, bi esl û bunyad
[342] Ibid, verses 7/36 321-7/37 322, pp. 167.
[343] Ibid, verse. 7/72 357-7/73 358, p. 170.

Xanî finds that his mountain milieu is something to be proud of. He clearly states that he derived his work from the folk tales of *Kurdewari* which is a sociological word meaning the lands where Kurds live and practise their way of life.

Martin Van Bruinessen once thought:

"Around 1600 CE we encounter the first written expressions of a Kurdish ethnic awareness. The poet Ahmed-i Khani lamented in the prologue to his famous epic *Mem u Zin*…the dividedness of the Kurds which had caused them to be dominated and ruled by Turks and Persians."[344]

Several years later he remarked that:

"The seventeenth century Kurdish poet Ehmedê Xanî prefaced his epic … poem *Mem û Zîn* with a section entitled *'Derdê me'*('our ills') in which he lamented the Kurds' division , which caused them to be under the rule of the Ottomans and Safavids, or previous empires." [345]

His main criticism of Khani at this point is that: "…with Khani we do not yet find an idea capable of inspiring a popular movement…"[346]

Bruinessen, (2003:5) thought of Ehmedê Xanî as a patriot, but not a nationalist, asserting,
> "Xani was not a nationalist: a 'political principle that the political and national unit should be congruent'. He deplored the division of the Kurds….and he saw that this division had caused them to live as subjects to a neighbouring state which, had they been united, they might have conquered themselves."[347]

Indeed in the discussion, he pointed out that Xanî had proposed a king simply to help unify the Kurds. In fact he recognised these empires or kingdoms as:

---

[344] Bruinessen, Martin van (1989). *The Ethnic Identity of The Kurds in Turkey in* Ethnic Groups in the Republic of Turkey; PA Andrews, R Benninghaus - Dr Ludwig Reichert Verlag. This essay was recently reprinted in his *Collected Articles* Analecta Isisiana, Istanbul, 2000. pp. 13-25 the quote is on p.19 of the latter edition and available on the web at; http://www.let.uu.nl/~Martin.vanBruinessen/personal/publications/Bruinessen_Ethnic_identity_Kurds.pdf p.6.
[345] Bruinessen, Martin van (1992). P. 267.
[346]Iibid.
[347] Bruinessen, Martin van (2003). Op. cit, p. 45.

"...multi-ethnic, and if Ehmedi Xani was thinking of a state form when he longed for a Kurdish king, his state definitely was not a national state either but another multi-ethnic state...,"[348]

In an important essay, Abbas Vali indicated that Xanî had been manipulated by Jemal Nebez to assert "...his definition of the concept of Kurdish nationalism..."[349] For him Xanî supplies two basic elements of Nebez's postulation.

"...that the idea of Kurdish nationalism is 'indigenous', having existed at least since the early seventeenth century, and ...that Kurdish nationalism since its inception has aspired to a *national* state."[350]

He recognised this as a primordial concept of nation and 'nationalism', equating it "with the political-ideological aspirations and outlook of [Kurdistan's] rulers".[351] However, Xanî was not writing for modern readers or writers. He was formulating, as will be seen below, an argument for his own times.

Vali later posed an interesting and very fundamental question: "Why did Xanî's quest for a Kurdish monarch signify nationalism?"[352] Yet it was one he had already answered when he stated that "in pre-modern societies systems of belief and value, arising from or associated with religion, tradition, lineage and kinship play a major role in the constructions of domination and subordination and the mechanisms of legitimation of power". [353] Indeed Vali conceived a nation in modernist terms:

"...the nation-state is the territorial state *par-excellence*..[it is where] conditions of sovereignty and the conditions of territorial centralism do coincide" And thus he believes that "These conditions are produced by and rest on the modern capitalist economy."[354]

At the age of forty-four years,[355] Xanî had a considerable awareness of Kurdish history, along with a consciousness of the psychology of the Kurdish people and their society.[356]   In his

---

[348] Ibid p. 45.
[349] Vali, Abbas (Spring 1996). "Nationalism and Kurdish Historical Writing", *New Perspectives on Turkey*, No 14, p. 36.
[350] Vali, Abbas (2003). The article in note 115 was reprinted as Vali, Abbas, (2003). Genealogies of the Kurds: Constructions of Nation and National Identity in Kurdish Historical Writing p.91, in Vali, Abbas, (Ed) Essays on the Origins of Kurdish Nationalism, California, p.79.
[351] Vali, Abbas (Spring 1996). Op. cit, 37.
[352] Vali, Abbas (2003). Op. cit, p.91.
[353] Vali, Abbas (Spring 1996). Op. cit, pp. 40-1.
[354] Vali, Abbas (2003). Op. cit, p.80.

prologues "*Kul û derdê me Kurdan*" (our Kurdish difficulties) and "*Çima bi Kurdî nivîsiye?*" (Why I wrote in Kurdish?) Xanî used *me* "us" thirty-four times. Without doubt by using "us", he meant Kurds collectively: I and You or with You.

Xanî at the time was more of a scholar, there is no evidence that his ideas had any impact on Kurdish mirs and chieftains. Nor were his ideas were strong enough for them to establish an ideology for national movement as Bruinessen, stated that "…with Khani we do not yet find an idea capable inspiring a popular movement…."[357] As has been stressed before, this was not what Xanî was attempting to do. Indeed it says much for the value and integrity of Xanî's poem that it has struck such a chord across all Kurdish people that it is *now* one of a number of unifying factors amongst them. Xanî does not elaborate an ideology; he explains a reality and presents a convincing case for unity.

Indeed Bruinessen's thinking on Xanî and the question of Kurdish identity appears somewhat flawed as will be discussed below. In one article he states that "because of a few famous lines in *Mem û Zîn*, he could not conclude that Xanî had "thought of a Kurdish state."[358] Hassanpour also shares the same views as Bruinessen, towards Xanî and stressed that "we cannot conclude from a few famous lines in *Mem û Zîn* that Xanî thought of a Kurdish state."[359]

Xanî's ideas about Kurds were not written in only "a few lines" as Bruinessen, and Hassanpour suppose, but they were referred to in no fewer than ninety-seven poetic verses; for example see the section *Our Problems;* ll. 5/1 189-5/46 234[360] and *why I have written in Kurdish* ll. 6/1 235-6/51 285.[361] The text refers in many other places to what we may now call Kurdish nationalism. In fact, *Mem û Zîn* as a whole should be analysed in its entirety, and its verses cannot be separated from each others. Hence, the best way to understand *Mem û Zîn* is to explore the full meaning of each verse with reference to its other verses, without which comprehension of it would be more difficult and could lead to misinterpretation.

---

[355] *Kurdistan*, newspaper, No. 2, 6th May, 1898, p. 4. SOAS, University of London, Shelfmark Per 9L 411082. Another run of these are at the British Library Newspaper Repository.

[356] Rasul, Dr. Izzadin Mustafa (1979). *Ahmadi Khani*, Arabic text, al-Hawadith Press, Baghdad, pp. 155-72.

[357] Bruinessen, Martin van (1992). Op. cit, p. 267.

[358] Bruinessen, Martin van, Ehmedi Xanis *Mem û Zîn* and its Role in the Emergence of Kurdish National Awareness, in Abbas Vali, edited, Essay on the Kurdish Nationalism, Mazda Publishers, Inc., California, 2003, p. 41.

[359] Hassanpour, Amir, (2003). Ehmedi Xani's *Mem û Zîn* and Its Role in the Emergence of Kurdish National Awareness, in Abbas Vali, Essays on the Origins of Kurdish Nationalism, ibid, p. 41.

[360] Yildirim, Kadri (2010). Op. cit, pp. 151-156.

[361] Ibid, pp. 157-162.

Xanî uses the word *dewlet* on three occasions to mean "power". He believed that one of the basic elements for the creation of a state is military force. He says:

Herçî bire şîrî destê hîmmet
Zebt kir ji xwe ra bi mêrî dewlet[362]

All those who managed to hold the sword in the hand of courage
Have established a government state for themselves with dignity

In another verse he says:

Ez mame di hîkmeta Xwedê da
Kurmanc di dewleta dinê da
Aya bi çi wechî mane mehrûm
Bilcumle ji bo çi bûne mahmûm [363]

I am astonished that, by God's wisdom,
The Kurds among all the world's states
Have stayed deprived [of their own state]
They are collectively dominated [by others].

The usage of *dewlet* in the above texts demonstrates that he means by it the existence of state powers as opposed to the characteristics of personal courage and non-state ethnic force. He is clearly hurt by the division of Kurdistan between the Ottomans and Safavids; therefore, Xanî's attitude reflects his thoughts towards the two mentioned states that imposed their imperial will against Kurdish wishes. His third mention of *dewlet* will be discussed in more detail later.

Xanî was conscious of the distinction between Kurds and other people, such as Persians, Arabs and Turks and emphasised this distinct identity in his writing; it is important to bear in

---

[362] Ibid, verse 5/23 211, p. 153. Professor Izzaddin Mustafa Rasul (1979). also interpreted dewlet as state. see his book Ahmadi Khani, Arabic text, al-Hawadith press, Baghdad, p. 98.
[363] Yildirim, Kadri (2010). Op. cit, pp. 5/28 216-5/29 217, p. 154.

mind that Xanî's approach to the national state reflects his particular circumstances and environment.

Certainly Xanî seemed to understand the desires and aspirations of his people. He bemoaned the lack of a Kurdish leader to the detriment of the Kurdish people. On the one hand, he blamed historic circumstances, namely the reality of domination by others, for the failure of the Kurds to settle their own destiny. On the other hand he blamed the lack of concern and consciousness by Kurdish princes. In fact, he blames the ruling class (Kurdish *mirs*, princes) for all the faults of Kurdish nation and not "poets and the poor."

An expression of self-identity, whether it is through language or from any other element may be a function of the elite. In his writings, Xanî represented Kurdish thoughts, and provided an expression for Kurdish aspirations. However, this remained the essence of his stance. He was perceptive enough to understand that his job was limited to the encouragement of Kurdism. To others he left the task of taking up arms against those Arabs, Turks and Persians whom he thought were the occupiers of Kurdish lands.

3.21 Poets after Xanî

The poets also provided evidence of cross-references occurring between the works of different Kurdish poets, even where written in different dialects and in different periods. This establishes the phenomenon of Kurdish literature as an important national heritage and political factor. Hajî Qadir Koyî (1815-1898) on occasion cited writings of *Mela* Mustafai Bêsaranî (1642-1701). Other poets included Mirza Ya'qub and Ahmad Bagi Komasi who were Hewramî. Mawlana Khalidî Naqishbandî, Nalî (1797-1869) and Kurdi wrote in Soranî as they originated from Silêmanî.[364]

Khana-i Qubadî (1704–1778)[365], was a very well known Kurdish poet, who wrote *Şirin û Xusraw* in 5526 verses. *Şirin û Xusraw* was an oral tradition of love and tragedy. Qubadi turned this into a written poem. He quite plainly stated that his work was written as an expression of his Kurdishness and part of his patriotic duty. Being proud of his Gorani-

---

[364] Xeznedar (2004). *Mêjui Edebi Kurdî*, Kurdish text, The History of Kurdish Literature: 14 -18th Centuries, Forth Volume, Aras Publishers House, Erbil-Kurdistan, p. 127.
[365] Xeznedar (2002). Op. cit, p. 73.

Kurdish mother-tongue, he lauded its merits in his work:

Rastan mwachan Farsi shakaran,

Kurdi ja Farsi bal shirintaran,

Pay chesh? Na dawran ai dinyai badkesh,

Mahzuzan harkas ba zuban wesh,

Ma'luman harkas ba har zubane,

Bwacho nazmi ja har makane[366]

The saying that "the Persian language is sugar" is true.

But Kurdish is much sweeter than Persian,

Why is it that, in the twists of this unfair world,

Those who use their own language are lucky?

All those endowed with a language

They write verses in that language anywhere.

For Qubadî, a good poem needed elements of both beauty and quality, sought after by anyone with reasonable taste and some poetic expertise. Qubadî emphasized quality and beauty in his Kurdish poems. He stressed that:

Ja kay khiradmand dl pasand mbo,	A wise man accepts things of high-quality,
Shirintar ja shahd shirai qand mbo,	Sweeter than pure sugar are good poems
Ja arsai dnyai dun bad farjam,	In this broader world,
Ba dastur nasm (Nizami) taqam,	According to arts of poetry of "Nizami',[367]
Ba lafz Kurdi, Kurdistan mamam,	I have written poems in Kurdish for all of Kurdistan,
Pesh bwan mahzuz, baqi wasalam.[368]	To make my people satisfied, this is all I want.

Khana-i Qubad Qubadî was proud of his linguistic heritage. The Kurdish people would cherish their linguistic national identity, which in time would help them to feel differentiated from others. Qubadî believed that Hewrami, his native dialect, should be used over and above

---

[366] Qubad-i, Khana (1975). Shirin u Xosraw, Kurdish text, The Masterpiece of the Eminent Kurdish Poet, Collation, Glossary and Introduction by Muhammad i Mela Karim, Kurdish Academy Press, Baghdad, p. 14.

[367] Nizami (1140-1203) was one of greatest and famous Persian who had great impact on Persian poets.

[368] Qubadi, Khana (1975). Op.cit, p. 15.

other regional languages; such as Arabic, Persian and Turkish. In the above verses, he stressed, moreover, that Kurdish should be used throughout Kurdistan. One interpretation of this could be seen as an indication, during Khana's lifetime, that Kurdish identity was already evolving; albeit a development that occurred whilst he lived in a region of the Erdelan Emirate, then under Persian dominance.

Some poets chose to write in two Kurdish dialects. For instance, Seyyid Ya'qub's (1802–1875) work was written in both the Kalhor and Soranî dialects.[369, 370] Feqê Qadiri Hemewend (1830–1889), was another Kurdish poet, who wrote in Hewrami dialect; following the example of his master Khana-i Qubadi. He expressed his pride in the use of the language. He insisted that when it was used, the same standards should be maintained as by those who produced masterpieces in the Persian language:

Chun Farsi biyan pandi hakiman,	As Persian became an example for wise men,
Ba lafzi Kurdi kardm tarjuman. [371]	I translated it to Kurdish words.

However, these were exceptions to the general rule of writing in only one Kurdish dialect.

3.22 Conclusion

Dimdim and *Mem û Zîn* are clearly, in both oral tradition and written literature, two powerful examples of the expression of Kurdish identity and desire for freedom from foreign occupation and domination. Both can now be found in different Kurdish dialects, and remain popular amongst the new generation, providing inspiration for nationalist campaigns. In *Dimdim*, Amir Khan attempted to continue his rule amongst Kurds in *Baradost* region. This brought him into conflict with Shah Abbas of Persia. They had different aims in governing the people. The Kurdish Amir wanted to preserve Kurdish autonomy. Dimdim is a powerful reflection of Kurdish identity, distinctiveness and determination to resist occupation and subjugation.

---

[369] Ibid, pp.77-88.
[370] Xeznedar (2002). Op. cit, pp. 115-117.
[371] Muhammad, Anwar Qadir (2004). edited, Cend Witareki Kurdnasi, Kurdish text, Few essays about Kurdology, Serdem Publishers, Silêmanî, p. 28.

Kurdish language as we have seen in this chapter was an important element in the process of the development of Kurdism. Historically, as we can see from the writings quoted in this chapter, Kurds maintained their ethnic distinctiveness from their rulers. Their attitude towards the Ottomans and Persians was one of hostility. They insisted on sustaining the vital elements of Kurdish life. They valued especially their way of life, language and literature.

Education in Kurdish *medreses* had played a significant role in Kurdish society. *Medreses* helped tie together Kurdish scholars and their *feqês* from different districts of Ottoman and Safavid Kurdistan. Kurdish identity was promoted through poems and during travelling and meetings. There were a few Kurdish scholars and poets who praised and promoted Kurdish language and culture, such as Melayê Cizîrî in the sixteenth century, which paved the road for Xanî to do the same.

The self-rule of Kurdish emirates and self-consciousness of being a Kurd prompted Sharafkhan to write a methodological history of his people. For the first time, he defined the words Kurd, Kurdistan and Kurdish language as historical realities. Although he wrote his work in Persian, his content was consciously Kurdist.

During the sixteenth century, the Ottoman and Persian Empires encouraged the Kurds to take their respective sides, whilst preventing them from becoming powerful in their own right. In Ottoman and Persian Kurdistan, the dominant languages were either Turkish or Farsi. The influence of these languages was concomitant with the imperial power of the two rival empires. This led to Xanî to establish the use of these languages for literature, wisdom, sciences and administration. Accordingly, Xanî identified the marginalisation of Kurdish language as a vehicle of knowledge and education as a salient indicator of Kurdish subjugation. Xanî found that the flourishing of Persian and Turkish civilizations, language and literature was the direct result of their having a *dewlet*. The Kurds' lack of *dewlet* was both a result of the occupation and domination of the Kurdish people and of lack of unity. Xanî thought that using Kurdish language for education and knowledge could provide a strong basis for Kurdish identity and differentiation from other groups. He wrote a small Kurdish-Arabic dictionary for Kurdish children first. However, in his project of writing *Mem û Zîn* in Kurdish he went much further. He made this a pretext to express his concerns about the whole Kurdish situation trapped between the oppression and wars of two empires on the one hand, and lack of unity and lack of awareness and enthusiasm for sovereignty by Kurdish mirs and governors on the other. He derived his poetical story from a known Kurdish oral tradition, expressing his concerns, views and vision for the future of his people. His use of Kurdish language is what has made Xanî's poem a pioneering seminal work. His realistic assessment of Kurdish woes and realities instead of producing an ideology is what makes Xanî both an inspiration and a point of unity for all the Kurds who proudly identify with his sentiments and dreams while understanding the complexity of his arguments.

Xanî was a scholar and a poet who expressed his thoughts and ambitions, but lacked the backing of figures of authority. His duties were giving advice, awakening people and encouraging them to achieve what other peoples had achieved. If Kurds had been free from the oppressive rule of the Turks and Persian and had been united under a king, with their own currency, fully developed language and culture, then Kurdistan would have had the foundations for the establishment of its own *dewlet* similar to those of the Turks and Persians. However, the thoughts expressed by Xanî over three hundred years ago about the specific situation of the Kurds and his working out of the elements that could help the Kurds to establish unity against the other and attain sovereignty, are advanced enough to be compared with modern ideas of nationalism. After Xanî, other Kurdish poets continued to write in Kurdish. Khana-i Qubadi and Feqê Qadiri Hemewend were among those who expressed their pride in the Kurdish language and their desire that it should be used more widely.

These works read individually and together, provided a strong base, context and background for Kurdism. They articulated Kurdish identity and the will to express freedom by using Kurdish language. They provide ideas, legends, symbols and collective memories that constitute the particular cultural heritage of Kurdish people.

Chapter Four

The Soran Emirate and its contribution to Kurdism

4.1 Introduction

This chapter deals with the rise of the Kurdish Emirate of Soran under the charismatic and powerful *Mir* Muhammad who later became Pasha (1813-1836). It will first present the background of the emirate, the process of the Pasha's military expansion and international reactions to his military adventures and then focus in detail upon his internal administration. It will present the necessary conditions that the Pasha created for the advancement of Kurdism and the emergence of the strong ideas associated with Kurdish patriotism and Kurdish self-awareness from which later Kurdish nationalism has emerged. This will be shown through the analysis of the works of two prominent scholars and an emerging Kurdish nationalist poet.

It will be argued that during the reign of Muhammad Pasha, Kurdism was based on the reforms to the Ottoman army which had begun during the reign of Sultan Salim and continued under Sultan Mahmud to include centralisation of the administration and education. At the very end of the Soran Emirate, these centralization policies played a negative role. The Kurdish language was a major element by which Kurdish scholars could identify with others, including dominant groups. The next element was locality; Kurds who were under the influence of the emirates were loyal to their tribal leaders and the Mir of their emirate. Thus, a long period of rebellion and revolts against central authority proved that Kurds did not have a serious sense of loyalty towards the Sultan and his government.

In this chapter, two features of Kurdism will be emphasised in relation to the Soran Emirate. Firstly, how Muhammad Pasha's government was able to safeguard Kurdish self-rule in the face of the centralization policies of the government and secondly, the important role played by Kurdish scholars and poets in fostering the notion of Kurdism. These individuals include *Mela* Muhammad Ibnu Adam (1750-1844) who lived during the reign of the Soran Pasha, Hajî *Mela* Abdullah Jelizade (1834-1903) whose writings were influenced by the notions of

Kurdish self-awareness which had emerged during the reign of Muhammad Pasha and Hajî

Qadiri Koyî (1815–1897) who wrote most of his work after the end of the Soran Emirate.

4.2 A short historical background of Rewanduz (Soran) and Muhammad Pasha

Soran, whose capital was Rewanduz, was one of the Kurdish Emirates which came into

existence towards the end of the sixteenth century. It was first mentioned in the *Sharafnama*

(completed in 1596) that the Soran dynasty was established by Kelos who had three sons. His

son Isa was brave, generous, and an influential leader who managed to gather people around

him and create local self-rule.[372] After the Battle of Chaldiran in 1514, the Ottomans

succeeded in dominating a large part of Kurdistan; however, the Soran Emirate remained in

existence until 1836.

After Chaldiran, Soran became a very influential emirate, against the wishes of the Ottomans.

In 1534, Sulaiman the Magnificent (1520-1566) recognised the rapid rise of the Soran

Emirate. To prevent it from becoming a force of resistance and a threat to his authority, he

killed Ezzaddin Shêr, the Soran prince, and gave its government to Husein Beg of the Yezidi

Dasini.[373]

The rule of the Yezidis did not last long. Seyfeddin, son of Mir Husein of Soran (with the

assistance of Bega Beg of Erdelan) regained power from Husein Beg of the Yezidi Dasini.

However, he was deceived and went back to Istanbul where he was killed by Sultan

Sulaiman,[374] After a while, Quli Beg, son of Sileman Beg, another prince of Soran (who left

Soran for Persia during the Yezidis' rule), was asked to return by the Soran tribes to assume

power.[375]

---

[372] Bidlisi, Sharafkhan (1343). *Sharafnama*, Persian text, edited by Muhammad Abbasi, published by Elmi, Tehran, pp. 352-3; Also see Rawlinson, Major H. C. (1841). "Note on a Journey from Tabriz, through Persian Kurdistan, to the Ruins of Takhti-Soleiman, and from thence by Zenjan and Tarom, to Jilan, in October and November 1838; with a Memoir on the Site of the Atropatenian Ecbatana", *The Journal of the Royal Geographical Society of London*, Volume Ten, p. 24 who stated that "the chief of Soran conquered the Rewanduz country between 400 and 500 years ago." By this account we understand that the existence of the Soran Emirate can be traced back to thirteenth or fourteenth centuries.

[373] Bidlisi, Sharafkhan (1343). Ibid, p. 356. Huzni, Husein (1962). *Mejui Mirani Soran*, Kurdish text, *History of the Princes of the Soran Emirate*, second addition, Kurdistan Press, Hawler, , p. 7. Yezidi (Ezidi in Kurdish) is a heterodox religion and exists only among the Kurds. It differs from Islam, the main stream religion of the Kurds. Yezidis speak Kurmanji and live mainly in Sinjar, Shaikhan and Ba'shiqe in Iraqi Kurdistan, their holy place being the Shrine of Sheikh Adi (d.circa 1075-January 1862) at Lalish, north-east of Mosul. There are also Yezidis living in Tor Abdin near Batman in Turkish Kurdistan. Some also live in Armenia, Georgia and Germany. Their main belief is the transmigration of souls. Yezidis are not considered "People of the Book", giving them a rather different legal status in the past from Muslims, Christians and Jews. According to Christine Allison in the past Yezidis have been described by people of other religions, and by European travellers as "devil worshippers. See Allison, Christine (2001). The Yezidi Oral Tradition in Iraqi Kurdistan, Curzon, London, p.26

[374] Bidlisi, Sharafkhan (1343). Ibid, p. 358.

[375] Ibid, p. 359.

Around 1813, Muhammad Pasha took control of Soran from his weakened father. Baillie Fraser recounted that his predecessor was "incapable of conducting the affairs of the tribe in [such] troublesome times." He quickly took the opportunity to gain supremacy and control over his native district, Rewanduz.[376] He was now unopposed and able to achieve his key objective: to become Pasha of the Soran Emirate, with its capital in Rewanduz.

At the beginning of the nineteenth century, after the Ottoman - Russian war in 1806-12, the Ottomans were very weak internally and externally. Later, the Ottomans became even weaker due to several serious events. Firstly, there was another war with Russia between 1828 and 1829 during which Kurdish emirates Botan, Hakkari, Soran, and Baban did not side with the Ottoman Empire. The Ottomans lost some territory in Anatolia including some parts of Kurdistan.[377] Secondly, there was the Egyptian expedition of Muhammad Ali Pasha under his son Ibrahim Pasha against the Ottomans and the Egyptian victory at Konya in October 1832.[378] When Sultan Mahmud II (1808-1839) came to power, he consciously and carefully followed in the steps of Sultan Selim III (1787-1807) to reform the Ottoman army. He managed to destroy Janissary corps, the old Ottoman army, and restored reform through attempting to establish the *Nizam-i Cedit* army. As a result of these circumstances, Sultan Mahmud II established "direct Imperial control in Eastern Anatolia, Armenia, and Kurdistan."[379] This situation encouraged Muhammad Pasha of Soran to resist and to extend his territories to gain stronger local power, by imposing his power on many tribes including Baradost, Surchi, Mamash and Shirwan.[380]

During the rule of Muhammad Pasha (1813-1836), a new phase of relations was instigated. Muhammad Pasha's era is generally seen as a Kurdish attempt to maintain Kurdish regional rule, distinct from the Ottoman Empire. Richard Wood, the British diplomat in Baghdad confirmed that Muhammad Pasha was very strong, writing: "Ravandooz Bey, the strongest of his opponents...the Pasha of Bagdad, confirmed as 'Miri Miran' or Pasha of One Tail, by the

---

[376] Fraser, J. Baillie (1840). *Travel in Koordistan, Mesopotamia, &c. Including an account of parts of those countries hitherto unvisited by Europeans, with sketches of the character and manners of the Koordish and Arabs*, Volume I, Richard Bentley, London, p. 64.

[377] Monteith, W. (1851). *Kars and Erzeroum with the Campaigns of Prince Paskiewich*, Brown, Green and Longmans, London, pp. 154, 221, 262-5 and 302. Allen, W. E. D. and Muratoff, P. (1953). Caucasian Battlefields: A History of War on the Turco-Caucasian Border, Cambridge University Press, Cambridge, pp. 31, 44.

[378] Longrigg, Stephen H. (1925). *Four Centuries of Modern Iraq*, Clarendon Press, Oxford, p. 274.

[379] Lewis, Bernard (1968). *The Emergence of Modern Turkey*, second edition, Oxford University Press, London, p. 104. For more details see Shaw, Stratford J., & Shaw, Ezel Kural (1977). *History of the Ottoman Empire and Modern Turkey, Reform, Revolution, an Republic, The Rise of Modern Turkey 1808-1975*, Volume II, Reform, Revolution, and Republic, Cambridge University Press, Cambridge, pp. 1-172.

[380] McDowall, David (2004). *A Modern History of the Kurds*, I. B. Tauris, London, p. 42.

Sultan's Commission."[381] Furthermore, Wood stated that the Soran Pasha was "Too powerful to be intimidated by the Pashas of Moussoul and Bagdad who in fact stood in awe of him."[382] McDowall suggests that "it was undeniable that he had - once the ruins of his punitive work had ceased to smoulder – imposed on his territories a level of law and order unknown for generations."[383] Van Bruinessen considers Muhammad Pasha of Rewanduz to be one of the Kurdish *mirs* who renewed the old glory of their emirates, extended the Soran territories and revolted against central authority.[384]

Muhammad Pasha was an educated man and aware of affairs beyond his region. Dr Ross who was sent to him by Major Taylor, the British resident in Baghdad on his demand found that the Pasha made many enquiries regarding education in England and also about religion in India and China. In addition, the Pasha wanted to know the relationship between England, Persia and Russia and on another occasion the Pasha asked about the uses and effects of medicine and cholera. Later Dr Ross found that Muhammad Pasha had guns and pistols in his tent. He saw that Muhammad Pasha had an old English double-barrelled gun and a rifle. Dr Ross also mentioned a sword, a telescope, an umbrella, a wooden bed, and carpets amongst Muhammad Pasha's possessions.[385]

Muhammad Pasha's successes, and those of Bedir Khan and the Baban Pashas, will be detailed in the next chapters. These laid the foundation for the development of 'Kurdism' in the early nineteenth century, not least for the inspiration they gave to Hajî Qadir, a poet who exerted influence on the Kurdish national movement which developed in the later half of the century. Most Kurdish clans were spread across the borders of several territories and kingdoms before the Soran Emirate expanded. An Emirate with extended borders gave the Kurds a voice through a semi-independent authority that provided them with control of their regional affairs.

Muhammad Pasha's ruthlessness helped his ascension to power. He also had ambitions to extend his national territories to rule a bigger part of Kurdistan. Fraser, recounting his travels in the region during the rise of the Pasha, suggested that a number of events led to the

---

[381] FO 78/277 From Richard Wood to Lord Ponsonby, Moussoul, No. 11, 28th June 1836. Jwaideh, Wadie (2006). *The Kurdish national movement: Its origins and development*, Syracuse University Press, Syracuse, New York, new edition, p. 56.
[382] FO 78/277 From Richard Wood to Lord Ponsonby, Moussoul, No. 11, 28th June 1836.
[383] McDowall, David (2004). Op. cit, p. 43.
[384] Bruinessen, Martin van (1992). *Agha, Shaikh and State*, Zed Books Ltd, London, p.176.
[385] Fraser, J. Baillie (1840). Op. cit, pp. 77-8.

consolidation of the Mir's military gains: "…the war between Persia and Russia, when the Prince Royal who had made some dispositions to crush the *Mir*, was forced to withdraw his troops in order to concentrate them against more formidable foes."[386]

Fraser showed how the *Mir* took advantage of the situation. He "…not only retook all the territory of which he had been deprived by the Prince", but also "obtained control over … the districts extending from Erbile (Arbela) to Kirkuk, inclusive, on the east of the Tigris."[387] In short, the Soran Emirate under Muhammad Pasha managed to rule a wide area "from Ushnei to the Tigris, and as far south as the lesser Zab, was subjected to his rule."[388]

It seems that the *Mir* of Soran was keen to establish a just and efficient Kurdish administration, managing to annex further territories. In 1830, Richard Wood in a letter to Norris (Chief Secretary to the government in Bombay) also described the *Mir*'s treatment of his subjects and his character: "[He]…is of distinguished personal courage and decision, his government is mild, his taxation light, his treatment of Merchants [*sic*] and artisans and soldiers is generous and enlightened; in case of robbery within his districts he repays their loss…"[389] Muhammad Pasha became so powerful that Ali Pasha of Baghdad recognised his power and sent him a special dress of investiture.[390] This will be discussed in the next section.

4.3 Effects of a Strong Army

As an ambitious man, Muhammad Pasha wished to build a strong infrastructure, and used his country's resources to build a strong army, enabling him to acquire the power to withstand both the Ottomans and Persians. He sought to establish a new system of recruitment that enabled him to form a strong army.[391] He ensured that the developing army had a plentiful supply of artillery and ammunition, which he achieved by founding ordinance works, placing his emirate in an enviable position.[392] They depended on no country but their own for the supply of all their wants. Everything they required was produced at home, and while their

---

[386] Ibid, p. 64.

[387] Ibid.

[388] Rawlinson, Major H. C. (1841). Op. cit, 1841, p. 24.

[389] IOR L/PS/9/91 p. 403.

[390] IOR L/PS/9/93. Major Taylor, R., the British Political Agent in Baghdad to Charles Norris the Chief Secretary to Government Bombay, Baghdad, 26th April 1832, p. 355. TBL, London.

[391] Huzni, Husein (1962). Op. cit, pp. 46-9.

[392] Huzni, Husein (1962). Iibid. Dr. Jamal Nabaz (1994). *al-Amir al-Kurdi*, Kurdish text, *The Kurdish Amir*, Published by Kurdish Academy for Science and Art, Hewler, p. 110. Dr. Jalili Jalil, (1987). *Kurdekani Empratoryeti Usmani*, Kurdish text, The Kurds of the Ottoman Empire, translated from Russian, annotations and presentation by Dr Qawis Qaftan, Al-Hurriah Printing House, Baghdad, pp. 141-2.

mountains formed impregnable defences against invaders, their rugged sides and valleys, with little effort, produced an abundance of everything they desired to cultivate, and also afforded a never-failing supply of wood, water, and pasture.[393]

Muhammad Pasha's concern with the army was described by two British army officers, Lieutenant Colonel Shiel and Major Rawlinson. Shiel was in Kurdistan in July and August 1836 and wrote: "It seemed to be the Mir's plan to retain his subjects in good order by taking a male from each family into his service."[394] Major Rawlinson also was travelling in Kurdistan in October and November 1836, he too understood that: "The Mir of Rowandiz [*sic*] brought them [tribesmen] under his sway; and taking a male from each family into his service, as was his usual custom, the Balik tribe contingent proved of great service to him."[395] The armed forces of the Soran emirate were so powerful that Muhammad Pasha took Herir, Erbil and Altun Kopri and established his power in those cities and forced the Ottoman Wali of Baghdad to recognize his rule.[396]

By the start of 1832, the strength of the troops of the Soran Emirate meant that they had advanced on the districts of Mosul, over which they then seized control, without the Baghdad government being able to resist.[397] By 1835, the British officer Major Taylor, the British Political Agent in Baghdad[398], estimated that the Soran army numbered "...not less than 80,000 mountaineers...the resources of a country scarcely penetrable by the enemy"[399], an apparent exaggeration.

For many years, such a presence caused regional powers to hesitate before they mounted an attack. In many cases, the army of the Soran Emirate was stronger than theirs and on occasions when they mounted campaigns, they sought out Soran's support. This led them to appease Muhammad Pasha and his expansionist ambitions.

Through his army, Muhammad Pasha wanted to show his sense of belonging to the Kurds. Hence, he purposely chose Kurdish ethnic costume for his army with the particular uniform

---

[393] Fraser, J. Baillie (1840). Op.cit, p.74.
[394] Lieut. Col. Shiel (1838). "Notes on a Journey from Tabriz, through Kurdistan, via Van, Bitlis, Se'ert and Erbil, to Suleimaniyeh, in July and August 1836", *The Journal of the Royal Geographical Society of London*, Volume Eight, p. 98.
[395] Rawlinson, Major H. C. (1841). Op. cit, p. 26.
[396] Longrigg, Stephen H. (1925). Op. cit, p. 285.
[397] IOR L/PS/9/93 Major Taylor, R. to Charles Norris, Chief Secretary to the Government of Bombay, Baghdad, 26th April 1832, pp. 354-5.
[398] IOR L/PS/9/99, Lt. Col. W. Taylor, Memorandum, Baghdad, February, 1836.
[399] IOR L/PS/ 9/99, p. 809.

worn by each soldier corresponding to his rank.[400] It is uncertain whether Muhammad Pasha

and his administration knew anything about the theory of Kurdism, but they certainly had a

sense of community and togetherness. Theories must reflect reality not the other way round;

indeed, Anthony Smith illustrates that people's thoughts and behaviour are more important

than ideology. He explains: "It [notion of identity] relates mainly to a sense of community

based on history and culture, rather than to any collectivity or to the concept of ideology."[401]

Here, the use of Kurdish costume by the Pasha for his troops' uniforms was at least an

assertion of his distinctive Kurdish identity and consciousness, simply because Kurdish dress

is part of Kurdish heritage which in Smith's words' "frequently provide us with clues about

thoughts, feelings and attitudes of communities."[402]

The Pasha of Soran attempted to regain "many lost portions of Kurdistan" and brought them

"into union with his Emirate."[403] The expansion and power of Soran was counted as a real

threat by all other powers in the region, especially the Ottomans and the Persians. According

to N. Turner, the British Consul General in Damascus, the Rewanduz Pasha "took thirty

villages from Persian territories."[404] The Ottomans were confronted by twin threats: the

Kurds and the Egyptians. Both Russia and Britain were also wary.[405] Two main options were

available for the Ottomans. They could either confront this danger or yield to it. They chose

the former. At an opportune moment, the regional powers decided to act in unison to defeat

Muhammad Pasha of Soran.

The Pasha of Rewanduz existed in a state of constant warfare with his neighbours. He paid

little attention, or regard, either to the Pasha of Baghdad (Ali Reda Pasha, 1831–1846) or the

Sultan at Constantinople.[406] He concentrated his efforts in developing an independent

Kurdistan. Therefore, he directed his forces against the Ottoman Empire and took over Upper

Mesopotamia, Erbil and Kirkuk.[407] To further consolidate the emirate, the Mir regained Harir

---

[400] Fraser, J. Baillie (1840). Op. cit, p. 51. According to Huzni, Muhammad Pasha introduced Kurdish costume for his military forces. Each regiment had some clothing which differentiated them from one another, for example: high ranks had cloth spun from goat's wool, with one white and one black stripe on their sleeves, with a special high hat. The infantry wore yellow *rank u chogha* (top and baggy trousers) and a khaki hat; Cavalry forces wore *rank u chogha* in various colours with a dotted pattern and so on. Huzni, Husein (1962). Op. cit, p. 51.
[401] Smith, Anthony D. (1999). *The Ethnic Origins of Nations*, Basil Blackwell, Oxford, p. 14.
[402] Ibid.
[403] IOR L/PS/9/97A Lt. Col. Taylor to the Secret Committee of the East India House-London, Baghdad, 26th November 1834, pp. 517-520. TBL.
[404] IOR L/PS/9.99 Turner, N. to the Secretary Committee, Damascus, 16th August, 1936, p. 177. TBL, London.
[405] IOR L/PS/9/100 In a long dispatch by N. W. Werry, the British Consul General in Aleppo to Lord Ponsonby, the British Ambassador at Constantinople on December 3rd, 1836 we find that the Soran Emirate became so strong that the Russians and British became wary about his power and attitude, pp. 833-854.
[406] Sykes, Lt Col Sir Mark (1915). *The Caliphs' Last Heritage: A short history of the Turkish Empire*, Macmillan and Co., Limited, London, p. 319.
[407] Soane, E. B. (1979). *To Mesopotamia and Kurdistan in Disguise*, arrangement with John Murray Ltd, London, p. 372.

from the Baban Emirate. He also added to his domains: Erbil, Altun Kupri, Koye and Raniya. In so doing he managed to establish the lesser Zab as Soran's frontier.[408]

In the beginning of the 1830's, the power of Rewanduz reached its strongest point and to some extent, the emirate could defend its territories. In a despatch by Major R. Taylor, the British Political Agent in Baghdad confirmed that the Rewanduz Pasha attempted to bring "lost portions of Kurdistan into union with this prince again."[409] These portions were Harir and Koye. Thus from 1833, the Soran Emirate, until its downfall, managed to maintain independence against both the Ottoman and Persia, in the process earning great respect by Kurds.[410]

Major Taylor thought that the Pasha had established a secure power base: "This Prince enjoys a splendid reputation, [with] a solid power [base] and so superior a mind that I will lose no time, nor spare any endeavour to attract his regard and attachment to our nation."[411] He also pointed out that the benign administration of Kurdistan by the Bey had drawn people under his wing.[412]

It is important to establish, that in the mind of at least one of his commanders Rewanduz Beg was struggling for Kurdish autonomy. Many years later, his brother, Rasul Pasha, conveyed to Frederic Millingen the idea that; "With an aspiring genius he had conceived the *grande idée* of emancipating his country from the authority of the sultans, and of consolidating the power of his family. Uniting the qualities of a conqueror and of a legislator, Mehemet Pasha succeeded in extending his sway over the neighbouring provinces of Kerkuk[*sic*] and Mussul [*sic*], and in gathering under his flag a large number of Koordish [*sic*] troops."[413] All the efforts of Muhammad Pasha were to make Rewanduz an influential centre of power, and therefore, he directed his forces against the Ottoman Empire and took over Upper Mesopotamia, Erbil and Kirkuk.[414]

---

[408] Al-Damaloji, Sidiq (1999). *Emarat Bahdinan al-Kurdiya*, Arabic text, *Badinan the Kurdish Emirate*, Second Addition, Aras Press, Erbil, p. 39.
[409] IOR L/PS/9/13, A despatch from Lt-Col R. Taylor, The British Political Agent to the Secret Committee East India House London, Baghdad, 26th November 1834, p. 518. TBL, London.
[410] Rawlinson, Major H. C. (1841). Op. cit, p. 25.
[411] IOR L/PS/9/91 Taylor, R., the British Political Agent to Charles Norris the Chief Secretary to the Government of Bombay, Baghdad, 23rd December 1830, pp. 366/9. TBL. London.
[412] Ibid, pp. 386/8.
[413] Millingen, Major Frederick (1870). *Wild Life Among The Koords*, Hurst and Blackett Publishers, London, p.185.
[414] Soane, E. B, Op. cit, p. 372.

Fraser recounted that Muhammad Pasha numbered Arabs amongst his tenants and that they preferred to live under his rule rather than to contest their former lands with another Arab tribe: "The country around Erbile is let out by the Pasha to the Sheikhs, in districts, after the manner of the feudal system. The Thye, or Taee Arabs", who had been driven across the Tigris by the more powerful tribe of Jebrah took refuge with Soran Emirate, and became subject to the Pasha sending "a large contingent to his army."[415]

Rasul Beg, the younger brother of Muhammad Pasha, when talking to Major Millingen many years after the collapse of the Soran Emirate, emotionally and sorely said "Times have changed". He proudly portrayed the glorious days of the Soran Emirate when he said: "I know that I am good for nothing; where are those days when, with lance in rest, I could crush a lot of ruffians under the hoofs [*sic*] of my horse? Now it is for them to rule the world."[416]

In the above statement, Rasul Beg expressed his sense of belonging to the Soran Kurds, when they were ruling themselves and were free from the power of the central government. He also articulated his hatred towards the Ottoman authorities. This proved that Kurds in the Soran did not integrate into the Ottoman state, because through many centuries of Ottoman rule, they could not build up a sense of community between the Kurds and the dominant ruler. Kurds remembered their happiness under Soran and other Kurdish emirates. Therefore, they did not welcome the Ottoman officials. Remembering the past is important for keeping one's own history in mind.

4.4 Some other important aspects of Soran Emirate

With the strong force that Muhammad Pasha established, he managed to produce stability in his emirate. He had some sort of *majlis* (council) to make decisions and to run his territory. Muhammad Pasha set up an administration with many notables and knowledgeable people.[417] Muhammad Pasha was the *mir* and commander of the Soran army, his brother Rasul Beg was his general-in-chief,[418] Ahmad Beg became *serhengi serhengan* (head of the colonels). There were six colonels in the Soran army, *wasta* (mastar) Rejeb, was responsible for artillery and

[415] Fraser, J. Baillie (1840). Op. cit, p. 74.
[416] Millingen, Major Frederick (1870). Op. cit, p. 188.
[417] Huzni, Husein (1962). Op. cit, p. 49. Nabaz , Dr Jemal (1994). Op.cit, p. 45.
[418] Millingen, Major Frederick (1870). Op. cit, p. 185. Fraser, J. Baillie (1840). Op. cit, p. 72. Huzni, Husein (1962). Op. cit, pp. 49.

ammunitions, *westa* Braymi Mawêli was chief of architecture, Hajî Mustafa Agha was chief trader. They met once a week to discuss Soran's affairs and make decisions.[419]

Furthermore, Muhammad Pasha was interested in the connection between different parts of his emirate. When he expanded the territory of Soran, he gave attention to building many bridges across the main rivers in different districts of Soran. Huznî, a Kurdish historian, has stated that Muhammad Pasha constructed fifteen bridges.[420] Nearly all of these bridges remain in position today over the rivers such as Rewanduz, Xelekan, Heware Kon, Nawprdan and Rayat. Another remarkable feature of his rule was the establishment of peace and security for his people both at home when travelling across his land. The Soran Kurds regarded this as an important tool for creating highly positive relations between the ruler and population. Taylor, a British resident in Baghdad at the time, observed that Muhammad Pasha of Soran's:

> "government is mild, his taxation light, his treatment of merchants and artisans and solders is generous and enlightened in case of robbery within his districts he repays the loss, and is so rapid and indefatigable of them, that he has succeeded in establishing a security of transit throughout his land quite unknown in any other portion of the tract of country between the Aras and the Euphrates and which has made it no eastern hyperbole to say, as the natives of these countries do, 'that you may travel through his territory in safety though laden with gold and jewels'."[421]

A very interesting division was made during Muhammad Pasha's era. He agreed with his *mufti* (Chief of Religion) *Mela* Muhammadi Xatê not to interfere in his affairs. In other words, the decision was to leave political affairs and the Soran Emirate administration to Muhammad Pasha, whilst placing religious affairs in the hands of *Mela* Muhammad.[422] Later in the next section, more detail will be provided relating to the role of *Mela* Muhammadi Xatê and the plight of Yezidîs.

---

[419] Huzni, Husein (1962). Op. cit, pp. 49-50.
[420] Ibid, pp.51-2.
[421] IOR L/PS/9/91 R. Taylor to Charles Norris, the Chief Secretar to Government in Bombay, No. 36, Baghdad, 23rd December 1830, pp. 386/8-386/9.
[422] Muhammad, Mas'ud (1974). *Hajî Qadri Koyî*, Kurdish text, Part 2, Published by Kurdish Academy, Baghdad, p. 108.

4.5 Effects of Expansion in Baghdad

A good relationship had already been established between the Pasha of Rewanduz and the Pasha of Baghdad before the expansion of the Soran Emirate. This caused Ali Reda to change his attitude towards Soran; particularly, when Muhammad Pasha took the Badinan territories.

The Pasha of Baghdad's antipathy towards Soran increased after Muhammad Bey had expelled several high-ranking Ottoman officials. Then the Wali's policy towards the Kurds involved removing what was left of their independence. Once Muhammad Pasha took Amedi, he caused Istanbul to have a negative attitude towards him, and caused the Baghdad Pasha's anger to be directed at him. Muhammad Rashid Pasha was chosen to be chief commander and Ali Reda Pasha of Baghdad was appointed to assist him. This led the two powers to consider acting in unison against Soran.[423] Kinneir, a British political agent, who was in Kurdistan from 1813–1814 stated: "the Pasha of Amedi was one of the richest and most powerful chiefs in Kurdistan." [424] Muhammad Pasha therefore moved to control Amedi which was a huge blow to Ottoman influence, because Amedi was an old hereditary Kurdish emirate. Indeed, the growing power of Muhammad Pasha became reasonably strong, especially in the eyes of the Ottoman Empire as it was dangerous for them.

4.6 Subjugation to Muhammad Pasha's Rule

Muhammad Pasha's own rivalry with other Kurdish emirates shows that his centralization aim, or his own leadership style, was paramount and took precedence over Kurdist aims. Muhammad Pasha had succeeded in bringing the Milli Kurds under his influence,[425] with incidents recorded in a dispatch sent from Baghdad, dated April 26 1832: "The *Bey* of Rewanduz has advanced against the districts of Mosul, and taken possession of a portion of them within a short distance of the city."[426] In order to exert his authority further, the Pasha insisted that he gained the allegiances of all those he subjugated: "The Mufti, Qazi, and principal inhabitants of the city"[427] were treated respectfully; whilst those who did not

---

[423] Longrigg, Stephen Hemsley (1925). Op. cit, pp. 285-6.

[424] Kinneir, John Macdonald (1818). *Journey through Asia Minor, Armenia, and Koordistan [sic], in the Years 1813 and 1814; with remarks on the Marches of Alexander, and Retreat of the Ten Thousand,* John Murray, London, p. 456. Amedi was an independent Emirate, with the Pasha being a subject of the Pasha of Baghdad (province of the Ottoman Empire).

[425] Until then the Milli Kurds had controlled Mosul and Mardin (part of Mesopotamia).

[426] IOR L/PS/9/93, Major Taylor to Charles Norris Chief Secretary to Government-Bombay, Baghdad, April 26th 1832, pp. 354–5.

[427] IOR L/PS/9/97A, Lt. Col.. Taylor, R., to the Secret Committee of the Court of Directors-East India House-London, Baghdad, 11th November 1834, pp. 423–5.

submit, had his wrath directed against them. He "burned the houses of…many of the principal people…who had refused to surrender".[428]

This however was not enough for him. In his self-aggrandisement he attempted to obtain the subjugation of key regional leaders to his rule, trying unsuccessfully to "summon, the Hajî Assad Beg, the Mutesselim, to his presence". This failed as "[the Hajî] declined obedience to the call."[429]

In contrast, Fraser, a British traveller, who visited Rewanduz, observed that Muhammad Pasha had a good reputation for justice and treated his subjects with fairness.[430] He also noted the moral change that the Pasha had brought to his emirate: "…for instead of being, as they were occupied by a nation, or rather nations, of robbers, who could not see a traveller pass without attempting to stop and strip him, and who…would cut a man's throat for an egg in his hand, there is now not a thief or theft in the country…"[431]

Muhammad Pasha was ruthless in his military campaigns and in establishing his personal family rule but once he succeeded in doing this, he was a fair, just and efficient ruler as witnessed by several European travellers. He understood that the Kurds needed a strong ruler to unite them and enable them to live as Kurds in their own country. This had serious implications with the Ottoman Empire and caused the Ottomans to hasten an attack on the Kurdish emirates in which Rewanduz was first to be attacked.

Muhammad Pasha was not a very careful man; therefore, the Soran army was often engaged in personal campaigns outside the best interests of the Kurds. On one occasion, Muhammad Pasha took the opportunity to attack the Yezidi Kurds for being of a different faith. In 1244 A.H/1828, Ali Beg of Dasini, the Yezidi Mir of Sheikhan, was involved in a longstanding feud with Ali Agha, a Kurdish chieftain. Ali Beg invited Ali Agha to his home. Ali Agha went with a few followers, but they did not manage to save their leader before Yezidi Mir Ali Beg's bodyguards killed his guest.[432] Ali Agha was the uncle of a very famous Kurdish scholar, *Mela* Muhammad of Muzuri, who went to Soran and asked Muhammad Pasha to

---

[428] Ibid, pp. 423–5.
[429] Ibid.
[430] Fraser, J. Baillie (1840). Op. cit, p. 80.
[431] Ibid, p. 65.
[432] Guest, John S. (1993). *Survival Among the Kurds*, A History of the Yezidis, The revised edition, Kegan Paul International, London and New York, p. 68.

retaliate against Ali Agha's killer. At the same time Sa'id Pasha of Amedi who had fled from his nephew Ismael Pasha, went to Rewanduz with *Mela* Muhammad of Muzurî and encouraged Muhammad Pasha of Soran to attack Yezidis and Amedi. Later, in 1247 AH-1831/2 C. E., the Soran Pasha attacked the Yezidî Kurds and killed a great number of them.[433] Some sources, such as John Guest, say that "Kor Muhammad's army swept on; killing all the Yezidis they could find."[434] In this incident, most probably the long time enemies of Dasini played a role in the attack against the Yezidis.

On the above occasion, the Soran Pasha "laid siege to Amadia itself and by availing himself of family friends and treachery, bribed his way into that important fortress from whence he directed his efforts with still greater vigour to reduce the remaining strongholds of the country."[435] In another instance, the army was mobilised to Soran's Eastern frontier to intimidate local Turkish officials. They aimed to replace officials with local chiefs. However, the Soran Pasha's strategy was flawed, as instead of helping him, it managed to further exacerbate the Ottoman Empire's opposition against him.

During the clashes between Yezidis and Muzuris, *Mela* Muhammadi Xatê played a destructive role when, upon *Mela* Muhammad of Muzuri's demand, he issued a *Fitwa* (religious statement or order) against Ali Beg of Dasini.[436] Huznî Mukiryani writes that "he heard from elderly people in Rewanduz that Ali Beg of Dasini was a very nice man, brave and well-mannered. He did not deserve to be killed. On the demand of a few extremist Muslim scholars who called upon the Pasha of Soran to ask Ali Beg of Dasinî to adopt Islam, he refused. As a result, he was killed by order of Muhammad Pasha of Soran. Then he attacked Sinjar and killed many Yezidis."[437] However, it seems that religion became a pretext for the Rewanduz Pasha to commit a massacre against his fellow Yezidis Kurds. The act of the Soran Pasha was a brutal shameful atrocity without justification.

---

[433] Huzni, Husein (1962). Op. cit, pp. 64-6.
[434] Guest, John S. (1993). Op. cit, p. 68.
[435] Ibid, pp. 68–9.
[436] Nebez, Dr Jemal (1994). Op. cit, p. 48.
[437] Huzni, Husein (1962). Op. cit, p. 66.

4.7 Soran Emirate as Focal Point of Kurdism

Apart from administration and building a strong army, during Muhammad Pasha's reign, *medreses*, scholars and poets, such as *Mela* Muhammad Ibnu Adam and Hajî Qadiri Koyî, played significant roles in promoting Kurdish self-awareness. This will now be discussed.

4.8 The role of *medreses* [schools]

One significant aspect of Kurdish political identity was the use of the Kurdish language. From the beginning of the nineteenth century, some intellectuals had put the Kurdish language in the heart of their written activities foregrounding its importance among other languages. These scholars, through the Kurdish language, had created a new ideology of Kurdism which was presented as the way to serve the Kurdish people.

The Pasha of Rewanduz had great respect for poets, artists and scholars. He helped them, through patronage and the provision of facilities, to teach 'Kurdishness'. Many of them such as *Mela* Muhammad Ibnu Adam, *Mela* Muhammdi Xatê, and others gathered around the Pasha, and he was able to establish a number of *medreses* (schools) and *mizgewt* (mosques) in his capital.[438] One pupil at these centres of learning was Hajî Qadiri Koyî. The pasha took Hewlêr. As he desired to spread education in his emirate, he ordered that every *mela* in mosques must start teaching *feqês* or leave the city.[439] This played an important role in raising teaching among Kurds. Sheikh Hidayatullahi Hewlêrî, a famous Kurdish scholar of his time, and others played a great role in this matter.[440]

During Muhammad Pasha's rule, Rewanduz became a focal point for 'Kurdism'. For these reasons: In the above mentioned era, Rewanduz and other parts of Balekayeti became a creative centre for Kurdish literature, social life and welfare.[441] Muhammad Pasha built mosques and *medresses*, developed education and supported *melas* [Kurdish Islamic scholars]. Hajî Qadiri Koyî witnessed education flourishing at that time, and says:

---

[438] Huzni, Husein (1962). Op. cit, p. 51. Nebez, Dr. Jemal (1994). Op. cit, pp. 60-1.

[439] Mudarris, Mela Abdulkarim (1979). *Yadi Mardan*, Kurdish text, *Remembering the great men, Mawlana Khalidi Naqishbandî*, published Kurdish Academy, Baghdad, p. 66.

[440] Ibid.

[441] Muhammad, Mas'ud (1974). *Hajî Qadiri Koyî*, Kurdish text, Hajî Qadiri Koyî: published by Kurdish Academy, part two, Baghdad, pp. 92, 108.

Ta te'inatiî kor u laĺ mabu

Le gelê dêyekan melay çabu[442]

Whilst the blind and the mute were alive

There were many good *Melas* in the villages

The "blind" is a reference to the Pasha and the "mute" to his brother who had a speech difficulty.[443]

Mas'ud Muhammad tells us that; "Hajî Qadir and his close friend Hajî *Mela* Abdullah were *feqês* [students] of *Mela* Muhammad Ibnu Adam (1750-1844), who was the leading Kurdish scholar of the Soran Emirate during Muhammad Pasha's time. From Ibnu Adam, Hajî Qadir and Hajî *Mela* Abdullah imbibed their conceptions of Kurdism. These thoughts were imparted before Hajî Qadir left for Istanbul."[444]

Ibnu Adam was a very well-known Kurdish scholar and poet of this time. In 1205 AH-1790 C. E., in an introduction to of one of his books, he mentions Kurdistan twice. First, he refers to *Wilejê* as a village of Kurdistan; second he mentions Abdulrahman Pasha of Baban, stating that its capital Silêmanî was *Meqeṟri Selteneti Kurdistan-* and Silêmanî was a centre for Kurdistan Sultanate.[445] This is a clear indication that at least a few Kurdish intellectuals were aware of the ideas of a fatherland and nation when Ibnu Adam praised Kurdistan and raised it to the level of Ottoman Sultanate. Kurdistan, to Ibnu Adam, was more than a place of birth; it had a political meaning and was an influential power, connected with territory. For Ibnu Adam, Kurdism did not conflict with Islam; in an Islamic state, a Kurd could express his Kurdism and at the same time express respect towards the Ottoman Caliph. Hence, he and other Kurdish intellectuals were Kurdist and Ottomanist at the same time.

From his poetry we understand that Hajî *Mela* Abdullah Jelizade first wrote in Persian, but after a while he stopped and began writing in Kurdish. Of this, he says:

Ba bikem tebdili wezn u qafye ṟewye u 'eruz

---

[442] Ibid, p. 109.

[443] Muhammad, Mas'ud (1976). *Hajî Qadiri Koyî*, Kurdish text, Hajî Qadiri Koyî: published by Kurdish Academy, part three, Baghdad, p. 354.

[444] Muhammad, Mas'ud (1974). Op. cit, p. 97.

[445] Ibid, p. 128.

Bem zimane hiçitr şi'rm le bo helnastê

Bikeme Kurdi zimani xome çaki têdegem

Xwaye tofiqm bidey min bende to mulasatî[446]

Let me change the metre and rhyme of my poetry

I cannot express myself any more by this language (Persian)

Let's make it Kurdish which is my own language which I understand very well

Oh God help me to progress it

In the above quatrain, Jelizade expresses his loyalty to the Kurdish language and declares that he feels the Persian language limits his expression. He pleads to God, as a Kurdish Muslim scholar, to be helped to develop Kurdish and to devote his time and his knowledge to it.

Beside his poetry, Jelizade wrote in prose as well, for instance the *Mewludname i Kurdî*. [447] This book was a religious book about the birth of the Prophet, but it was important because it was written in prose and it was unusual at that time because it was written in the Kurdish language. *Mewludnamei Kurdî* was regarded as an outstanding literary work for two reasons. First, it was written in prose, making its meaning more accessible than if it had been written as a poem. Second, as it was about the birth of the Prophet, it attracted the attention of both literate and illiterate Kurdish people and above all it represented a desire to develop the scope of Kurdish literature.

This stream of Kurdish consciousness indicates that Kurdism existed among the Kurds before the news of the French revolution reached Kurdistan and before Hajî Qadir went to Istanbul.

4.9 Hajî Qadirî Koyî (1815–1897)

Hajî Qadir was a leading Kurdish poet of the nineteenth century and his Diwan was published in 1925.[448] He lived the first half of his life in the Soran Emirate. His influence spread throughout Kurdistan, and he was considered a great nationalist thinker. He had a close

---

[446] Ibid, p. 139.

[447] Jelizade, *Mela* Abdullah (1966). *Mewludname i Kurdî, Kurdish text, The birth of the Prophet, Kurdistan Press, Hewler.*

[448] Said, Abdulrahman (1925). Published by, *Komele Şi'ri Hajî Qadiri Koyî, A Collection of Hajî Qadir's poems,* Dar al-Alsalam Press, Baghdad.

friendship with his contemporary Kurdish intellectuals and scholars such as *Mela* Abdullah Jelizade, Keify, Amin Agha and Ibrahim Haidari.[449]

The specific historical conditions which Hajî experienced in his early life, his friendships and the impact of Baban poets influenced his work in formulating his idea of Kurdism. He often praised Nali, Salim and others who established the Soranî dialect poetry during the first half of the nineteenth century, in his Diwan.[450] The impact of his teachers, in particular, *Mela* Muhammad Ibnu Adam and his travels through both parts of Kurdistan added to his own personal intelligence and awareness. All these experiences must have given Hajî formative elements of a strong and passionate romantic nationalism to take to the Bedirkhans. His discovery of the nationalist message of Ahmadi Khani was only one revealing indicator of his strong nationalist thoughts to which he has given vivid expression in his poetry.

Martin van Bruinessen suggests that "the first person to recognise a nationalist message in *Mem u Zin* was the southern Kurdish author Hajî Qadri Koyî.... who had a great influence on Kurdish national awareness", even more so after his death. Van Bruinessen points out "He must have known from personal experience the government of the last great ruler of Soran."[451]

Hajî certainly treasured the memory of the last Kurdish Emirates and the rulers asking:

Kuwa wali Senenduj, begzadey Ṛewanduz,
Kuwa wali Baban, miri Jezire u Botan.[452]

Where are the governors of Sanandaj, and the prince of Rewanduz?
Where are the governors of Baban, and the ruler of Jezire and Botan?

Van Bruinessen also suggests; "These last great Kurdish rulers... must have made a strong impression on the young Qadir. Their ultimate defeat...gave rise to a romantic nationalism in Hajî Qadir, and to a nostalgic idealisation of the feudal past."[453] Jwaideh states "Hajî Qadir of

---

[449] Muhammad, Mas'ud (1974). Op. cit, p.167.
[450] See chapter 6 for more details.
[451] Bruinessen, Martin van (2003). *Ehmedi Xani's Mem u Zin and its Role in the Emergenceof Kurdish Awareness,* in Abbas Vali (Ed) *Essays on the Origin of Kurdish Nationalism,* Mazda Publishers, Inc, Costa Mesa, California, p. 47.
[452] Ibid, p. 44.
[453] Ibid. p.47.

Koyî was known for his intensely patriotic poems and for that reason is considered one of the fathers of Kurdish nationalism."[454]

For three decades of his life, Hajî lived during the period of existence of three of the Kurdish emirates and lived on for a further half a century following their collapse. In 1866, Hajî moved to Istanbul, which gave him an opportunity to contrast his national outlook with that of other countries. Much of Hajî's work abounded with several key themes: praise, romance, the natural habitat of Kurdistan, the state, nationalism, and the conflict between positive and negative practices, his attitude toward *Melas* and Sheikhs and the occupation of his country.[455]

Hajî received ideas of Kurdish consciousness from his teacher, *Mela* Muhammad Ibnu Adam,[456] a pioneering Kurdish scholar who commonly used terms such as 'Kurds' and 'Kurdistan'. Ibnu Adam promoted the Kurdish language according to his Islamic opinion, seeing no contradiction between Islam and the expression of Kurdishness. Ibnu Adam was a renowned scholar[457] who was keen to further Islamic knowledge; taking care to distinguish between truth and falsehood. He had no compunction about standing against the unjust.[458]

Ibnu Adam questioned the silence of his fellow Kurds at the destruction of the Soran Emirate;

Hewran kirde gaĺe gaĺ
Mikael 'etoş dey
Tutn u maşan brşêne
Deba noş bête ser dey
Romi 'ewa peya bun
Kutubxanan deken tey[459]

Clouds thundering
Mikael (Michael) you do the same

---

[454] Jwaideh, Wadie (2006). Op. cit, p.24.

[455] Hajî Qadiri Koyî, (1969). *Diwani Hajî Qadiri Koyî*, Third edition, Hewler Press, Hewler. Ghalib, Orkhan (1997). "Hajî Qadir Koyî: The Nationalism Theorist", *Melbend Magazine*, No. 84, November, London, p. 24.

[456] Isma'l, Zuber Bilal (1977). "Muhammad bin Adam al-Balaki, Arabic text, Muhammad Adam al-Balaki", *The Journal of the Kurdish Academy*, Volume 5, Baghdad, p. 450, 467.

[457] Ibnu Adam was one of the most well-known Kurdish scholars in his time, he taught Hajî .

[458] Muhammad, Mase'ud (1974). Op. cit, p. 121-2

[459] Ibid, p. 118.

Rain over tobacco and beans

And make us suffer even more (literary expression: "add nine to ten")

Romis have dismounted here and destroy libraries

An interpretation of the above poem could take into consideration that Ottomans were alien to Kurds in Kurdistan. *Mela* Muhammad Ibnu Adam, a famous Kurdish Islamic scholar in his time distinguished Ottomans by their customs which showed that they were a dominating people and had a negative attitude towards Kurds. This accusation of a Kurdish intellectual against the Ottoman army suggests that the Ottomans did not only plunder and kill people but they also destroyed libraries and *medreses* [schools]. It is clear that the Ottoman army acted as an occupying rather than friendly force.

Ibnu Adam had a positive impact on Hajî Qadir, helping him to perceive the Kurdish political situation in its historical and social contexts. From his early days, Hajî was in conflict with reactionary *Melas* and Sheikhs who were trying to adhere to traditional thoughts and old fashioned attitudes in the Kurdish community.

Hezdekey têbgey le bêdynî
Bibe derwêşi şêkhekan behewes[460]

Do you want to understand non-religion?
Then you should become followers of Sheikhs.

Hajî graduated from mosques and *medreses*, and he lived in a Kurdish Islamic society, but he never followed religious men who used religion for their interests. Instead he stated that "the clergy were all traitors."[461] Hajî condemned those clergymen who betrayed poor people. In a couplet Hajî says:

Xaneqaw şêx u tekyekan yekser
Pêm blên nef'yan çiye 'axir
Xeyri te'limi tembeli kirdin
Jem'i emlak u xezne kokrdin

---

[460] Hajî Qadiri Koyî, (1969). *Diwani Hajî Qadir Koyî, Collected Poems*, Giwi Mukryani (Ed.), Third edition, Hewler Press, Hewler, p. 35.
[461] Hassanpour, Amir, (1992). *Nationalism and Language in Kurdistan, 1918-1985*, Mallen Research University Press, San Francisco, p. 92.

Def'eye emtihanyan naken
Têbgen zehrin yane tryakin[462]

All kind places such as *Xaneqa* and *tekye*

Tell me what their benefits are

Apart from teaching laziness

They were used for collecting money and getting more properties

They should be examined

To find out if they are poison or hashish

Hajî Qadir saw the destruction of three Kurdish emirates; Soran, Botan and Baban by the Ottomans. He observed how the Ottomans used their influences against the Kurds. From his early days, he was always critical of negative traditions amongst his people and worked for their re-awakening. Thus, he critically assessed social conditions within the Kurdish community, seeking out the practices restricting development within his society. This enabled him to alert his fellow Kurds to these impediments.

He observed how many religious men in Kurdistan used their position to advance their personal interests. He recognised that, in this manner, such religious men were a reactionary force within Kurdish society.

Êma bêxireteen u bê 'areen,
'ewei neixwênduwe le me'areef,
Qeid u tezbib u şerh u haşyakan,
Bune seddi me'areefi Kurdan.[463]

We are a disgrace and shameful,

Those who are too illiterate to know

Poor interpretations and footnotes,

Have become barriers to Kurds' enlightenment

---

[462] Hajî Qadir Koyî, (1969). Op. cit, p. 89.
[463] Ibid, p.112.

Hajî spent his life from 1270 to 1279 A. H. and 1853-1862 C. E. in Persian Kurdistan.[464] During that time, he travelled through the Persian part of Kurdistan and perceived the Kurdish situation under Persian rule. From his experience and Kurdish confrontation with Persians, he learnt that ruthlessness and suppression were the Iranian attitude towards the Kurds.[465] Hajî said:

Qed semi'na min munadi, mate (şah)
Le'netullahi 'eleihi mateşa [466]

We heard an announcer saying: the Shah is dead
May God's curses be upon him, as many as you wish.

Muhammad Shah was the Persian Qajar Shah who did not treat Kurds well, and died in 1848.[467] In this verse, all Hajî's ethnic and sectarian feelings accumulated against the Persian king. Hajî therefore attacked the oppressive Persian rulers in Kurdistan. It could be interpreted that Hajî had the same negative thoughts towards the Ottomans who were another dominant power over Kurdistan. Furthermore, Hajî had extensive knowledge about the negative impact of the Ottoman Empire against the Kurds which later he strongly condemned and called for the liberation of the Kurds under such dominant powers.

In this sense, it would be reasonable to consider that Hajî's famous teacher, Ibnu Adam, was within Hajî's very well-known circle of friends. His Kurdist thought developed over the forty five years he spent travelling through Kurdistan. It is also important to recognize that most of Hajî's poems in his Diwan were written in Kurdistan. Regretably, his work in Istanbul was burnt and only a few of his poems reached Kurdistan.[468] Therefore, it is possible to deal with Hajî's work as a production of his national status.

Although Hajî Qadir was a Kurdish Muslim scholar, he constantly called for a secular state and strongly believed in the separation of political and religious influences. Thus, he condemned the reactionary forces within his society and believed that such forces hindered his society's advancement and progress; so much so that these forces should be swept away.

---

[464] Muhammad, Mase'ud (1976). Op. cit, pp. 146,162.
[465] Ibid, p. 141.
[466] Muhammad, Mase'ud (1974). Op. cit, p. 173.
[467] Sykes, Percy M. (1915). *A History of Persian*, Vol. II, Macmillan and Co., London, p. 439.
[468] Muhammad, Mase'ud (1974). Op. cit, p. 62.

In 1866,[469] Hajî Qadir left Kurdistan for Istanbul. There, he established a friendship with Bedirkhan Pasha, the last powerful ruler of the Botan Emirate. Hajî became a tutor to Bedirkhan's children.[470] The new vistas of Istanbul allowed Hajî Qadir, to move around and learn more readily (in comparison to his relatively limited environment in Kurdistan). This also provided him with the opportunity to observe the advancement of European nations. He could also observe the rise of their nationalist movements, and their developing education systems.[471]

Hajî Qadir believed that his own people needed to take similar steps towards freedom. He felt obliged personally to make a contribution towards the liberation of the Kurdish people from the Ottoman Turks. He deduced that the Turks, since they were powerful within the Ottoman Empire, could use their influence to impose their nationalist ideas over non-Turk *millets* (nations), including the Kurds.

This led Hajî Qadir to develop an idea for the establishment of a Kurdish state. He proposed its foundation should be based on several principles: i) the postulation of equal rights for all citizens of Kurdistan. ii) the participation of all people in a general armed uprising against the Turks and iii) a collective responsibility for their administration. Such a call for civic rights and equality was years ahead of the development of the Iranian constitution introduced in 1906 and the Young Turks Revolution in 1908. In a long poem, Hajî writes:

Lem beineda ittifaqê peydabken be merdî ,
Ferqi nebê şwan u jutyar u mir u gawan [472].

We should unite together as brave men,

Let there be no discrimination between shepherd, peasant and prince.

As a modern theorist, Hajî Qadir called for the promotion of thought, education, and culture in order to build political and social consciousness among his people. He wished for his

---

[469] Muhammad, Mase'ud (1973). *Hajî Qadri Koyî*, Kurdish text, Part 1, Published by Kurdish Academy, Baghdad, p. 115. Isma'l, Zuber Bilal,.Op. cit, p. 463.

[470] Sejadi, Ela'edin (1971). *Mejui Edebi Kurdi*, Kurdish text, The History of the Kurdish Literature, Second edition, Maearif Press , p. 343.

[471] It has been suggested that he was thinking in 'Kurdish' terms before he became aware of the French Revolution, Jalil, p. Jalil bases his supposition on documents apparently now inaccessible to scholars. If this is, in fact the case, some arguments offered by 'modernist' historians of nationalism might be open to questioning.

[472] *Hajî Qadri Koyî* (1969). Op.cit, p.96.

people to feel the burden of their oppression and to join the struggle for their freedom. He therefore placed the existence of both internal and external consciousness amongst the fundamental elements of such a development. Kurds were urged by him to study and learn the new sciences, history and sociology. He drew their attention to political and administrative theories circulating in Europe:

'ddie'ai hiç sanae'êk naken,

Taku neixwênn, imtihani naken,

Boçi fermuyeti Neyii 'emin,

'utlobu 'el-'lme welew bi 'el-Sin,

To were fennê fêrbe, çita lewe ,

Gawre, hindwue, yaxu jwue.[473]

They cannot discuss any science or knowledge,

Until they study and examine it,

The honoured Prophet said,

Learn knowledge even if it was in China,

You, come and embrace learning,

Care not whether your teacher be a Christian, Hindu or Jew.

Hajî Qadir endorsed those Kurdish Emirates which had been destroyed by the Ottoman Turks. He condemned the Ottoman Empire, calling it an "aggressor" and an "occupier". Hajî advocated a secular Kurdish state rather than an oppressive religious Empire. Reminding Kurds that:

Hakim u mirekani Kurdistan,

Her le Botanewe heta Baban,

Yek be yek hafizi şeri'et bun,

Seyyidi qewmu şêxi millet bun. [474]

Our Governors and Princes of Kurdistan,

from Botan to Baban,

____

[473] Ibid, p.90.
[474] Ibid, p.101.

Each one a guardian of the law

Seyyids of strength and sheikhs of our people

When the Kurdish emirates were dismembered, both powers, the Ottoman Turks and the Iranians, were brutal in their suppression of the Kurds; Hajî Qadir illustrated the equal ruthlessness shown by both occupiers of Kurdistan:

du hazar jin fesadkran lemla,
bune katili ewanitr lewla.[475]

This side raped two thousand women,
The other side killed so many more.

Hajî Qadir was not a Pan-Islamist at the expense of Kurdish interests. He admired Western nationalism and called upon the Kurds to follow its path in the establishment of a Kurdish state. He endorsed the struggles of those who had already gained independence from the Ottoman Empire, such as Bulgarians, Serbians and Greeks, and urged fellow Kurds to follow their path. He wrote:

Binware se'y u xiret esta lenaw ewrupa,
Xoyan xeznedarin, xoyan tebib u sultan,
Bulxar u Sirb u yonan, hem 'ermen u Qerebax,
Her pênjyan be te'dad nabin be qeddi Baban,
Serpaki musteqillin kullêki dewletêkin,
Sahêbi jeyş u rayet, 'erkani herb u lêdan.[476]

Look at how the Europeans, through their striving and enthusiasm,
Have become owners of their treasury, healers and sultans (rulers)
Bulgarian, Serb, Greek, Armenian and Karabakh,
Their combined population is less than Baban,
Yet all now are independent, having their own states,
With armies, flags, science and other symbols....

---

[475] Ibid, p. 101.
[476] Ibid, p.45.

Hajî Qadir's usage of a generalised language of struggle indicates his belief that Kurds would not appreciate the Hajî or understand the reason for their lack of development until they had been released from the Ottoman Turks. That they supposedly represented the Islamic Caliphate did not soften his blows:

Ta le jêr bari Ŗomiyan nemrin,
Zehmete qedri beyti min bigrin.[477]

If you don't die under the weight of the Ottomans,
Will you never appreciate my entreaties or understand my poems?

Hajî Qadir noted that the Kurdish population was estimated to be four million. Yet from amongst them, no leader had yet emerged to guide them towards independence. For this, he blamed the Kurdish people in general; and also in particular Kurdish *Melas* and Kurdish Sheikhs.

Kurêki wa nebu hestête serpê,
Bizanê khelki çon kewtune serpê.[478]

There was no talented man to lead an uprising,
Look at how other peoples grabbed their independence.

Be qisey sade birsi têr nabê,
'emele 'zzetî din u dunya.[479]

The bellies of the poor are not filled by words,
It needs hard work and struggle for a people to advance in this life and beyond.

Hajî Qadir focused on people's ability to alter their own circumstances. He believed passionately that the main factor for social change was the force of the people. When people believe in a cause and prepare themselves for its accomplishment, they can achieve their

---

[477] Ibid, p.92.
[478] Ibid, p.114.
[479] Ibid, p.116.

goals. In his view, Kurds could gain independence and inter-Kurdish unity, which would enable them to resist and overthrow the occupying forces.

It was clear that Hajî Qadir presented a collective idea of unity in the minds and hearts of his people, arguing for the assumption of a real union between all individuals to mobilise the entire strength of the Kurdish nation. The destruction of the Kurdish emirates, in the mid nineteenth-century, was believed by him to have provided an opportunity for the Ottomans and Persians to attack Kurdish people.

Hajî Qadir vigorously promoted and defended the Kurdish tongues; he believed language was a very important factor in keeping a nation alive. Moreover, it was presumed by him that barriers of communication, amongst members of a nation, would create difficulties for them in establishing a state of their own. Hajî Qadir also recognised the Kurdish language as a most beautiful tongue; the Kurdish people were chastised for their lack of devotion to it.

Melên fesaheti Kurdi be Farsi naga,
Belaxetêkî heye hiç zimanê pêi naga,
Le bê te'esubi Kurdane bê ṛewaju beha.[480]

It cannot be said that the beauty of Kurdish is less than Persian,

Our language has a beauty unmatched by any other,

Because of the Kurds' lack of national solidarity it has remained without value.

The Kurdish language was considered an important element contributing towards the culmination of Hajî Qadir's project of a national movement. Kurds were asked to show interest in their language and to respect it. His perception was that it was an essential element for unity and understanding amongst them all. This resulted in him attacking those Kurds who did not speak Kurdish, using derogatory expressions towards them:

'eger Kurdêk zimani xoy nezanê,
Muheqqeq dayki hize babi zani.[481]

---

[480] Ibid, p.25.
[481] Ibid, p.71.

If a Kurd does not know his own tongue,

Certainly, he/she must be the child of a whore and an adulterer.

Hajî Qadir believed that the Kurdish language would act as a unifying factor amongst his people. He believed that all Kurdish people possessed a shared literature and culture. He appealed:

Bibne yek le te'lim u le nusin,
Jil u berg u ziman u ṛesm u 'aiiyn.[482]

Let our learning and letters unite us,

Let us share one tradition, one language and one religion.

To advance their language and educate the people, Hajî Qadir promoted the founding of a newspaper many years before the first one was eventually published in April 1898. He saw such a project as a means of general communication, hoping to use it as a vehicle to encourage Kurds to think seriously about their identity. He reminded them that the rise of the European press had been a major element in European advancement.

Sed qa'ime u qeside kes naikṛê be pulê,
Ṛojnam u jeride kewtune qimet u şe'n.[483]

Hundreds of lists and poems have slight value,

Newsprint carries more weight and gravitas.

Hajî understood that to establish a Kurdish state both language and culture were
required on the one hand, whilst power or force were required on the other. The first
one represented by *qelem* (the pen) and the second represented by the sword. He said:

Seyf u qelem şerikin lem 'esreda, drêxa
Şirm qelemtrashe w kalaninye qelemdan[484]

---

[482] Ibid, p.18.
[483] Ibid, p. 141.
[484] Ibid, p. 45.

Sword and pen are sharing in this time; alas
My sword is a pen sharpener, and my scabbard is a pen case

In the following verse, Hajî shows his love for the Kurdish people and their language. The only reason he gave praise to God was to show his adoration and his respect for Kurdism.

Me'lume boçî Hajî medht deka be Kurdî
Ta kes nelê be Kurdi nekrawe medhi barî [485]

It is certain that why Hajî praised you oh God
Was so that no one could say that God was not praised in Kurdish

Another facet of Hajî Qadir's theory was his belief that a people's homeland is fundamental to a people's survival, emphasizing that the Kurdish people had inhabited Kurdistan for a thousand years. He believed that when Kurds had government, they were ruling over Kurdish people and their land. He felt land to be an important element in the establishment of a Kurdish state. In a verse of one of his long poems, Hajî said:

Kuwa ew demei ke Kurdan azad u serbexobun
Sultani mulk u millet xawendi jeysh u 'irfan[486]

Where is the time when Kurds were free and independent?
They were ruling their land and their people and had their army and knowledge

He believed in the unity of Kurdistan. On many occasions he talked about the boundaries of Kurdistan. Sometimes, as in this poem, he appears to have become a little carried away with his delineations of its extent.

Waseti pane pazde ṛoj ṛêya,
Piṛ le re şmaĺ u xane u dêya,
Bedrêjyi le qaf ke ṛaburdun,
Ta be şiraz u Isfehan Kurdin.[487]

---

[485] Ibid, p. 74.
[486] Ibid, p. 44.

From the middle, Kurdistan is fifteen days walk away,

It is full of tents and villages,

In length, from the Caucasus Mountains,

To Shiraz and Isfahan are Kurds.

Hajî believed that Kurds had once possessed a state and a king with an army and wisdom; he therefore stressed that independence had a great impact on people's development. Expressing sorrow for Kurds because they had lost their state, he did not mention when and how they lost it. He remained optimistic that the Kurds would re-establish their state, but only if they united together and acquired tools such as artillery and guns with which to fight their enemies:

Kuwa 'ewdemey ke Kurdan 'azad u serbexobun,

Sultani muĺk u millet, xawendi jeiyş u 'irfan,

Joşêk biden weku heng, tegbir biken be bê deng,

'esbabi şeṟ peyaken, top u tfeng u hawen.[488]

When was the time when Kurds were free and independent?

Masters of their land, owning military might and science,

Swarm like bees, silently draw plans,

Get tools for fighting, such as guns and artillery.

When talking about a unity of land and history, Hajî Qadir stressed that without the possession of a Kurdish state, no unified people could be protected. He argued that if the Kurds did not struggle for their own state, then the occupying forces would succeed in the division of Kurdistan. Were this to happen, their movements would be severely restricted:

Wa rêgetan debestn elati Jaf u Biĺbas,

Ger mrdun le germên, memnu'e bçne kwêstan. [489]

Tribesmen of Jaf and Bilbas, Your movements

---

[487] Ibid, p. 100.
[488] Ibid, p. 44.
[489] Ibid, p. 43.

Are fettered, should you die, the enemy would detain you here.

Hajî Qadir also appreciated the need to establish a strong defensive force to act as a guardian to any fledgling Kurdish state. He found however that his fellow Kurds did not know and would not listen to him. Hajî believed that he completed his duty as a man of the pen through his poems as much as he could, but he sorrowed for his lack of use of the sword. He stated loudly:

Be şir u xame dewlet payedare,
'emn qeĺemm heya şir nadiyare,
Ne beydaxi heya ne tepĺ u kursi,
'ewendei pêykra bêçare nusi,
Wezifei xom bejêhêna temami,
Be şiri dewlete millet nizami. [490]

A State may be held by pen and sword,

I have a pen, but the sword remains sheathed.

I have no flag, no drum and no chair,

I have written as much as I could,

I have done my all duties,

It is by force that the state could be regulated.

Hajî Qadir was not alone in his sentiments, as many other Kurdish poets expressed their national feelings in verse such as Sheikh Reza Talebany, as discussed in Chapter Six.

4.10 European and regional powers

Muhammad Pasha of Soran proved that a very important centre of Kurdish power had emerged which rivalled and affected the power and interests of regional and international players.

---

[490] Ibid, p, 19.

At the time several European powers vied to gain influence in the region. The Russians had led several campaigns, as they wanted to increase their interests in the Asian continent. Richard Wood[491] mentioned in a letter to Richard Norris that the Russians tried to influence the region, saying that "the Persian Court" and probably "all Persian conquests" were "used for the attainment of Russian ends." [492]

Moreover, in order to gain part of a territory in Azerbaijan, the Russian Deputy, in the Districts of Sauj Bulag [Mahabad], made a demand for supplies of forage and even submission.[493] In support of the Russian demands, Kurds had sent a force of over two thousand troops to accompany those of the Prince Royal of Persia to "…be sent against the Turkumans bordering Khorasan."[494]

According to Wood, this demand had "excited the attention of the Curdish [*sic*] Nobles subject to this Pachalik [*sic*] that they referred to the Pacha for instructions how to act in case of similar demands on them."[495]

4.11 British Concerns in the Region

The British, with significant interests in India, were keen to maintain just one regional power in order to protect their key trading route from Bombay to the Mediterranean Sea, which happened to go through the Soran Emirate. They were concerned with any changes to the status quo and anything that could affect the European balance of power.

There is no doubt that the British established a good relationship with the Soran Emirate and correspondences were exchanged between the two sides.[496] In reply to the letter sent by Sir John Campbell, the British Ambassador to Persia, to Muhammad Pasha of Soran, Muhammad Pasha expressed his warm friendship to the British and expressed his wish to fulfil the British interests in his region. He stated that

---

[491] Richard Wood (1836). The British Consul in Aleppo, was sent to Rewanduz in 1836 by Ponsonby the British Ambassador at Constantinople to motivate Muhammad Pasha of Soran to surround to the Ottoman army. " Richard Wood to H.E. the Lord Ponsonby KB-Constantinople, Ravanduz Castle, near the Persian frontier, Sept. 3, 1836, FO 78/277, p. 226. See whole dispatch pp. 221-227. TNA, London, Kew Gardens. See also IOR L/PS/9/100, pp.686-8, TBL, London. See appendix B for full report.

[492] IOR L/PS/9/91 (1830) Op. cit. p. 395

[493] IOR L/PS/9/91 R. Taylor to Charles Norris, Chief Secretary to Government in Bombay, No 36 of 1830, Baghdad 23rd December 1830, p. 386/11.

[494] Ibid p. 386/13.

[495] Ibid p. 396.

[496] IOR L/PS/9/97A. From a letter written about November 1834 by Muhammad Pasha of Rewanduz we learnt that there was a relation between British and Rewanduz. See: Letter from Muhammad Pasha Am*ir* of Rewanduz to Sir John Campbell, pp. 793-795. TBL, London.

"I take the advantage of the opportunity to reply to your friendly communication, and I will hereafter look forward with much anxity and pleasure to the prospect of hearing frequently of your welfare, and that will honour me with our commands, and you may be assured that I will do all in my power to fulfil your wishes, whatever they may be."[497]

It seems it was on the basis of this relationship that Taylor expressed his delight for the victory of the Rewanduz Pasha, and said that his informant "entertained strong hopes of the Pasha's success as he was well fitted to cope with such ... enemies". It was confirmed that, "the Turkish troops of Baghdad under the Kahayah, who has reached the suburbs of [Baghdad] together with the remains of his army, an event which had thrown this Government in the deepest embarrassment."[498]

Despite this memorandum, Britain's foreign policy aimed to avoid any regional expansion that may have fragmented or destabilised the Ottoman Empire. Even Taylor realised the significance of the movement initiated by Rewanduz Bey, particularly, in terms of the regional impact the Emirate then posed. He observed, "...even in the heart of Assyria, a formidable rival to the power of both Turk and Persian was started by the Rewanduz Bey, the most extraordinary political and not least powerful Kurdish prince of the time. "[499]

Two years later, Taylor in a letter acknowledged the power of the Soran Emirate and the Pasha's influencial on the Kurds and others. Taylor observed that there was "unexpected success of Muhammad Pacha [*sic*] of Curdistan [*sic*] against the Curdish tribes who long held the part of Mesopotamia between Mosul and Mardin in powerful an almost undisputed possession."[500]

The British maintained pressure to ascertain that their position was made clear to key regional players; on occasion, political advisors were dispatched to ensure their policy was protected at all costs. Their primary aim was to ensure that the status quo of two regional powers was maintained within acceptable limits and they supported actions which enabled this policy. The British policy in the east of the Ottoman Empire was ultimately antipathetic to Kurdish

---

[497] Ibid, p. 795.
[498] IOR L/PS/9/97A. Taylor, R., the British Political Agent in Turkish Arabia to the Secret Committee of the East India House dated 11th November 1834, pp. 423-425.
[499] IOR L/PS/9/91 R. Taylor to Charles Norris, Chief Secretary to Government in Bombay, No 36 of 1830, Baghdad 23rd December 1830, pp 386/5-6.
[500] IOR L/PS/9/97A Lu. Col. R. Taylor to Secret Committee East India House-London, 11th November 1834, Baghdad, p. 423.

interests. Layard, the Under-Secretary of the Foreign Office wrote, in April 1832, to Granville [British Foreign Secretary] explaining that the policy of Britain was to "…maintain the Turkish Empire in its present state until the Christian population may be ready to succeed the Musulman. My conviction is that it is possible to do so; and that this policy is the only hope of a favourable solution to the Eastern Question."[501] Evidence for this can be seen in a letter that was written, in September 1832, to the Persian Shah by Sir Campbell. The letter was written when the Persians sought action against the expansion of Soran Emirate in an effort to regain occupied territory. Moreover, a communication was sent by Sir Campbell, which asked him to plead with the Sultan in Istanbul and say that if the Ottomans did not act against Rewanduz Pasha, then he would not protest against any action taken by the Persian authorities.[502]

From 1833, Britain established independent relations with the Bey of Rewanduz in order to make sure its objectives were met. Taylor wrote to the Chief Secretary of the Bombay Government in this regard, expressing his concern for the Bey's activities in the region, which by this time were significantly impacting upon the regional powers. In a letter dated March 15 1833, Taylor suggests that the:

"Curdish [*sic*] Provinces are an endless source of anxiety to this Pachalik
[of Baghdad] from the increasing intrigues of the Persians with its
restless chiefs who have just reason to complain of this line of conduct
in their neighbours. Being on the most friendly terms with the Chiefs of
Curdistan [*sic*] I have written confidentially to the Bey of Rewandooz at
the request of the Pacha simply to prepare his mind for His Royal
Highness's communications."[503]

In 1834, a letter was sent to the Iranian Foreign Affairs minister in Persia from the deputy British ambassador, which gave Britain's support for any joint action made by both the Ottomans and the Persians in order to push the Soran Emirate back to its original borders.[504]

---

[501] Waterfield, Gordon (1963). Layard of Nineveh, John Murray, London, pp. 235-6.
[502] Mirza Salih, Ghulam Muhsin (1365). Isnadi Rasmi dar Rawabiti Syasi Iran ba Inglis u Rus u Othmani, Persian text, Official Documents regarding political links between Iranian, England, Russia and the Ottoman, Volume 2, Ta'rikh Iran publisher, Tehran, pp. 143-4.
[503] IOR L/PS/9/95 Lt. Col R. Taylor, P. A. Turkish Arabia, to the Chief Secretary to Government of Bombay, Baghdad, 15th March 1833, p. 241.
[504] Iranian Foreign Ministry (1369). Unit of publishing documents, Guzidai Isnadi Syasi Iran u Othmani, Persian text, Selected Political Documents regarding the relations between Iran and the Ottoman, Volume 1, Tehran, p. 529-530.

Lord Palmerston expressed concern about two developments in the region, the expansion of Egyptian power and Russian expansion. Palmerston[505] was worried lest the Egyptian campaign troubled British interests in the Ottoman Empire. If Muhammad Ali managed to establish Egypt as a new Empire in the region it had the potential to cause the fragmentation of the Ottoman Empire.

Russia wanted to extend its influence in the region, particularly into Asia Minor, which was then controlled by the Ottoman Empire and Persia. This had a considerable impact on Britain's foreign policy towards the region, and helped to shape their attitude towards the territories of Kurdistan. Thus, the British preferred that the Soran Emirate remained in an unexpanded state so that it acted as a buffer zone to keep Russian ambitions in check. There were concerns that if the Russians became the dominant power in the region they would threaten British interests.[506]

4.12 The Effects of the Soran Emirate's Expansion on Persia

Persia started to take into serious consideration the future of the Soran Emirate, after the borders of Kurdistan had been extended to a point that could potentially have led to their influence within Persian territory. To counter this, they decided they should consider building a better relationship with the Ottoman authorities.

In 1829, Amir Nizam (a powerful official in the Qajar court) sent a letter to Muhammad Rashid Pasha [the Ottoman Grand Vazir, from 1829–33], where he expressed his anxiety and anger about the actions of the Soran Pashas who had taken many Persian Kurdish villages, which included some areas of Mukiryan including some villages in Lajan, Sauj Bulag and Sardasht.[507] Muhammad Pasha of Rewanduz had offended the Shah of Iran by making inroads on the side of Salmas and Uromiyah.[508]

In a letter to Charles Norris, The Chief Secretary to the government in Bombay, the British agent in Baghdad, Major Taylor, noted that in 1830 the two most influential regional events

---

[505] He was British Foreign Secretary, 1830–41 & 1846–51.
[506] O. Shea, M. T. (1994). The Question of Kurdistan and Iran's International Borders, in K. McLachlam, *The Boundaries of Modern Iran*, London, p. 53.

[507] Nasiri, Dr Muhammad Raza (1367). Isnad u Makatibati Ta;rikhi Iran-Qajar, Persian text, Documents and correspondences of Iranian Qajar History, Volume 2, Kaihan Publisher, Tehran, pp. 127-9.
[508] Ibid, p. 809.

were: "...the invasion of Curdistan [*sic*] by the troops of Abbas Mirza,[509]...and the arrival and subsequent death of Derweesh Mohamed (*sic*) Sadiq Effendi."[510], [511]

According to Wood, in the same letter, with regards to the invasion of Kurdistan the British "...claimed preference in consideration whether viewed as an isolated event or connected... particularly with our vital interests in this Pachalik and its neighbouring territory under Turkish dominion". Wood's major concern was how this affected the Ottoman Empire. He observed that the Kurds at the time "...appear to be by no means favourable to the permanent retention of power by Mahmood Pacha [*sic*]..."[512]

According to some other British officials and travellers such as Fraser, "the Meer [*sic*] of Rewandooz (*sic*), thought fit to overrun, and appropriate a considerable portion of the territory to himself."[513] This indicates clearly that the Mir was capable of ruling the Soran Emirate and of improving Kurdish self-rule.

Rawlinson writes that the Rewandi tribe and dynasty led by Muhammad Pasha, the *Mir* of Rewanduz, was "regarded by all the Kurds with great respect."[514] Here it may be understood that Muhammad Pasha was generally accepted as a respectable ruler among the Kurds.

Wood was also somewhat concerned about the Persian intentions and of their long-term influence in the region stating that: "...how is it possible not to feel the utmost anxiety at the operation of the Persians in Curdistan [*sic*] and not to exert the utmost influence and effort so as conduct affairs as to exclude their troops from Soolamaniah [*sic*] as early as possible."[515]

4.13 Persia's Role in the Downfall of the Soran Emirate

Whilst the machinations of Wood[516] played a major part in the downfall of the Rewanduz Emirate, the role played by Persia should not be entirely overlooked. To Persia, dissolution of the Rewanduz Emirate had significant importance. The Persians sent two of their highest

---

[509] The then Prince Royal of Persia.
[510] The late Defterdar Effendi or Chancellor of the Exchequer, at the Sublime Porte.
[511] IOR L/PS/9/91 Letter and enclosures from Richard Wood (1830) to Charles Norris, Chief Secretary to the government in Bombay, p. 386.
[512] Ibid, p. 389.
[513] Fraser, J. B. (1840). Op. cit, p148.
[514] Major Rawlinson H. C. (1841). Op. cit, p.25.
[515] IOR L/PS/9/91 Letter and enclosures from Richard Wood (1830) to Charles Norris p. 401
[516] See the appendix A & B for details.

ranked princes to command the Persian forces: the brother of the Shah and Melik Hassan Mirza [the son of the late Shah] who led the Persian expedition against the Rewanduz Kurds.

The Christian missions in Persia played a role in the collapse of the Soran Emirate as well. When Persian troops returned from the battlefields against Soran, both Persian princes commanding the Persian forces visited a Christian school in Orumiya on their return.[517] There was evidence that in 1829, Amir Nizam, a powerful man in the Persian Court, sent an official letter to the Ottoman Grand Vazir asking for cooperation between both empires to root out the Soran Emirate. The letter advocated the elimination and destruction of Muhammad Pasha of Rewanduz; it stipulated securing boundaries between states to prevent further conflict; it advocated receiving four thousand tomans [Persian currency] as compensation and releasing all prisoners in Rewanduz; and it finally called for the occupier [Muhammad Pasha] to withdraw from Lajan, Mukri and other places in Persia. [518]

Below, it will be shown how the Ottomans and Persians collaborated against the Soran Emirate and brought it to destruction. The Ottomans needed to keep control over their disparate territories, so they placed governors over Baghdad and Egypt. They made flawed decisions in their choice of candidates. After a while, the governors used the opportunity to their own political advantage by expanding their influence and power. Muhammad Ali would take any opportunity to increase his influence. On one occasion when Egypt was told by central government to provide troops, the Pasha stipulated that in return he wanted Anatolia.[519] However, later he rebelled against the Ottomans, using Egyptian troops to invade Syria.

The military successes of Muhammad Pasha of Rewanduz were opposed by the Constantinople authorities. Thus, the Ottomans prepared to retaliate against him. The Pashaliks of Baghdad and Mosul were weak and had serious domestic problems after the deposition of Dawood Pasha.

---

[517] Grant, Dr. (1837). Latter October 18th 1836, Visit of two Princes to Oorumiah and to the School, *The Missionary Herald* , Volume XXXIII, 1837, p. 251.
[518] Amir Nizam, Muhammad Khani Zangana (1367). A letter from to Muhammad Rashid Pasha, in Dr Muhammad Reza Nasiri, *Isnad u Mukatabati Ta'rikhi Iran* (Qachari), Persian text, Iranian Historical Documents and Correspondents (Qachari), Part 2, Kayhan Publisher, Tehran, 1367, p. 127.
[519]Shaw, Stanford J. & Shaw, Ezel Kural (2002). *History of the Ottoman Empire and Modern Turkey: Reform, Revolution, and Republic, The Rise of Modern Turkey 1808-1975*, Cambridge University Press, Cambridge, p. 31.

4.14 The Effect of Muhammad Ali of Egypt and his campaigns

In the beginning of the nineteenth century, the weakness of the Ottoman Empire could no longer be ignored by the officials. The Empire needed to consolidate its grip on power again. Sultan Mahmud II (1808-1839) decided to do whatever he could to introduce a program of reform in his empire to prevent further disturbances in his state. Apart from military and administrative reforms, another feature that the Sultan was determined to control was the powerful hereditary governors and princes who were seen as unreliable to the empire.

To further his expansionist aims, Muhammad Pasha used the weakness of the Ottoman Empire and its inability to maintain control to his advantage. This, in effect, he destabilised the Empire further in his favour. He attempted to make pacts with the rebellious governor Muhammad Ali Pasha of Egypt against the Ottoman Empire. According to a dispatch dated 5th Sebtember 1836, by Turner, the British Consul Genral in Syrian, stated that Muhammad Pasha of Soran "had appealed to Ibrahim Pacha [*sic*] to have his territory placed under the Egyptian Government."[520] However, his decisions did not always lead to the desired results. Muhammad Pasha underestimated the reaction of the Ottoman Empire and European Powers; previously Russia had already been contacted by the Egyptians and this incensed the British. Thus, during July and August of 1836, both collaborated, sent troops to entrap him and placed the Soran Emirate under siege. News of Muhammad Pasha's intentions incensed both the Ottoman and Persian authorities, particularly due to his continued incursions in their territory.

4.15 Regional Powers action to eliminate the Soran Emirate

The Persians often sought opportunities to oppose the Soran Emirate, according to a despatch sent by Henry Ellis (23rd May, 1836). On one occasion, Persia suggested co-operating with Turkey in an opportunity to act against Rewanduz, but Turkey rebutted their suggestion and warned them, "don't interfere in the Ottoman affairs!"

---

[520] IOR LP/S/9/100, Turner. N., Consul General in Syria to Secret Committee of East India House-London, 16th August 1836, Damascus, p. 177.

However, during the siege of the Soran Emirate, various forces understood that combined action could be beneficial to all parties in dealing with the Soran Emirate, who had at some point put pressure on their territory.

At this point the Ottomans, who had been weakened by various campaigns, recognised the benefit of co-operating with Persia, which would enable them to surround the territory from both the Ottoman and the Persian frontiers of Kurdistan. They agreed to provide support to the Persian campaign, and they sent troops under the command of Prince Karaman Mirza and the Amir Nizam.[521]

Moreover, other Emirates, such as the Baban Emirate, who were disaffected by Muhammad Pasha's treatment of them, sent a contingent with the Persian army, who had been attacked by Muhammad Pasha of Soran between 1823 and 1826. Lieutenant General Shiel was in Kurdistan when the Ottomans attacked Rewanduz. He documented evidence of how the Persians helped the Ottomans to subdue the Kurds: the road was prepared by the Persians to enable better access of [Rashid Pasha's] canon.[522]

The regional powers craved an opportunity to crush the Kurdish Emirate. They were keen for a restoration of Kurdistan to its ancient relation with the Emirate, and to its former boundaries with Persia.[523] To this end, a plan was concocted by Ali Reda Pasha for the subjugation of Kurdistan. Ali Reda Pasha was the first Turkish Wali of Baghdad who was backed by Ince Bairaqtar Muhammad Pasha in this regard.[524] Furthermore, Rashid Pasha, the Turkish High Commander to end the Rawanduz Emirate, believed that:

> "Rawanduz was a clear threat to the Sultan's supremacy in Asia. And that only his capture or geath would make the Pashalics of Mosu and Bagdad [*sic*] safe against

[521] IOR LP/S/9/99 John McNeill, 12th September 1836, Op. cit, p. 369; raised points that included: i). removal of bases taken by Muhammad Pasha; ii). returned borders to original limits and make sure peoples there not effected again; iii). claim back 40,000 Tumans taken from people by M. Pasha; iv). Released prisoners taken to Rewanduz; v). Withdrawal of Muhammad Pasha's troops from Lajan, Mukri and other places occupied by him.

[522] Lieut-Col Shiel, J. (1838). "Notes on a Journey from Tabriz, through Kurdistan, via Van, Se'ert and Erbil, to Suleimanyeh, in July and August, 1836", *The Journal of the Royal Geographical Society of London*, Volume Eighth, p. 67.

[523] IOR L/PS/9/92 Major Taylor to Sir Charles Norris, Chief Secretary to Government of Bombay, Basra, 16 November 1831, p. 715.

[524] Ali Reda Pasha was the first Turk who became the Ottoman waly of Baghdad (1831-1841), during his governorship he tried very hard to bring Kurdish rulers in Southern Kurdistan to be under his authority. Inceh Bairaqdar Muhammad Pasha who was also the first Turk to become the Ottoman waly of Mosul (1835-1844) and always had negative attitudes against Kurdish self-rule. See Sulaiman Saigh, *Ta'rikh al-Mosul*, History of Mosul, al-Salafiya Press, Cairo, 1923. See also Nawwar, Dr. Abdulaziz (1968). *Ta'rikh al-Iraq al-Hadis*, The History of New Iraq, published by Dar al-Katib al-Arabi, Cairo.

Persian infringement from the east and the molestations of Ibrahim along the Euphrates in the west."[525]

This aim was shared by Wood who managed to win over Muhammad Pasha of Soran "by an appeal to his loyalty to the Sultan, and use him in the creation of a strong Turkish *bloc* in Mesopotamia, with Bagdad [*sic*] as its centre of gravity."[526]

For the various powers, other positive outcomes of their aim meant the Soran Emirate no longer interfered in the affairs of regional or European powers and no longer carried out incursions into their territory. Events out of Muhammad Pasha's control caused him to surrender and led to the eventual demise of the Soran Emirate.

The ending of the Soran Emirate took a long time, costimg the Ottoman Empire two thousand men.[527] In other words, keeping Kurdish local-rule was at the heart of the conflict between Kurdish Emirates and the Ottoman Empire. Therefore, for some time after removing Muhammad Pasha, the Ottoman Sultan reinstated the *Mir* of Rewanduz in the government of his native province in Kurdistan and later the *Mir* of Rewanduz received the Nishan [medal].[528] Wood believed that giving a medal to Muhammad Pasha meant that he would be reappointed in his position. Especially after his removal from power, Kurdistan was thrown into disorder.[529] During his stay in Istanbul, he was so respected by the Sultan that he accompanied him to the mosque.[530]

4.16 Reactions of the European Powers

Concerns over the effects on regional interests if the rebellion had succeeded may have led to the Ottoman Empire being toppled: it meant the local issue became an international incident. Unfortunately, for Muhammad Pasha his strategies had made few friends in the international community.

---

[525] Cunningham, A. B. edited by (1966). *The Early Correspondence of Richard Wood, 1831-1841*, published by Royal Historical Society, London, p. 13.

[526] Ibid, p. 14.

[527] IOR L/PS/9/102 Ponsonby the British Ambassador in Istanbul to Viscount Palmerston the British Foreign Secretary, May 9, 1837, p. 121. TBL.

[528] Ibid.

[529] Correspandance p. 120

[530] Ibid

Muhammad Pasha of Soran knew the importance position of the British and on hearing news of the Pasha's potential Egyptian-Kurdish campaign and just before the siege of Soran, the British Embassy at Constantinople sent one of his diplomats Richard Wood to Rewanduz, the capital town of Soran. Wood was alarmed by two possibilities. First, he was concerned that the defeat of the Ottoman army by the Soran Emirate. Second, he was concerned that this would leave a vacuum which could be occupied by Persia and Russia after the collapse of the strong Kurdish local rule. He had information which reached him from Persia that an irregular battalion of Russians in the service of the Persia was almost certain to reach Kurdistan.[531] Therefore, Woods exerted influence over Muhammad Pasha to protect their self-interest. The Pasha still believed that his emirate army was invincible and he became "obstinate and determined to resist" the imminent arrival of the Ottoman Empire.[532] Wood realized that strong local forces in the region such as Soran and foreign powers, especially Russia and Muhammad Ali of Egypt, would be the three vital elements threatening the Ottoman Empire. Therefore, British policy and British political representatives in that region backed the Empire against these three. The Soran Emirate became a victim of British policy in the Ottoman Empire.

Wood understood that the Pasha's position was now untenable as all the Kurdish towns had been garrisoned, with the combined forces now closing their grip on Rewanduz. He convinced the Pasha to retreat. Wood was then dispatched in order to bear influence over the Pasha and to ascertain a favourable outcome. Wood later played a key role in convincing the Pasha of Soran to submit himself to the Ottoman forces. He stated: "The Pasha's submission to the Porte being the great object to be obtained…"[533] The British preferred that the Pasha surrendered to the Ottomans rather than the Persians, as "surrendering to the Persians meant later, if he returned from exile, he would still pose a threat to the Ottoman Empire."[534]

According to Taylor, surrender to the Persians was considered more satisfactory by the Ottomans because if the Pasha had handed himself to the Ottomans, then he could have

---

[531] Cunningham, A. B. (1966). Op. cit, p. 105.

[532] IOR L/PS/9/92 Major Taylor to Sir Charles Norris, Chief Secretary to Government of Bombay, Basra, 16 November 1831, p. 682.

[533] FO 78/277, Richard Wood to Lord Ponsonby at Constantinople, Revanduz castle near the Persian frontier, No. 14, Sep 3rd, 1836, p. 226. See whole dispatch, pp. 221-227.TNA, London, Kew Garden. See also IOR L/PS/9/100 p. 691. See whole dispatch, pp. 679-695 in IOR L/PS/9/100.

[534] FO 78/277, Richard Wood's report.

become "a formidable opponent" to "the Russians…should they ever attempt to execute one of their avowed plans of carrying their power down to the Persian Gulf."[535]

The release of Rashid Pacha's army would in turn

> "leave … [his] .. forces … free to oppose the ambition…of Muhammad Ali & Russia" whilst "it will be a great advantage to our interest should His Majesty's Government think fit to prosecute any plans… to have at Rewandooz a chief who thinks he owes his life and liberty and power…to the English Ambassador."[536]

The Pasha at the time was convinced that his best interests would be met if he surrendered to the Persians. Wood's priority was to consider British interest first and foremost, so he influenced Muhammad Pasha to take the alternative action and surrendered to the Ottomans. Wood later in a communication stated how he "…justly increased his fears by pointing to him the duplicity of the Persian Court, and by preventing his flight thither, without compromising either His Majesty's Government."[537] The success of his approach was later relayed to Palmerston in a communication from Lord Ponsonby.

John White also wrote about the capture of Muhammad Pasha to Lord Ponsonby, and concluded in this communication that the Persians sought to cover damages from previous expansion of Soran into their land and of the British support of that aim:

> "There is reason to hope that Rashid Pasha has every disposition to facilitate the adjustment of the claim for cooperation which the Persian government has preferred on the ground of injury done to its territories by the Mir…a portion of the claim had been liquidated by the Mir himself previous to capture, and the remainder will it is to be hoped be paid from the captured property."[538]

By this time, the Pasha was more concerned more about his imminent safety than the future of his people. Wood, to achieve a favourable outcome, made it seem as though he had given advice only with the Pasha's primary concern in mind. Wood interposed:

---

[535] IOR L/PS/9/102, p. 121.
[536] Ibid, p. 121-2, p.467.
[537] Ibid, p. 693.
[538] FO 60/43 Letter from John McNeill to Lord Ponsonby, dated September, 11th 1836. IOR LP/S/9/99: pp. 213–216.

"I trust that if I have promised him Your Lordship's interpositions with the Porte…I have not acted contrary to your Lordship's wishes."[539]

By the end of the conversation, the Pasha presumed that he had been offered the guarantees that he desired for his own safety. The Pasha falsely perceived the final outcome would be more favourable for him, thus Richard Wood succeeded "to prevent the flight of into Persia of the Kurdish Chief, and to induce him to surrender to the Sultan's General."[540]

However, Wood had other objectives in mind, to make sure his own interests were met. Rashid Pasha "immediately sent an officer with some Kurdish 'Mollahs' [*sic*] to renew his assurances of protection and to confirm the promise of 'Muhuily Koran' or a Koran bearing his seal (equivalent to a solemn oath)" The envoy promised, moreover, that the Pasha wished to reinstate him, protesting that he only wished to see the Ottoman commander for one hour and recommended that he pay attention to "what I had said to him respecting his flight into Persia". He declared feeling "great gratification in having it in my power to announce the close of this war the seventh day after my arrival at Revanduz, by overthrowing the Rebel's Hopes."[541]

According to the British, Muhammad Pasha of Rewanduz held the false notion that "he was the only competent person to rule over Kurds and protect the frontier of the Ottoman Empire from Persian violation." He also believed that in all likelihood the Turkish commander would recommend his reinstatement to the Sultan. In fact he never returned back to Rewanduz.[542] There is evidence to suggest that Muhammad Pasha stayed in Istanbul for more than a year and finally fell victim to a plot. His death was confirmed at the Porte on 11th November 1837 by the Undersecretary of the Interior Ministry to Richard Wood.[543] In his letter dated 15th November 1837, Lord Ponsonby confirmed that Muhammad Pasha was murdered.[544]

---

[539] FO 8/277, , Sep 3, 1836, Richard Wood to Lord Ponsonby at Constantinople, Revanduz castle near the Persian frontier pp. 224-5.

[540] FO 8/277 Lord Ponsonby to Lord Palmerston, despatch No. 184, Therapia, 12th October 1836, p. 217.

[541] FO 78/277 Richard Wood to Lord Ponsonby about his dealings with the Pasha of Soran, Op. cit, pp. 225-6.

[542] Ibid. Also in Richard Wood to Lord Ponsonby at Constantinople, Revanduz castle near the Persian frontier and in IOR L/PS/9/100, p. 687.

[543] Cunningham, A. B. (1966). Edited by, *The Early Correspondence of Richard Wood 1831-1841*, The Royal Historical Society, London, p. 128

[544] Ibid.

4.17 The Soran Emirate's Contribution to Kurdism

Muhammad Pasha's unrivalled position enabled him to reorganise Soran's domestic affairs so that he could strengthen his grip on power, and enable him to raise followers to prepare for future struggles. Thus the cornerstone of a Kurdish political administration could now be established. This meant that local distinctions could be replaced with a wider Kurdish identity, which gave the Kurds in the emirate just one central authority and voice. Muhammad Pasha used both diplomacy and force to strength his power base. According to Dr Mortiz Wagner, Muhammad Pasha established friendships with both Nurullah Beg, the Mir of Hakkari and with Bedirkhan Pasha of Botan, who supported the Soran Pasha.[545] Dr Mortiz Wagner observes, "Accordingly, the Bey of Rewanoz [*sic*] requested the more powerful chief, Bedar Khan [*sic*], ruling over all the clans of Bodhan [*sic*] (meant Botan), to share in the exploit."[546] Therefore, during his rule, Muhammad Pasha never attacked the Hakkari and Botan emirates. Furthermore, the Soran Pasha made allies with tribal leaders, such as the chief of Muzuri in Badinan.[547] The Pasha was welcomed by local Kurds when he took the Solduz region in Persian Kurdistan. Local Kurds were suffering from paying high taxes to Persia and at the same time supporting Rewanduz troops.[548] It is significant of Kurdism that the Pasha intended to gather Kurdish chiefs around his rule without resorting to physical force.

Muhammad Pasha expanded the Soran Emirate primarily with his interests in mind; he seemed to have failed to consider how his actions might have affected the interests of both the regional and external players. His military expansionist tendencies included campaigns against rival Kurdish Emirates especially Baban.

Consequently, in the long term, Muhammad Pasha's policy of territorial expansion earned him more enemies than friends, which in effect proved a hindrance to the Kurdish cause. Thus, they opposed his aims and the benefits he received from expanding the Soran Emirate in the first place.

---

[545] Wagner, Dr. Mortiz (1856). Travels in Persia, Georgia and Koordistan; with sketches of the Cossacks and the Caucasus, Vol. III, Hurst & Bleckett, Publishers, London, pp. 260-1.

[546] Ibid, p. 261

[547] Askander, Sa'd (2008). Qiyam al-Nizam al-Amarati fi Kurdistan wa squtihi, Arabic text, The establishment of the Kurdish emirates system and its downfall, published by Binket Jin, Silêmanî, p. 180.

[548] Khalfin, Dr N. A. (1969). Struggle for Kurdistan, Kurdish Question in the International Relations during 19th Century, Arabic text, translated from Russian by Dr. Ahmad Osman, Al-sha'b Press, Baghdad, p. 51.

Having a powerful and influential emirate, which was backed by a strong army, meant that the regional powers adopted a policy of appeasement and "wait and see" until it was in a weakened state. On one occasion, such a gesture even bestowed Muhammad Pasha with titles and riches. However, the emirate still posed a substantial threat to the stability of Ottoman Empire, which eventually led to the combined action to bring it down.

Once his strength had diminished and it was no longer strong enough to resist, the disparate powers capitalised on its now weak position; this enabled them to exploit the Egyptian-Kurdish Pact, which meant that Muhammad Pasha was prevented from being able to disrupt the regional status quo any longer.

Normally the regional empires had strained relations. However, Muhammad Pasha's long-term actions forced the regional powers to put aside their differences to lessen Soran's threat to the regional stability. This temporarily brought them closer together so they could achieve their objective to mount an effective challenge against their enemy. This, in turn brought about the fall of the Soran Emirate and in turn the capitulation of Muhammad Pasha, leading to his eventual demise.

The overthrowing of the Soran Pasha, did not improve the situation for the Ottoman Empire. Muhammad Pasha's legacy was that Kurds in Soran, as in other parts of Kurdistan, refused the Ottoman direct rule. In a dispatch by N. W. Werry, the Consular in Aleppo to Lord Ponsonby, the British Ambassador in Constantinople, observed that "the Koordish [*sic*] population, the most active and warlike opposed to the Sultan's Pachas [*sic*], is ready to embrace if they cannot maintain their former de facto independence."[549] The representative of the Wali of Baghdad, appointed to govern Rewanduz, could not put the Ottoman's policy into practice and did not stay long under Soran Kurdish pressure. Therefore, the Ottoman returned the governorship of Rewanduz to Rasul Pasha, the *mir*'s brother, who tried to regain the former glory of the Soran under the Pasha of Rewanduz. This made Najib Pasha of Baghdad remove Rasul Pasha by force; then the emirate ended for ever.[550]

---

[549] IOR L/PS/9/100 Copy of a despatch by N. W. Werry, the British Consular in Aleppo to Lord Ponsonby, Aleppo, December 3rd, 1836,
[550] Nawwar, Dr. Abdulaziz (1968). Op. cit, p. 109.

4.18 Conclusion

The expansion of the Soran Emirate helped to bring the Kurds closer together. A strong army gave them security and peace. People paid less tax than in the other parts of the Ottoman Empire. Muhammad Pasha successfully recruited tribesmen from all over his emirate to serve in his troops. Muhammad Pasha's aim ultimately failed after ten years because of various tactics, coincidences and events. Muhammad Pasha was determined to succeed in expanding his Emirate, regardless of the consequences. His actions often seemed somewhat flawed; thus by his strong-handedness he managed to alienate disparate Kurdish Emirates and clans, instead of uniting them into a single entity, and giving them a single voice and authority.

To bring local rulers under central control, from 1826 the *Nizami Cedit* (New Order) in the Ottoman Empire started to enforce direct rule over all the territories. In doing so their central administration imposed its rule over all the minorities of the Empire. As a consequence, the old multi-ethnic Ottoman System was destroyed. The military reform and later *Tanzimat* or "Reform" not only abolished Kurdish emirates, but became a bludgeon with which they could suppress the Kurdish people as well.

Moreover, the Ottomans and Persians had no desire to see a powerful Kurdish ruler. The European powers such as Russia, Britain and France did not want another regional power in the region such as Muhammad Pasha of Soran. The British policy in the east of the Ottoman Empire was apathetic to Kurdish interests, which had a major impact in the final demise of Soran Emirate and Muhammad Pasha. They were primarily concerned to maintain the regional status quo so that the balance of power remained in equilibrium in Europe, and British interests in India were maintained.

The Ottomans tried to strengthen their authority and control by reforming their army and centralising power in the Empire. However, the size of the army had an impact on its strength. The Ottomans relied on governors to exert their rule over the distant territories, such as Egypt and Baghdad. Unfortunately, their choice of administrators was flawed as they used their posting as an opportunity to expand their regional influence, which in effect managed to further weaken Turkey's grip on power. This was opposite to Ottoman's initial intentions.

Muhammad Pasha attempted to form pacts with these governors, recognising how, with their help, he could attempt to further destabilise the Ottoman Empire. However, he ultimately managed to alienate them, which also mitigated his aims. Furthermore, outside influences conspired against him, which also prevented him from achieving his goal. The *Mir* of Soran's failure to consider how his stratagems would affect the interests of the international community meant that although the Soran Emirate had been in existence for some five hundred years, the *Mir* managed to bring about its collapse in only ten.

For the Ottoman Empire, the fall of Rewanduz had two main effects. First, if the Pasha surrendered to the Turks, he would no longer interfere with them but he could be used for future defence against their enemies. Second, the opportunity enabled the Ottomans to finally achieve their main objective: Rewanduz never regained or recovered its power. In fact, there is documentary evidence that the British envoy to Soran Emirate, Richard Wood, working on behalf of both the British government and the Ottoman Commander Rashid Pasha, had a decisive role in preparing and implementing the treacherous plot which undermined the authority of *Mir* of Soran and persuaded him to surrender to the Ottoman forces on the promise of retaining his position as the governor of Rewanduz. [551]

Besides working on strenthening his army and implementing security and administration in his emirate, Muhammad Pasha promoted education in *medrese*, and had respect for scholars and *melas*. He showed generosity and kindness to them during the period of the Soran Emirate when Kurdish language and literature was instrumental in developing Kurdism by using Kurdish language. The most famous Kurdish scholars in the Soran Emirate, such as *Mela* Muhammad Ibnu Adam and Hajî *Mela* Abdullah Jelizade, wrote in Kurdish. Ideas of Kurdish consciousness became an important ideological force for resisting occupation and calling for revolution and liberation. Hajî Qadiri Koyî became the most nationalistic Kurdish

---

[551] A dispatch by Richard Wood to Lord Ponsonby KB- British ambassador in Istanbul, states proudly how he managed to deceive the Kurdish Mir, dissuaded him from siding with the Persians and persuaded him on false promises to surrender to the Turkish army of Rashid Muhammad Pasha. The following is only a short quotation from a long dispatch he has written to the British authorities detailing his treacherous plot that brought down the Kurdish pasha. He writes: " By the movement, which brought the Turkish troops within four hours of Revendous (Rewanduz), the Rebel was astounded, the desertion of his men followed; and his efforts for defence were paralysed, and I went even so far as to prove to him that the every Position of Rewanduz was untenable and that he must seriously think of submission. He abandoned consequently his Works in despair, and in their crisis intelligence reached him of Rashid Pasha's approach. As I had his Highness's word that, provided Muhammad Pasha threw himself on his mercy, he would not only spare his life, but would recommend his (the Rebel's) restoration to the Sultan, as the only Person competent to rule over Mountains, and to protect the Frontier from Persian encroachments. I trust that if I have promised him Your Lordship's interposition with the Porte in favour of his life as a further inducement for him to submit, and put an end to intestine contention which has so long devastated their devoted country, I have not acted contrary to Your Lordship's wishes." Richard Wood to H.E. the Lord Ponsonby KB-Constantinople, Ravanduz Castle, near the Persian frontier, Sept. 3, 1836, FO 78/277, p. 226. See whole dispatch pp. 221-227. TNA, London, Kew Gardens. See also IOR, L/PS/9/100, pp.686-8, TBL, London.

poet to give expression to these ideas in a language that was, and is, understood by all sections of Kurdish society from intellectuals to peasants. He developed the theory of nationalism as revolutionary, progressive and secularist. He clearly identified the goal of national unity of land and people, and statehood as the only way for the liberation of his people and the revival of the past glories of the Kurdish nation. All the experiences and thoughts which he learnt from Baban, Erdelan and Soran must have given Hajî formative aspects of a strong and passionate romantic nationalism that he took to the Bedirkhans. This means that Hajî played a great role in connecting three Kurdish emirates together, at least through literature.

Chapter Five

The Botan Emirate and the Development of Kurdism in the time of Bedirkhan

In this chapter, the development of Kurdism in the era of Bedirkhan Pasha (1821-1847) in the first half of the nineteenth century will be examined. Bedirkhan's character and his ideas about establishing a powerful Kurdish Emirate will be discussed. His implementation of internal policies, administration, his military's aim, economics, security and justice will be explored; the role of Kurdism within this context will be explained. Furthermore, the development of the notion of Kurdism during the period of rule of Bedirkhan and how this was achieved will be addressed. Literature, particularly *lawiks* (Kurdish folkloric songs), and their influence upon the development of Kurdism will be discussed. Finally, it will be argued that Bedirkhan's connections with the Nestorians became a crucial pretext for the Ottoman Empire and the European powers, especially those of Britain, to end Bedirkhan's rule and topple the Botan Emirate. Bedirkhan's legacy and its impact on future generations of Kurds will be examined.

5.1 The rise to power of Bedirkhan Beg

Bedirkhan, Pasha of Botan, was and remains one of the best known Kurdish personalities and leaders among Kurdish intellectuals and Kurdish people in general. He was born in 1802 in Cizire[552] and became a *mir* (prince) of the Botan Emirate in 1821.[553]

Bedirkhan was only eighteen when he came to power in 1821. He was the last *mir* of the Botan Emirate and became the most powerful ruler in northern Kurdistan. He quickly showed a desire to create a centralised power base under his direct control.[554] From the beginning of his rule, he sought to maintain his power. According to Joyce Blau, "Bedirkhan

---

[552] Sejadi, Ela'din (1959). *Shorshakani Kurd wa Kurd u komari Iraq*, Kurdish text, Kurdish revolutions, Kurds and the Republic of Iraq, Ma'arif Press, Baghdad, p. 44. Nezan, Kendal (1993). *The Kurds under the Ottoman Empire*, in A people without a country, Edited by Gerard Chaliand, Interlink Publishing Group, Inc., New York, p. 20.

[553] Nezan Kendal (1963). Ibid, p. 21. Shamzini, Aziz (2006). *Julanawai rzgari nishtmani Kurdistan*, Kurdish text, translated from Arabic by Farid Asasard, published by Centre for Kurdistan Strategy Studies, Silêmanî, p. 107. Sherko, Blach (1986). *Al- Qaziya al-Kurdiya mazi al-Kurd wa hazirihim*, Arabic text, The Kurdish Question: their past and present, published by Rabitat Kawa, Beirut, p. 51. Blach Sherko is a pseudonym of Celadet Amin Ali Bedirkhan (1893-1951) the grandson of the Bedirkhan Pasha who was one of the nationalists actively involved in Kurdish politics, journalism and cultural movements. Bruinessen, Martin van (1992). *Agha, Shaikh and State*, Zed Books Ltd, London and New York, p. 178.

[554] Hururi, Salah M. (2000). *Emarat Botan fi 'ahd al-Amir Bedirkhan 1821-47*, Arabic text, The Principality of Botan During the Rule of Prince Bedirkhan 1821- 47, A Political and Historical Study, MA Dissertation, Mukryani Publisher, Erbil, Kurdistan, pp. 50-1.

Pasha was struggling for Kurdism, working to unite the land of Kurdistan, and desired to establish a Greater Kurdistan which was the aspiration of Kurdish people."[555]

During this period, Bedirkhan was able to take advantage of a number of problems which confronted the Ottoman Empire.   Parts of the Empire had begun to break away from a centralised rule, and the leaders faced interference in their internal affairs from European powers.

Bedirkhan appears to have been attempting to gain independence from the Ottomans for some time.[556] Before the Russo-Ottoman war (1828-9), Bedirkhan had brought under his government most of the Kurdish peoples in Northern Kurdistan, and established strong contact with both Christians and Yezidis.[557] This made him confident about approaching the Ottomans.   Therefore, during the Russo-Ottoman war (1828-9), the Ottomans submitted a request to Bedirkhan for support, asking for a detachment of troops to aid them in their fight against the Russians. Bedirkhan stubbornly refused to come to their aid.[558] Lieutenant Colonel Shiel, whilst in Cizire during the summer of 1836, described the position of the Botan Pasha towards the Ottoman Empire as follows: "...for several years Bedirkhan had refused to pay tribute or acknowledge subjection to the Sultan..."[559]

In 1838, the Ottoman army under Rashid Pasha attacked Bedirkhan and his allies. After a long siege, the Ottoman commander took Cizire, the Botan's capital,[560] and destroyed the city and looted all they could.[561] According to the German High Commander who was with the Ottoman army during the operation named Multke, the army killed great numbers of women and children.[562] Consequently, to avoid further defeat and to conserve his army for a better opportunity, he had to support the Ottomans temporarily. Information about Bedirkhan's early career is sparse. Two writers, Ozoglu and Jwaideh, agree that in 1838, "Bedirkhan aided the Ottoman forces in stabilizing...Cizire" and a year later

---

[555] Blau, Joyce (1998). *Introduction written for Malmisanij, al-Bedirkhaniun fi Ciziret Botan*, Arabic text, The Bedirkhans of Cizire Botan, translated from Turkish by Dlawer al-Zangi and Gulbehar Bedirkhan, Amiral Press, Beirut, p. 8.
[556]van Bruinessen, Martin (1992). Op. cit, p. 179.
[557] Safrastian, Arshak (1948). *Kurds and Kurdistan*, The Harvill Press Ltd, London, p. 55.
[558] Ibid. Bruinessen Martin van Op. cit, p. 179.
[559] Shiel, Lieut. Col. J. (1838). "Notes on a Journey from Tabriz, through Kurdistan via Van ...." *The Journal of the Royal Geographical Society of London*, Volume Eight, p. 87.
[560] Bruinessen, Martin van (1992). Op. cit, p. 179.
[561] Jelil, Jelili (1987). *Min Ta'rikh al-Emarat al-Kurdiya fi al-Epratoriya al-Othmaniya fi al-Nisf al-Awwal min al-Qarin al-Tasi' al-Ashar*, Arabic text, History of Kurdish Emirates in the First Half of the Nineteenth Century, translated from Russian by Muhammad Abdo al-Najjar, Beirut, p. 100.
[562] Yahya, Abdufatah Ali (1992). "Al-Kurd wa al-Kurdistan fi Rasa'l Field Marshal Helmuth von Multke", Kurdish text, Kurds and Kurdistan in the Field Marshal Hemlton Karil Moltka, *Govari Nuseri Kurd*, Number 4, p. 14.

"was appointed an honorary captain in the Ottoman army and participated, at the head of a contingent of Botan troops, in the battle of Nisib...After the Ottoman defeat, Bedirkhan retired with his men.....[and] taking advantage of Turkish weakness...began to strengthen his forces."[563]

In 1839, the Ottoman army was defeated badly in the Battle of Nisib at the hands of the Egyptian forces under the command of Ibrahim Pasha.[564] Bedirkhan Pasha took part in the battle and saw the crushed Ottoman army. This was an opportunity for Bedirkhan to realise his ambitions; he started to develop his emirate and to extend it to include surrounding Kurdish princes and chieftains.

It is true that Botan was not an independent state, but when Bedirkhan became strong he kept a distance with Ottoman Walis in the region. He did not allow the Ottoman Walis to interfere in his affairs and rather challenged the central power. Evidence shows that Bedirkhan tried to establish greater power in Kurdistan against the Ottoman Empire. In a despatch by Vice Consul Rassam to Sir Stratford Canning British Ambassador at Constantinople, on 16th July 1843, he states that:

> "Report states that the object of Mahmood [*sic*] Khan's visit to Bider Khan Bey was in order to secure assistance of the latter chief against the Ottoman authorities of Van."[565]

The Tanzimat, as has been well-established, brought about fundamental changes in the structure of the Ottoman Empire. It is held that:

> "[the] period of sustained legislation and reform that modernised Ottoman state and society, contributed to the further centralization of administration, and brought increased state participation in Ottoman society." [566]

---

[563] Ozoglu, Hakan (2004). *Kurdish Notablesand the Ottoman State*, State University of New York Press, Albany, p.71. Jwaideh, Wadie (2006). *The Kurdish National Movement: Its Origins and Development*, New Addition, Syracuse University Press, Syracuse, New York, p. 63.

[564] Noel, E. M. (1920). *Diary of Major E. M. Noel, C. I. E., D. S. O., or Special Duty in Kurdistan: From June 14th to September 21, 1919*, Printed and Engraved by Superintendent, Government Press, Basrah, p. 53.

[565] FO 195/228 C. Rassam to Sir Stratford Canning His Majesty's Ambassador at Constantinople, No 3, Mousul, July 16th, 1843.

[566] Shaw, Stanford, and Shaw, Ezel Kural, (2002). *History of the Ottoman Empire and Modern Turkey, Reform, Revolution, and Republic, The Rise of Modern Turkey 1808-1975*, Vol. II, Cambridge Uneversity Press, Cambridge, p.55. Quataert, Donald (2000). *The Ottoman Empire, 1700-1922*, Cambridge University Press, Cambridge, p.64. McCarthy, Justin, (1997). *The Ottoman Turks*, Longman, London and New York, p. 295.

A member of the Bedirkhan family, Celadet Emin Ali Bedirkhan recalled that,

> "Sultan Mahmud II of Turkey introduced a new policy that aimed at centralizing administration and curtailing the powers of the semi-autonomous tribal chiefs. The arrival in Botan of strange Turkish officials, who interfered with what, had hitherto been the prerogative of their prince, caused discontent among the Kurds, and…rebellion began to smoulder."[567]

The policies pursued by Bedirkhan Pasha helped in developing the notion of Kurdism in the Botan Emirate. Through the forging of alliances with other Kurdish leaders, Bedirkhan Pasha carved out an area of influence that left him in a position where he could begin to seek an autonomous area for Kurds. He can be seen, in several ways explained later in this chapter, to have attempted to maintain a degree of autonomy from the Ottomans. He pursued a number of administrative reforms and a modernisation of the army. All these served to strengthen his position as a leading power in the region. Kurdish people in Medyat, Merzan and Sert, were not under his government, but,

> "were he inclined to resistance, would assist him [Bedirkhan], would show that he is not prepared to defy the authority of the Sultan. He is an ambitious man, no doubt, and would wish to preserve the powerful influence he appears to have acquired over all the chiefs of Koordistan [sic], but what he seems to desire most, is that some notice should be taken of him at head quarters."[568]

The revolt is held to have taken place between 1842 and 1847.[569] During its course, two assaults were made on the Nestorian Christians. The second of these, in 1846, led to Bedirkhan Pasha's downfall. "England, supported by France, protested vigorously to the Porte.…at the insistence and with the support and blessing of these two great powers, the Porte finally decided to suppress Bedirkhan-an action it had long contemplated." He defeated the first army sent against him and "after this success, he decided to sever all connections with the Ottoman Empire. He proclaimed the independence of his state and coined his own money."[570]

Mr Laurie, in his letter of 13th April 1844, writes,

---

[567] Bedirkhan, K. A. (1952). "In Memoriam…", *Journal of Royal Central Asian Society*, Vol. XXXIX, p.91.
[568] FO 195/228 The Consul of Moussul's report of a visit to Bedr Khan (*sic*), Moussul, July 10th 1844. Enclosed in Sir Stratford Canning's dispatch No. 169 of 1844, pp. 297-317. See appendix D for the full report.
[569] Bruinessen, Martin van (1992). Op. cit, pp. 179-80.
[570] Jawadieh, Wadie (2006). Op. cit, pp. 72-3.

> "What will be the result of this outrage cannot be known as yet; but it will be undoubtedly being productive of important results and that soon. The Porte will either be obliged to send an army and subdue him to more than his present nominal allegiance, or his growing power will soon set his superiors utterly at defiance. The Koords are all devotedly attached to him, and many associate his name with that of Sultan in their prayers at the mosque."[571]

It is unclear how the situation would manifest itself. The Porte could either challenge his growing influence, or have his power increase, with the help of the many Kurds loyal to him.

His position has been interpreted somewhat differently by Ozoglu, who states the Ottomans were "powerful enough to interfere with internal politics of the Botan emirate if necessary."[572] However, dispatches and other reports from the period indicate otherwise. When, in September 1843, Sir Stratford Canning, the British ambassador to Istanbul, attempted to help the Nestorian Christians in the Botan Emirate, he was told that Bedirkhan was so powerful that the Ottoman government could not challenge his rule. The Ottoman Porte "expressed its readiness to comply with his Excellency's wishes as far as it was able, but it declared that it was not strong enough to enter into a contest with the powerful Khoordish [*sic*] Chiefs."[573] It is interesting to consider whether this might have been a diplomatic refusal to help Christians, or whether the Ottomans really had very limited power in Botan.

It seems that there is other evidence that might suggest that the Ottoman Empire was powerless to confront Bedirkhan's influence. A letter, written by the missionary Dr Grant, dated 4th November 1843 stated that the Porte could not provide protection to Nestorians in Kurdistan, so there needed to be a plan to remove them to other parts of the empire where they could be protected.[574]

Concerns about the growing power of Bedirkhan were also expressed by Mr. Laurie, who wrote,

> "The Porte will either be obliged to send an army and subdue him to more than his present nominal allegiance, or his growing power will soon set his superiors utterly at

---

[571] Laurie, Thomas (1844). "Letter dated April 13, 1844", *The Missionary Herald*, August 1844, Vol. 40, 263-6, p. 508. Amman.
[572] Ozoglu, Hakan (2004). Op. cit, p. 71.
[573] FO 78/2698 Sir S. Canning, No. 203, September 17th, 1843. pp. 3-4. The National Archive, Kew Gardens, London.
[574] Grant, Dr. (1844). "Letter dated Nov.4, 1843", *The Missionary Herald*, Vol. XL, No. 3, March, 1844, p. 83.

defiance. The Kurds are all devotedly attached to him, and many associate his name with that of the Sultan in their prayers at the mosque."[575] The Kurds had no respect for the Ottoman state; as demonstrated by their assault on the defeated Turkish soldiers from battle of Nisib.[576]

The Ottoman army was weakened by liquidation of the Janissaries, the Empire was threaten and exploited by Muhammad Ali of Egypt.[577] This threat provided Bedirkhan with a brief window of opportunity, enabling him to form a confederacy with other Kurdish chiefs, thus further extending the Kurds' power base.

The defeat of the Ottoman army in Nisib was taken as an opportunity by the Kurds to express their negative attitude towards the Ottoman Empire, hence, Kurds desired to see the empire in weakness,

> "almost simultaneous to demise of the sovereign…Their feelings had long been irritated by the indiscreet violence of the government in forcing them from their mountain-homes into the ranks of the army."[578]

Reverend Thomas Laurie admitted that,

> "Bedirkhan Bey, a friend of the emir, was a chief in the prime of life, of commanding influence among the tribes, and full of ambitious schemes, aiming at nothing less than entire independence of the Sultan, the subjugation of the Mountain Nestorians, and the union of all Kurdistan under his single sway."[579]

Indeed, it is impossible to know what was really meant by the expression "all Kurdistan" used in the above quotation. It has been understood that for Bedirkhan, Kurdistan was much wider than the Botan Emirate. Bruinessen suggested that this opinion made him expand his authority to control the regions between Diyarbekir-Mosul and the Persian boundary.[580]

[575] Laurie, Thomas (1844). "Letter dated April 13, 1844", *The Missionary Herald*, Vol. XL, No. 8, August, 1844, p. 264.

[576] Laurie, Thomas (1853). *Dr Grant and the Mountain Nestorians*, Johnstone and Hanter, Edinburgh, p. 88.

[577] Joseph, John (1961). *The Nestorian and their Muslim Neighbors*, Princeton University Press, Princeton, New Jersey, p.49.

[578] Southgate, The Rev Horatio (1849). *Narrative of a Tour through Persia, Mesopotamia, and Armenia*, Published by James M'Glashan, Dublin, p. 329.

[579] Laurie, Thomas (1853). Op. cit, p. 85.

[580] Bruinessen, Martin van (1992). Op. cit, p. 180.

Contemporary documents illustrate that Bedirkhan had aspirations to have wider power than just his base in Botan. He knew that the Botan Emirate was a small portion of Kurdistan; he sought to extend his power over greater parts of Kurdistan.

With the Tanzimat reforms, the Ottomans intended to increase their power and influence over their disparate territories. However, the Ottomans came under increasing attack by regular incursions of Mohammad Pasha of Rewanduz, who was keen to expand his territory and influence. The Ottomans' power was gradually being undermined. To re-establish their authority they attempted to subjugate all the Kurdish emirates one by one. In this way the Porte then added the emirate of Botan to the Pashalik of Mosul.

Mohammad Bairakdar, Pasha of Mosul, had managed to convince the Porte to create two Pashaliks in the region. He argued that if they placed Botan directly under his control, he could help the Sultan to increase the revenue collected from Kurdistan. Thus he tried to assert influence over the whole of Botan, and the mountain tribes including those of Bedirkhan.[581]

According to Ozoglu[582], Bedirkhan believed that it was only when the Ottoman government started their *Tanzimat* (reforms) that the Kurdish emirates lost their semi-autonomy.[583] As he did not want his emirate to have such a fate, his objective was to hold onto his autonomy at any cost. Missionaries in the area believed that "Bedirkhan Bey was an ambitious man, and had been gradually extending his dominions on every side, till he had become the most powerful chief in Kurdistan."[584]

Hakan Ozoglu has presented the view that Bedirkhan was not antipathetic towards the Ottoman Empire, although he challenged it. He suggests only that, "Bedirkhan was agitated by the attempt to divide his emirate administratively."[585], stating that "Bedirkhan revolted to keep his emirate administratively intact."[586]

---

[581] Ibid, p. 183.
[582] Ozoglu, Hakan (2004). Op. cit, pp. 65-6.
[583] This led to all governing powers being centralized by the state: inaugurated during the reign of Sultan Mahmud II (died. 1839).
[584] Laurie and Smith (1845). "Cause of the late invasion", *The Missionary Herald*, Vol. XLI, No. 4, April 1845, p. 122.
[585] Ozoglu, Hakan (August 2001). "Nationalism and Kurdish Notables in the Late Ottoman-Early Republican Era", *International Journal of Middle East Studies*, Vol. 33, Number 3, p. 398.
[586] Ibid.

5.2 Administration of Botan under Bedirkhan Beg

The administrative reforms introduced by Bedirkhan helped to strengthen the position of the Emirate. He first removed any officials who had failed to demonstrate skills that were useful in governing the state although he sought to maintain the position of the religious classes whose support he wished to maintain. However, he recognised the value in individuals who devoted their lives to religious purposes; such individuals managed to retain their place aside the ruling power.[587]

George Percy Badger and his English missionary colleagues travelled from Mosul to Diyarbekir, writing that:

> "Wherever we travelled we found that the fame of this chieftain was extolled by the Coords [*sic*], who regarded him almost in the light of a second Mohammed. From what I gathered from the villagers, it appears that he used to sent costly presents to the Moollahs [*sic*] in the different provinces under his jurisdiction, to remit the taxes of such as could not pay them, to distribute largesses to the poor, and to give to any Mussulman [*sic*] who had no means of purchasing arms, a sufficient sum to provide himself with a firelock, sword and shield."[588]

The twentieth century writer Jwaideh, referring to a report by Dr Austin Wright and Edward Breath, upon their visit to Bedir Khan in the Missionary Herald (November, 1846: 381), suggests,

> "His person as well as his activities were tinged with a charismatic quality…In his own eyes, as well as in the eyes of his followers, his success bore the stamp of divine approval."[589]

It appears that Bedirkhan did indeed challenge the highest authority of religion in the Ottoman Empire, the Sheikh ul Islam of the state. In a despatch from Rassam to Sir Stratford Canning, one learns that Bedirkhan acted independently by appointing a Qadi [Islamic judge] in Botan without reference to Constantinople. Rassam declared that:

---

[587] Lutfi, Bedirkhan (1992). *al-Amir Bedirkhan*, Arabic text, translated from Turkish by Ali Saydo al-Gorani, Damascus, p. 11.
[588] Badger, George Percy (1852). *The Nestorians and their Rituals with the Narrative of a Mission to Mesopotamia and Coordistan in 1842 to 1844*, Part I, Joseph Masters, London, pp. 304-5.
[589] Jwaideh, Wadie (2006). Op. cit, p. 65.

> "I further beg leave to suggest to your Excellency whether it would not be advisable to lay the conduct of the Cadi of Jazeerah [*sic*] before the Sublime. The person holding this office has been appointed by Badir Khan Bey without any authority from the Sheikh ul Islam, which is an infraction of one of the most sacred laws of the Turkish Empire."[590]

Another writer Derek Kinnane believed that Bedirkhan planned in 1843 to establish an inclusive Kurdish Government that reached out and included a, "...considerable confederation which he headed...", his movement "...was the first uprising that might be called nationalist in a modern sense..."[591] Bedirkhan established different departments in his administration such as The Emirate Consultation Board, religion, treasury, army and others departments.[592]

Some observers such as Khalfin a Russian scholar noted that Bedirkhan "...did not discriminate between the religions or sects in Kurdistan."[593] Yet the missionaries, Wright and Breath who travelled throughout Kurdistan and visited Bedirkhan, acknowledged another side to Bedirkhan. In regards to his treatment of those he found, Wright and Breath who visited Bedirkhan in May 1846 acknowledged that:

> "The guilty under his government find no escape. Bribery, favouritism, &c., which too often, in these countries, pervert the course of justice, and nullify the force of law, are unknown here."[594] One aspect of his Kurdism was that he established law and order among the nomad tribes, and encouraged an end to their nomadism.[595]

It is interesting to consider why Bedirkhan might have encouraged an end to nomadism. One possibility is that he wished to control them better, another that he wished for them a more stable and ordered life and regarded settled peasant life to be more advanced than nomadism.

---

[590] FO 195/228 Rassam C. the Vice Consul at Mosul to Sir Stratford Canning British Ambassador at Constantinople, No. 1, Moosul, 13th January, 1844.

[591] Kinnane, Derk (1964). *The Kurds and Kurdistan*, Oxford University Press, London, p. 23.

[592] Bedirkhan, Lutfi (1992). Op. cit, p. 12.

[593] Khalfin, Dr. N. A. (1969). *al-Sira' ala Kurdistan*, Arabic text, *Struggle for Kurdistan*, Translated from Russian by Dr. Ahmad Osman, al-Sha'b Press, Baghdad, p. 60.

[594] Wright and Breath (1846). "Visiting Bedirkhan", *The Missionary Herald*, Vol. XLII, No. 11, November, 1846, p. 381.

[595] Bedirkhan, Lutfi (1992). Op. cit, p. cit, p. 13.

Stevens, the British Consulate in Mosul, witnessed the leadership skills and social power of Bedirkhan when he visited Derghuleh, the winter residency of Bedirkhan in 1844. 190 of the 250 families there were Kurds, with others being Armenian, Syrian and those from Bedirkhan's other territories. According to Canning (1844), they lived in "comfort and happiness, forming a striking contrast with misery one meets with in the villages of Moussul [*sic*] and Diarbekir."[596]

5.3 Bedirkhan, Botan and the Economy

Before the ascent to power of Bedir Khan, Kurds were suffering from two great impositions on them by the Ottoman government: heavy taxes and forced military service.[597] Therefore, many Kurdish peasants from other regions migrated to Botan to live in peace and harmony under Bedirkhan's rule.[598]

During the era of Bedirkhan, Kurdistan's economy also improved. In the villages, the plains and fields began to flourish. There were many signs of Bedirkhan's independence. He struck money in 1842, and ordered prayers to be said for him in the Friday congregational prayers.[599]

The most notable step that Bedirkhan took was the minting of a coin in 1842 with the writing "Amir Botan Bedirkhan" on one side and on the other side "1258 AH-1842 CE". His mint was at Cizire, a town he had established as his capital.[600]

The Botan Kurds had a desire to maintain the power to collect their taxes; subsequently they were keen to retain it, rather than handing the full money collected to the Ottomans. According to Safrastian, "they did not wish to pay taxes to the defeated Rumi [Ottomans] and desired to govern their hereditary areas according to their own ideas."[601]

---

[596] FO 195/288 The Consul of Moussul's report of a visit to Bedr Khan, Moussul, July 10th 1844. Enclosed in Sir Stratford Canning's dispatch No. 169 of 1844, pp. 297-317.
[597] Khalfin, Dr. N. A. (1969). Op. cit, p. 58.
[598] Ibid, p. 60.
[599] Sherko, Blach (1986). Op. cit, p. 55. Jalil, Jalili (1987). Op.cit, p. 135.
[600] Sherko, Blach, ibid, p. 55. Malmisanij (1998). p. 39. Nazif, Sulaiman (1958). *Ta'rikh al-Nuqud al-Iraqiya*, Arabic text, The History of Iraqi Currency, Baghdad, pp. 123-8. Sejadi, Ela'din (1959). Op. cit, p. 45.
[601] Safrastian, Arshak (1948). *Kurds and Kurdistan*, The Harvill Press Ltd, London, p. 50.

Bedirkhan made ample provision for those who were in need. It was reported that in Dergule, the winter residence of Bedirkhan, situated twelve miles east of Cizire "heralds were sent through the surrounding countryside to summon the lame, the blind, the poor of every class" to attend Bedirkhan's residence at a given time. The Beg distributed gifts among them, dispensing his largesse according to their needs, where "each individual, upon receiving his portion, raised his eyes towards heaven, and invoked the blessing of God upon his generous benefactor."[602]

Bedirkhan distributed lands to the poor and to those peasants who migrated to Botan. In return they were obliged to pay a small sum in taxation. They were also obliged to pay a small tax on their cattle.[603] He instituted a special land law where every peasant paid a small sum of money to obtain land titles and thereafter peasants paid very little tax to the Botan Emirate.[604] The tax the peasants paid to Bedirkhan in his emirate was 3% less than the tax paid to the Ottoman state.[605] This can be seen as a concrete step in the promotion of agriculture. As another condition of their land rights, peasants were required to obtain a horse, gun and pistol. By such a measure, Bedirkhan encouraged his people to form a civil militia for the defence of their lands.[606] From time to time he met with an assembly of his people to discuss their problems.[607] In this way he supported the flourishing of agriculture. Bedirkhan also used Botan's geographical position which lay along the trade road to Aleppo, Mosul and Trabzon.[608] He taxed trade caravans who passed through his region.[609] He also benefited from Van Lake for transport and connections with allied chiefs around the lake.[610]

5.4 Bedirkhan Pasha: Modernizer of the Army

Bedirkhan modernized his army. He transformed the army from units organised as tribal 'commands' to a "specialised" standing regimental army in which he provided for both

---

[602] The Missionary Herald, a monthly published in Boston by the American Board of Commissioners for Foreign Missions, Vol. XLII, No. 11, November, 1846, p. 381.

[603] Dantsig, B. M. (1981). *Rahaltul Rus fi al-Sharq al-Awsat*, Russian Travelers in the Middle East, Arabic text, translated with commentary by Pro. Marouf Xeznedar, published by Dar al-Rashid, Baghdad, p. 240.

[604] Khalifin, Dr. N. A., (1969). Op. cit, p. 60

[605] Mantik, Yusuf Ahmad (2005). *Bedirkhaniyekan malbateki khebatkar*, Kurdish text, Bedirkhans: A Family of the Resistance, Published by Soran, Hewler, p. 14. *Malmisanij*, (1998). *al-Bedirkhaniun fi Ciziret Botan*, Arabic text, The Bedirkhans of Cizire Botan, translated from Turkish by Dlawer al-Zangi and Gulbehar Bedirkhan, Amiral Press, Beirut, p. 37.

[606] Khalifin , Dr. N. A. (1969). Op. cit, p. 60.

[607] Bedirkhan, Salih (1991). *Muzakarati*, Arabic text, *My Memories*, translated by Roshin Badir Khan, Published by Dlawer Zangi, Damascus, p. 76.

[608] Hururi, Salah M. (2000). Op. cit, p. 83.

[609] Rauf, Emad Abdulsalam (1975). *al-Mosul fi al-Ahd al-Uthmani*, Arabic text, *Mosul during the Ottoman period*, al-Najaf al-Ashraf, to see more about trade caravans, see pp. 235-280.

[610] Jalil, Jalili (1987). Op. cit, p. 125. Kinnane, Derk, (1964). Op. cit, p. 23.

cavalry and infantry forces. In order to provide overall leadership he appointed Tahir Memo a General Commander of his army.[611] To develop his forces, he instituted a levy requesting that every tribe should provide one hundred of their best men for the Kurdish Army;[612] but as well as conscription, he went further still to open the ranks of his army to anyone who was willing to join.[613]

By doing this, the tribesmen no longer went to war under their leaders, but only under the General Commander of the Botan emirate army. The *Mir* was General Commander of the entire Botan army and he took a personal role in leading his forces which meant that by the end, he led the Kurdish troops in most of their engagements with the Ottomans.

This helped to consolidate the *Mir*'s power by reducing the overall power of the tribes;[614] these forces would now be loyal to him and his Emirate of Botan, rather than their local chiefs. By taking their best armed men, this arrangement cemented his power and led to any potential challengers being weakened. However, this had a deeper implication,[615] as it introduced the concept of his forces having a wider loyalty to Botan in general.

Bedirkhan believed that the European method of armaments was superior; thus, he decided to arm his soldiers along European lines. This he achieved by establishing two factories for the production of gun powder in Cizire,[616] where he employed European experts to make ammunition. As he wanted control of this process, he started to send Kurdish students to Europe in order for them to learn modern processes of manufacture.[617]

Bedirkhan also employed many Armenians as military advisers including Stephan Manŏglyan, Houhannes, Chilktryan and *Mir* Marto.[618] They were not obliged to convert to Islam. Assyrians also enjoyed privileged positions in Bedirkhan's army; they fought bravely on the side of the Botan troops in their battle against Rashid Pasha's army who attacked Cizire.[619]

---

[611] Hururi, Salah M. (2000). Op. cit, p. 77.
[612] Bedirkhan, Lutfi (1992). Op. cit, p.12-14.
[613] Khalifin, Dr. N. A. (1969). Op. cit, p. 59
[614] Bruinssen, , Martin van (1992). Op. cit, p. 179.
[615] Ibid, p. 179.
[616] Malmisanij (1998). Op. cit, p. 34. Sherco, Blach, (1986). Op.cit, p. 52.
[617] Shamzini, Aziz (2006,). *Jolanaway Rizgari Nishtimani Kurdistan*, Kurdish text, *The National Kurdistan Movement*, Translated from Arabic by Farid Asasard, The Centre of Kurdistan for Statically Studies, Silemani p. 108.
[618] Malmisanij (1998). Op. cit, p. 39.
[619] Jalil, Jalili (1987). Op. cit, p. 101.

In instituting these reforms, Bedirkhan demonstrated that he understood two serious obstacles to the liberation of Kurdistan: a lack of unity had hindered Kurdish nationalism, and arms manufactories were needed in Kurdistan.[620] There is evidence to suggest that Bedirkhan established a powerful army which became too great in number. According to a dispatch by *Mr* Wellesley, the British military attaché, Bedirkhan was said to have had "60,000 men at his call, and to inhabit fastnesses almost unapproachable". For that reason the Ottoman Government defused the expedition against Bedirkhan as it did not have "sufficient troops to ensure success."[621]

Bedirkhan also concentrated on developing his army. In his report, Stevens, the British Consul in Mosul in 1844, visited Bedirkhan and witnessed Bedirkhan's well- organised army, stating,

> "On one side of Bedr Khan [*sic*] Bey's tent were drawn up about 300 men, all dressed alike, in dark jackets, red trousers, and long hanging sleeves of the same colour. On the other side an equal number, but blue trousers and sleeves. They all standing with their hands resting on their daggers, from the handles of which hung a string of beads, with which all these bigoted Koords of the Shap sect are provided."[622]

The troops presented themselves in a Kurdish style, each resting their hands on a dagger hung with a string of beads, a style still adopted in many parts of Kurdistan today. It seems that Bedirkhan wished to present to Stevens a uniformed army, with its own distinctly Kurdish style of dress. Bedirkhan wished Stevens to understand that he had his own way to rule his emirate and could receive foreign diplomats without going back to Constantinople to first ask permission to do so.

Stevens visited Bedirkhan in June 1844, and wrote about the strength of Botan's army who continually stood against the Ottoman army under Muhammad Rashid Pasha and finally defeated the Ottoman army. Stevens reported that Bedirkhan's forces,

> "proved a serious annoyance to the army of Koordistan [*sic*] under Rashid Mehmed Pasha, who thrice attempted to force the passage, but failed with great loss, and

---

[620] Sherko, Blach (1986). Op. cit, p. 51.

[621] Mr. Wellesley to Lord Palmerston, dispatch No 101, Buyukdery, October 29th, 1846. FO 78/2699.

[622] FO 195/288 The Consul of Moussul's report of a visit to Bedr Khan, Moussul, July 10th 1844. Enclosed in Sir Stratford Caaing's dispatch No. 169 of 1844, pp. 297-317.

retreated each time to Gezireh [*sic*]. The forth attempt succeeded but with great bloodshed."[623]

This stand and other confrontations against the Ottomans suggest that when Bedirkhan was powerful, he challenged the Ottoman Empire and considered Kurds to be distinct from other Ottoman peoples.

5.5 Consolidation against the Ottomans

In 1840, when the American missionaries were in the region, Bedirkhan contracted an alliance with various regional Kurdish tribal leaders and established "an almost independent Kurdish confederacy under his own rule".[624] Dr Aziz Shamzini stressed that it was Bedirkhan who in 1839 called Kurdish princes and chiefs to act together against the Ottoman Empire's policy towards Kurds.[625]

Unity among Kurds was a factor of Kurdism promoted by Bedirkhan. In 1828-29, "he sent envoys to other Kurdish notables and local leaders urging them to unite and work jointly in defending Kurdistan and its self-rule."[626] Many Kurdish leaders came forward, such as Khan Mahmud of Van, Nurullah Beg of Hakkary, Khalid Beg of Khizan, Sharif Beg of Mush and Husein Beg of Qaris, Kurdish notables and Islamic scholars also entered the alliance, the Khan of Erdelan Emirate from Persian Kurdistan as well as others who collectively established "The Holy Allied Agreement."[627] According to Rassam, the British Vice-Consul in Mosul, Bedirkhan was in contact with some other Kurdish leaders in Persian Kurdistan to work together against the Ottoman Empire. Rassam asserted that "Messengers are continuingly going and coming between Bidr Khan [*sic*] Bey and the Kurdish Ameer [*sic*] of Salamas including within the Persian Frontier."[628]

This enabled them to act as a single entity, against a common enemy.[629] The conditions were as follows:

₆₂₃ Ibid.

₆₂₄ Joseph, John (1961). Op. cit, p. 49.

₆₂₅ Shamzini, Aziz (1968). *Al-Harakat al-Taharuriyat lil-Sha'b al-Kurdi*, Arabic text, PhD thesis, Kurdistan, p. 57. Malmisanij, (1998). Op. cit,, p. 40.

₆₂₆ Sherco, Blach (1986). Op. cit, p. 51.

₆₂₇ Ibid, p. 52. Joseph, John (1961). Op. cit, p. 49.

₆₂₈ FO 195/228, C. Rassam to Sir Stratford Canning His Majesty's Ambassador at Constantinople, No 3, Mousul, July 16th, 1843.

₆₂₉ For more details see: Sherko, Blach (1986). Op. cit, pp. 38-9.

1. To revolt together against the Ottoman Empire.[630]

2. To provide a regional territory for every Kurdish prince.[631]

3. To bolster their protection, by renewing old castles and building new ones, to increase numbers of their fighters and to arm their fighters well.[632]

4. To support each other in counteracting the aggression of outsiders.

In 1838, when Bedirkhan was under siege from Ottoman forces, Khan Mahmud attempted to rescue him with large armed forces of 20,000 Kurds, Armenians and Assyrians, but they were prevented by the Ottoman army from getting to the battle field.[633]   At the end of 1842, Bedirkhan Beg and Ziner Beg, planned and instigated a joint campaign to renounce Ottoman subjection, along with the ex-governor of Amadia, Ismael Pasha. Together they marched to the frontier of Berwari district, where they invited various regional tribal Kurdish chiefs to participate.[634]

Even after this failure, Bedirkhan remained strong in the region. Two missionaries, who both visited Bedirkhan, assessed his power and character thus:

> "His power extends from the Persian line on the east to far into Mesopotamia on the west, and from the gates of Diarbekir to those of Mosul; and his fame is wide spread. While [we] were with him, nearly every chief in northern Koordistan [*sic*] came to make their respects to him bringing him presents of money, horses, mules and other valuable property. Even the Hakkary Bey, higher in rank, and once more powerful than he, and Khan Mahmud, seemed to think themselves honoured by being in waiting upon him."[635]

The coalition of the Kurdish *mirs* and Kurdish chieftains during the Bedirkhan's time and his legacy formed a potential nucleus of Kurdism which might be interpreted as proto-nationalism.

[630] Jalil, Jalili (1987). Op. cit, p. 120. Safrastian, Arshak (1948). Op.cit, p. 50.

[631] Ibid, p. 120

[632] Zaki. Muhammad Amin (1947). *Mashahir al-Kurd wa Kurdistan*, Arabic text, Translated by Saniha Muhammad Amin Zaki, Kurd and Kurdistan Notables, al-Sa'adat Press, Baghdad, p. 137.

[633] Safrastian, Arshak (1948)p. 51.

[634] Badger, Rev. George Percy (1852). *The Nestorians and their Rituals: with the narrative of a mission to Mesopotamia and Coordistan in 1842-1844 and of a late visit to those countries in 1850*, Vol. I, Joseph Masters, London, p. 188.

[635] Wright and Breath (1846). "Visiting Bedirkhan", *The Missionary Herald*, Boston, Vol. XLII, No. 11, November, 1846, p. 381.

5.6 Obstacles

The factors that led to the demise of Bedir Khan's Emirate were not of his own making, but due to the influence of agencies external to the region who exploited a Christian sect for their own purposes.

5.7 The Christian-Nestorians and other Christian groups in Kurdistan

There were various Christian groups in Ottoman Kurdistan who preserved and developed a separate religious existence: Nestorians, Syrian, Jacobites, and Armenians were among them. These Christian sects each sustained a high level of particularity in their relations with the Kurds and other Muslim groups in Kurdistan.

The so-called Nestorians (Church of the East) were famously tribal, lived in many towns and villages of Kurdistan although their concentration was greatest in Hakkari in Turkish "Kurdistan". The remaining quarter of the Nestorians lived across the border in Persian Kurdistan, mostly around the city of Urmia.[636]

Visitors were unsure about the actual status of the Nestorians. Some thought they owed much of their freedom and independence to the tolerance of the Amir of Hakkari, under whose jurisdiction they lived. However, their freedom was only tentative, as their voice on the council of the Hakkari tribes was provided on a promise that they would supply "...a contingent of armed men in times of crisis..."[637]

Baillie Fraser described the Nestorians as follows: "They amount to better than fourteen thousand families, which constitute a sort of commonwealth of their own, separate from the rest of the world", who

"yield neither obedience nor tribute to any foreign authority, and, though professing, as some say, a nominal adherence to the head of the Hakkaree [Hakkari] Koords who

---

[636] Coakley, J. F. (1992). *The Church of the East and the Church of England*, Clarendon Press, Oxford, p. 11.

[637] Brant, James (1841). H. B. M. Consul at Erzerum, Communicated by Viscount Palmerston, G. C. B., "Notes of a Journey through a part of Kurdistan, in the Summer of 1838", *The Journal of the Royal Geographical Society of London*, Volume Tenth, p. 351.

lives at Jalamerick [Jolamerg], are, in reality, subject to none but their own chief or chiefs." [638]

This was reiterated by Smith, who noted, confusingly, that due to their independence the Nestorians did not pay tribute to the Kurds, it led them becoming known as the Ashiret; yet this meant they could "…exact tribute from the Kurds who lived amongst them…"[639]

When Lieutenant Colonel J. Shiel travelled through Kurdistan in July and August 1836, he found good relationships existing between Kurds and Orthodox Armenians:

"The Kurds highly value the Armenians, whose industry is a source of profit; they treat them well too; better at all events than the Persians among whom it is not uncommon to carry off their daughters and force them to turn Mohommedans [*sic*]."[640]

He added that,

"A Kurd, the chief of a village, once boasted to me, that he had just enticed an Armenian priest to settle in his village; 'for now' said he 'When I invite Christians to establish themselves here, and they inquire about a priest, I am able to say to them, here you have him.'"[641]

However, Henry James Ross gave a different account about the state of the relationship between Kurds and Christians. He stated:

"Generally [they're] at war with each other and with their neighbours the Koords [*sic*], the Nestorians were always prepared for raids; their rooms were hung with arms, and a shot echoing in the narrow valleys called out every male above fifteen to the strife – even children of ten or twelve frequently handled their rifles with effect. A small annual tribute of about 2s was paid by every grown man to the

[638] Fraser, J. Baillie (1840). *Travels in Koordistan, Mesopotamia, &c. Including an Account of Parts of those Countries Hitherto Unvisited by Europeans, with Sketches of the Character and Manners of the Koordish and Arab Tribes*, Vol. I, Richard Bentley, London, pp. 59-60.
[639] Smith, Eli (1833). *Researches of the Rev. E. Smith and Rev. H. G. O. Dwight in Armenia: Including a Journey Through Asia Minor, and into Georgia and Persia, with a visit to the Nestorian and Chaldean Christians of Oormiah and Salmas*, Vol. I, Published by Crocker and Brewster, Boston, p. 218
[640] Lieut. Col. Shiel, J. (1838). "Notes on a Journey from Tabriz, through Kurdistan via Van, Bitlis, Se'ert and Erbil, to Suleimaniyeh, in July and August, 1836", *The Journal of the Royal Geographical Society of London*, Volume Eighth, p. 57.
[641] Ibid, p. 57.

Kurdish Mir, or Chieftain of Hakkari, whom they acknowledge as their supreme head, but in time of war they were led by their own Maliks or hereditary chiefs."[642]

This somewhat uneasy balance was disturbed by the arrival of Christian missionaries in the region. When they first visited Sheikh Tahir of Nehri, the most celebrated Kurdish saint, the Sheikh received them,

> "As he knew Persian, we were able to converse freely with him. We explained to him our object in visiting his country, and assured him that we had no connection with Government-(agents of which he suspected us to be the evening before) that our design was one of simple benevolence, and related merely to the spiritual interests of the Nestorians. He then assured us of his kind regards, and compensated by his cordiality for the coldness of our first reception. He moreover gave us a paper, certifying that we were his friends, and that any persons who should trouble us or any of our native helpers in any way, would meet with his displeasure."[643]

Whilst Henry Rawlinson a few years later was passing through Kurdistan, he wrote that the Kurdish Beg (Nurallah Bey) was away on business in Bashkala to tender his allegiance to Hafiz Pasha,[644] where he met his envoy; during his absence, as he was on such good terms with the Nestorian Patriarch Mar Shimun, he had deputised him in his stead.[645]

Bedirkhan himself tried to persuade Mar Shimun not to take the side of the Ottoman Empire against Botan Emirate and offered him safety and freedom with Christian's followers and his power, but the Patriarch refused the offer. In a despatch by Stevens to Canning, he illustrated the matter that:

> "Bedr Khan [*sic*] Bey sent the following message to Mar Shimon [*sic*] a few days since. He warned the Patriarch against listening to proposals made by (Osmanlee's) who he said were notorious for lying, that if Mar Shimon [*sic*] would put himself in Badr Khan Bey's hands, he should be reinstated in the mountains and all his affairs settled to his satisfaction. Mar Shimon [*sic*] replied that having thrown himself on the

---

[642] Ross, Henry James (1902). *Letters from the East 1837-1857 BY Henry James Ross*, edited by Janet Ross, J. M. Dent and Co, London, letter to his wife, dated: 19 November 1847, pp. 61-2.

[643] Ibid, p. 57.

[644] Nurallah went to Erzerum in order to barter independence in return for a appointment from his Ottoman superior: "...deeming it wise to make such voluntary overtures as would strengthen his hold as the immediate head of the Hakkary tribes..." – from J. Joseph, John (1961). Op. cit, p. 53.

[645] Ross, Henry James (1902). Op. cit, p.64.

protection of the Sultan he would abide by whatever decision His Highness' Government should come to regarding him."[646]

This indicated that Bedirkhan was concerned about unity of his people. Clearly, he was not a fanatical person and had no intention to harm the Christians, a pretext the European used to topple Bedirkhan and the Botan Emirate.[647]

5.8 Consequences of British Influence

The Nestorian Patriarch, Mar Shimun, applied in 1842 for "…a clergyman of the Church of England to assist them…" to help them establish new schools for the instruction of children.[648] The man chosen was George Badger,[649] whose selection was commended by the Church:

> "…whom we have charged to salute your Holinesses in our name, and assure you of our goodwill towards you, and our hearty desire to render you all assistance in our power…we earnestly commend him to your Holiness, and request you to receive him as a brother…"[650]

The choice of Badger proved disastrous for the Nestorians. Badger was later accused of conspiring with the Patriarch against Kurdish interests. It was said that Badger recommended the patriarch should,

> "…not seek the friendship of the Kurds, but to apply for aid, if he needed it, to England, which, he said, was able and willing to grant him the fullest protection…"[651]

Incursions began in a small way when the British Vice-Consul at Samsun spoke to Bedirkhan Pasha. The Pasha told him, "Some Nestorians entered my territory, and killed two men", in return, Bedirkhan put to death two Nestorians "according to the established custom among

---

[646] FO 195/228, R. W. Steven to Sir Stratford Canning His Majesty's Ambassador at Constantinople, Moussul, March 23rd, 1844.

[647] Jwaideh, Wadie (2006). Op. cit, p. 66.

[648] "…Understanding that you have expressed the desire that we would send you a clergy of our Church, who might assist you in the establishing of schools for the instruction of children, and make known unto us more particularly the things which you stand in need…": from Badger, George Percy (1852). The Nestorians and their Rituals with the Narrative of a Mission to Mesopotamia and Coordistan in 1842 to 1844, Vol. 1, Joseph Masters, London, p. xvi.

[649] FO 881/3003, Confidential, Memorandum Respecting the Persecution of the Nestorian Christians by the Turks, Persians, and Khoordish Chiefs. December 2, 1876, p.2.

[650] Badger, George Percy (1852). Op. cit, p.xvi.

[651] Joseph, John (1961). Op. cit, p. 62.

Koordish tribes". Later, the Nestorians escalated affairs by murdering four Kurds; Bedirkhan "retaliated" by killing eight Nestorians.

The Kurdish Pasha had also been asked by "the Hakkari Chief" for his assistance in punishing the Christians who had raided several Kurdish villages. The British Vice-Consul agreed to his request, but before Badir Khan and his people attempted to leave the garrisons at Usheetah, which were under the command of Zeynel Beg, the castle was surrounded by Nestorians who cut off all their supplies and kept them nine days without water. An attack was then made on the Kurds there, and as a result several of them were killed by Nestorians.[652]

Seemingly emboldened by their contacts with Western Missionaries, the Nestorians began to increase in confidence. By the time James Ross reached the area in 1847, the hostility appeared mutual; as he stated in his observations about the situation between the Nestorians and Kurds:

"the Tiyary Nestorians frequently descended in strong parties to the neighbouring districts… and plundered the Koordish and Christian villages indiscriminately…they spared the lives of their fellow-Christians, while they invariably murdered as many of the Koordish men as they could, but respected the women."[653]

It was this behaviour that Bedirkhan was determined to stop.

Once Bedirkhan's forces had descended on the Tiyari region, the patriarch feared for his safety; so he fled, taking refuge at the British Vice-Consulate, in Mosul.[654]

As a result, British Officials began to place heavy pressure on the Porte. They urgently demanded the Porte to send an envoy to Bedirkhan to prevent any further outrages from taking place.[655] Indeed, the British managed to gain an order from the Porte to end

---

[652] Ibid, p. 13.
[653] ibid. p.62.
[654] FO 78/2698 Sir S. Canning to Lord Aberdeen, despatch No. 179, Buyukdery, August 17th, 1843.
[655] FO, 881/3003 Confidential despatch from Mr. Rassam to Mr. Wellesley, October 19, 1846, p. 17.

Bedirkhan's authority[656] and to establish the Sultan's authority over the Kurds: The Ottomans desired this also.[657]

During the summer of 1843, Messrs Laurie and Smith visited the mountain Nestorians to ascertain their condition and prospects; they were concerned about potential Kurdish harassment of the Nestorians should the Kurds be placed under a Turkish Pasha, with potentially independent rule of themselves:

> "Should this scattered and down-trodden people be placed under the government of a Turkish pasha, their external circumstances will at once undergo a decided change…But while the lawless Koords can harass and destroy them at their own pleasure, there can be no adequate encouragement for continuation of this branch of the mission."[658]

Laurie speculated that the British tried all means to end Bedirkhan and his powerful emirate, although the Porte assured Canning that "the Nestorians were the aggressors."[659]

The British Foreign Secretary, Lord Aberdeen, instructed Stratford Canning to state to the Turkish Government that the British demands on the Porte were these:

> "Restitution of the Nestorian prisoners; evacuation of the country invaded and occupied by Bedirkhan Beg and the Koodrish [sic] Chiefs who acted with him; assistance in rebuilding the destroyed houses against the approach of winter; delivery of two boys, whose release had been ordered before, to the Nestorian Patriarch; and grant of the Porte's protection to the Patriarch on a suitable agreement being made with him."[660]

Canning also co-operated with his Russian counterpart in Constantinople in sending a protest to the Porte demanding that any joint assault made against the Nestorians, by combined Kurdish forces, should be *prevented;*[661]

---

[656] Ibid p. 18.

[657] Badger, George Percy (1852). Op. cit, p. xii.

[658] Laurie and Smith (1845). "Visit of Messre Laurie and Smith to Ashete and Julamerk", *The Missionary Herald*, Vol. XLI, No. 4, April 1845, pp. 116-7.

[659] FO 78/2698 Sir S. Canning to Lord Aberdeen, despatch No. 203, Buyukdery,September 17th, 1843.

[660] FO 78/2698 Lord Aberdeen to Sir S. Canning, despatch No. 139, November 4th, 1843.

[661] FO 78/2698 Sir S. Canning to the British Commissioners at Erzeroom, Buyukdery, September 13th, 1843. Enclosure in Sir S. Canning to Lord Aberdeen, despatch 208, 1st October, 1843.

"the combined attack of the Persian and Turkish Koords [*sic*] upon the Nestorian Christians, appears to have been well-suited to the occasion, and in concert with the Russian Envoy, I have made a corresponding representation upon the subject to His Excellency the Minister for Foreign Affairs."[662]

Later in a despatch dated 28th September 1843, Sir S. Canning sent instructions to Rassam, the British Vice-Consul in Mosul informing him that the Ottoman Foreign Affairs Minister assured him that,

"reiterated orders ....[for]....the evacuation of the Christian districts occupied by the Koord [*sic*] Chiefs....had been prepared for those purposes to the Pashas of Arzeroom and Mosul, and also to the Pasha of Diyrbekir."[663]

Canning also added,

"...our interference is friendly in its character, that it requires to be managed, especially by you [The Vice-Consul in Mosul] with delicacy and discretion, that it might be inconvenient, if not impracticable, to enforce it by adequate means, and that the Turkish authorities, with every proper disposition, may find it indispensable to temporise with a Chief so powerful and disobedient as Bedirkhan."[664]

Accordingly, the Porte sent a Commissioner (Kemal Effendi) to Mosul to settle the matter; he arrived there in February 1844.[665]

In an interview between Sharif Pasha and Bedirkhan, the Turkish envoy told the Kurdish Chief that "all Europe, and England in particular, felt an interest in the Nestorians", their Ambassador impressed on the Porte to do something.

Sharif Pasha told Bedirkhan,

"You perhaps fancy... that the English have no right to interfere in these matters, but you are not aware that Treaties exist, and are constantly made between the Porte and the Governments of Europe, which give the latter a right to remonstrate on these occasions."[666]

---

[662] Ibid, Sir Stratford Canning to British Commissioners, September 13th, 1843.

[663] FO 78/2698 Sir. Stratford Canning to C. Rassam, Buyukdery, September 28th, 1843. Enclosure Sir S. Canning to Lord Aberdeen, in despatch No. 208, Buyukdery, October 1st, 1843.

[664] Ibid, FO 78/2698 Sir. Stratford Canning to C. Rassam, Buyukdery, September 28th, 1843.

[665] FO 881/3003 Confidential, Memorandum Respecting the Persecution of the Nestorian Christians by the Turks, Persians, and Khoordish Chiefs. December 2, 1876, p. 8.

[666] FO 195/228 R. W. Stevens to Sir Stratford Canning, Nestorian Affairs, Moussul, May 18, 1844. Inclosure in Sir S. Canning to FO, Despatch No. 126, June 17, 1844.

Bedirkhan was told by Sharif Pasha that he should leave the Christians alone or face the consequences. Either the Ottoman government would punish him, or England would ask the Porte to give them permission to do it themselves.[667]

It was not until after news of war and massacres became widespread in England that the British Government used the incidents as a pretext to take a more active interest in Kurdistan and its environs.[668] On this ground, Layard admitted that the British put pressure on the Ottoman Sultan to overthrow Bedirkhan Pasha.[669] The British and the Ottomans aimed to end the Botan Emirate for their own interests. For the British, eliminating Kurdish self-rule was important in order to prevent Russia from expanding southwards towards the Mediterranean and gaining influence over the Ottoman Porte. For the Ottomans, deposing Bedirkhan's authority was essential and was within framework of the reform and centralization.

5.9 Other Powers and Bedirkhan of the Botan Emirate

In 1834, Rashid Pasha, who had subjugated most of the Kurdish princes, turned his attention to Bedirkhan of Botan. At the same time, Ibrahim Pasha, the Egyptian commander in Syria, moved forward and entered Anatolia on his way to Istanbul. The Ottomans thus had to deal with the Egyptian expedition which was a more serious threat than Bedirkhan. In these circumstances, the Ottomans expressed their good will towards Bedirkhan, gave him an official rank of Pasha in the Ottoman military and called on him to mobilize against Egyptian forces. Bedirkhan, however, was impressed with the success of the Egyptians against Constantinople. He took this opportunity to expand his influence and Botan territories further; he took control of the regions from Mosul and Diyarbekir to the border line of Iranian Kurdistan.[670]

He became so powerful that the Ottoman Porte admitted that they had no party strong enough to engage with him.[671] Indeed, during the battle of Nisib[672] in 1839, the Ottomans recognised

---

[667] Ibid, FO 195/228 R. W. Stevens to Sir Stratford Canning, Moussul, May 18, 1844.
[668] FO 881/3003 Op. cit, p. 1.
[669] Layard, A. H. (1852). Popular Account of Discoverise at Ninevah, Jine Murray, London, p. 122.
[670] Wright and Breath (1846). "Visit of Messrs Wright and Breath to Badir Khan Beg", *The Missionary Herald*, Vol. XLII, No. 11, November, 1846, p. 381.
[671] FO 78/2689 Sir S. Canning to Lord Aberdeen, despatch No. 203, September 17th, 1843.
[672] Nisib is often referred to as "Nezib".

that his participation might prove invaluable – appointing Bedirkhan as an Honorary Captain of their army.

Even so, the Turks were defeated by the forces of Ibrahim Pasha. Despite, "the ruling Emir Badrkhan [*sic*] [having to] withdraw his contingent to Diyarbakir, and thence to Jezira..."[673] he realised this was only a "...setback to the Turks..."[674] who were now weakened. Thus, an opportunity opened, which he turned to his favour to fulfil his territorial ambitions, when "...he proceeded to extend his frontiers to include the Hakkary..."[675]

Sharif Pasha, the Wali of Mosul, in 1844 helped to nourish the prosperity of Bedirkhan's emirate further; he demanded so many new taxes that many peasants were forced to flee their lands for Bedirkhan's safe haven.[676] These events alarmed the Porte who feared that the remaining provinces of Kurdistan might also come under Bedirkhan's rule. Omer Pasha was appointed Marshal of Anatolia with orders to raise an army to march against the Kurdish *Mir*.[677]

Persia was in serious trouble as it lacked any serious command or structural organisation; the various divisions of the Persian army were mostly scattered around the various tribal enclaves,[678] with only a handful under the direct command of the prince:

> "...only the regular Persian army was organised by his royal highness prince Abbas Mirza, under the immediate command of Major Hart [British Officer]...[with] the present available forces...amount to about fifty thousand men.".

Thus it would be impractical to organise, the disparate forces in order to maintain, an effective defence should an invasion occur.

Persian problems did not end there, as Persia lacked proper organisation of supplies and in some cases food. Any invader would have to seek resources from their own supply lines, or "...subsist by plundering the whole line of the country for which they passed..."[679]

---

[673] Noel, Major E. M. (1920). *Diary of Major E. M. Noel, Special Duty in Kurdistan: From June 14th to September 21, 1919*, Government Press, Basrah, p. 53.
[674] Ibid p.53.
[675] Ibid p.53.
[676] FO 195/228 Stevens to Canning, 8th March 1844. Rassam to Canning, 13th January 1844.
[677] Noel, Major E. M., (1920).Op. cit, p. 53.
[678] Mignan, Captain R. (1839). *A Winter Journey through Russia, the Caucasian Alps, and Georgia; Thence Across Mount Zagros, by the Pass of Xenophon and the Ten Thousand Greeks, into Koordistan*, Vol. II, Richard Bentley, London, p 167.
[679] Ibid, p 174.

However, Persia's stance against the Kurds was directed by Persian loyalty to any European invading power, which might provide an opportunity to increase Persian influence or autonomy. Fraser, in a meeting with Bedirkhan, noted his intention.

> "[That any]…invaders in advance would be joined by various tribes is quite certain, that so disconcerted were the tribes…that if one thousand men of any European nation were to make their appearance… [such as] Russia, France or England… they would be joined by one thousand Kurds…."[680]

In this regard, Persia made a very positive approach by supporting the western missions in Iranian Kurdistan. Smith and Dwight reported to the American Board that,

> "To the Nestorians of Oroomiah [*sic*] we would especially direct your attention. That Abbas Mirza [sic] would, without doubt, patronize missionary efforts for their improvement, and in fact for the improvement all of his Christian subjects."[681]

The weakened Persian state meant their stance in terms of the Kurds has often been very minimalist; preferring indirect forms of control:

> "Some of [Kurdistan's] south-eastern districts have occasionally paid a small tribute to Persia for pasturing their flocks and herds in Erdelan free from molestation;"[682]

However, this was at a cost, as they were unable to control the more disparate elements:

> "…but the whole disciplined army of the prince royal of Persia has never been able to reduce subjection those numerous, fierce and predatory chieftains of the western frontiers who assert their independence…"[683]

Sometimes the Kurds would take property or flocks, which they chanced upon during their travels when they trespassed into Persian territories, or, as they would see it, when they made incursions there. Unfortunately this had become a habit for some, enough for the Shah to consider an attack on some of the Kurds in his care.

> "It is now stated that the King has ordered that all the Koordish [*sic*] chiefs in this region be seized, and their castles demolished…" This is a consequence of "…murders and …outrages they had committed on the Persians."[684]

---

[680] Ibid, p. 174.
[681] Perkins, Rev Justin (1843). *A Residence of Eight Years in Persia among the Nestorian Christians with Notice of the Muhammedans*, Published by Allen, Morrill & Wardwell, New York, pp. 25-6.
[682] Russia the Caucasians p. 228
[683] Ibid.

Furthermore, there were considerable concerns that the Turks might use the Kurds in war against Persia, considering some of their territory straddled Persian lands, "…and being Sunnis in common with the Kurds in Turkey…"[685] In addition the "Shah [was] angry that his name [was] not revered unlike that of the Kurdish chief. Also Kurdish herdsmen had taken flocks from Persian holdings." This all became enough to convince the Shah to attack the Kurds.[686]

The Ottoman Empire twice attacked Bedirkhan Pasha. The first time was in 1838.[687] When the Ottoman expedition was sent to Kurdistan to fight against Muhammad Pasha of Rewanduz, the Kurds made a tough stand in return. Bedirkhan's forces resisted the Turkish army under Rashid Pasha, killing some of his forces.[688]

In retaliation, the Turkish army destroyed many villages and their surrounding plains and fields between Diyarbakir and Cizire. [689] Three months after the attack on Cizire by Rashid Pasha, Lieutenant Colonel Shiel described the situation in the town as,

> "The most complete desolation existed in the town; it was almost in ruins, and it was only after a long search that we were able to find a wretched hovel to pass the day in; no inhabitants were to be seen; it absolutely contained none, excepting a few hundred sickly miserable soldiers."[690]

On arrival at Ain-ser, Shiel recorded the devastation left by the Turkish forces;

> "The plain abounded in villages, but many had been destroyed by Rashid Pasha three months before, in his passage from Diyarbakir to Cizire, in consequence of opposition to his troops by the Meer of Botan."[691]

5.10 The Ottoman attack against Bedirkhan and his downfall

---

[684] The Patriarch-War against the Koords, *The Missionary Herald*, Vo. XLI, April 1845, No. 4, p. 410.
[685] Ibid.
[686] Ibid, p. 411.
[687] Bruinessen, Martin (1992). Op. cit, p. 179.
[688] Lieut. Col. Shiel, J. (1838). Op. cit, p. 76.
[689] Ibid, p. 85.
[690] Ibid, p. 87.
[691] Ibid, p. 85.

It seems that Bedirkhan believed that Kurds were a different entity in the Ottoman Empire and that Turks were "strangers" among the Kurds. This belief was reflected on the Ottoman officials and their authorities in Kurdistan. In a letter to R. W. Steven, the British Vice-Consul, he expressed his beliefs and his sense of identity as a Kurd and that Kurds are unrelated to Turks and that he desired a separate future independent of them. Nearly three hundred and thirty years of Ottoman presence in Kurdistan was not enough to make Kurds feel that they were true Ottomans. While the Ottomans were moving towards a policy of centralization, the Kurds were shifting in the direction of separation. In the following part of his letter to Steven, Bedirkhan states that:

"I may inform you that the people of our country are Koordish [*sic*] mountaineers, wanting in politeness unacquainted with the respect due to officers in the employ of the Sultan, and are strange to the customs of the Ottomans and people of the cities. This arises from all the people of our country being deficient in sense, knowledge, and politeness, which makes us ashamed, and that being the case, we feel certain they will not be attractive to you, but I beg you will excuse them, and not hear me ill will for it."[692]

Day by day, the relations between Ottomans and Kurds deteriorated. Muhammad Pasha of Mosul, nicknamed Ince Bayraktar, managed to convince the Ottoman Porte to add both Badinan and Botan to his control, with Botan being transferred from Diyarbekir to Mosul in 1841.[693] However, he failed to convince Bedirkhan to submit to his rule. Instead, Bedirkhan's answer was confrontation, increasing his fortifications in readiness of any impending attack by the Pasha.[694]

Joseph Perkins, the American missionary, at that time living amongst the Nestorians, recorded the Nestorians and his own feelings about the imminent demise of Bedirkhan:

"We trust that the result of this conflict (Turkish expeditions against) will be a great relief to the mountain Nestorians in their political relations; and, what is of far more

---

[692] FO 195/228, No. 149, Dated 5th June 1844. See appendix C for the detail of this letter.
[693] Badger, George Percy (1852). Op. cit, p. 183.
[694] Ibid, p. 84.

importance to us and to them, that it may also open to us a wider and more effectual door for missionary labours among them."[695]

This time the Botan Emirate was toppled. The pressure exerted by the European powers offered an opportunity for the Ottoman Empire to act against Bedirkhan. They were willing to do this because he had a long history of defying the Ottomans and had established his independence and for the sake of the European nations, especially the British.

It could be seen that for the majority of the time, the Ottoman and Persian authorities were in political agreement against Kurds. especially at the height of their power. The two states prevented the Kurdish *mir* from intersecting the boundary of the Ottoman and Persian territories. Any treaty agreed between the two states had as its objective to put pressure on the Kurds. This was evident from the conclusion of their treaty in 1847:

> "The Turkish and Persian governments have recently ratified a treaty, by the terms of which each is to restore subjects of the other that cross the boundary, when demanded; a treaty hastened probably, on the part of the Porte, to provide against the flight of the obnoxious Koordish [*sic*] chiefs into Persia."[696]

Henry Ross believed that the pressure exerted by the European powers was the decisive factor in precipitating the Ottomans to eliminate the Emirate,

> "At length the representatives of the Great Powers at Constantinople brought such pressure to bear on the Sultan that he ordered the formidable Meer to be deposed as well as Khan Mahmud, the rebel chief of Van. Troops were collected at Kharpoot near Diarbakir, and Osman Pasha, the Seraskier, a renegade Croat, assumed the command. He completely routed the Kurds on the banks of the Tigris, and Bedirkhan Bey fled with a few horsemen to his stronghold Arrak Kala. About the same time the Erzerum troops were victorious over Khan Mahmud and Zeynel Beg on the banks of the river Sert. The Serasker besieged Arrak Qala and after some days Bedirkhan Beg surrendered and was sent to Constantinople with his chief adherents and his counsellors the Moolahs [*sic*]."[697]

---

[695] Perkins (1847). "Letter dated May 29th, 1847", *The Missionary Herald*, Vol. XLIII, No. 10, October, 1847, pp. 348-9.
[696] Ibid, p. 349.
[697] Ross, Henry James (1902). Op. cit, pp. 68-9.

After huge pressure by the Ottoman troops, with the collaboration of the Nestorians at home, Bedirkhan Pasha was surrounded, and defeated. He was permitted to take into exile with him two hundred personal belongings and it was with these that he was chiefly instrumental in quelling the Greek rising in 1856.

In recognition of this service, he was recalled to Constantinople where he was allowed to remain. In the year 1866, he moved to Damascus where he resided until his death in 1870 at the age of sixty five. He was buried in what was then the Kurdish village of Salihiyeh, an hour from Damascus. His tomb is near to that of the most famous of all Kurds, Salah ed Din.[698]

Nurullah Beg did not submit and fled to the borders of Persia. A local Missionary thought that "Norullah Bey…is undoubtedly destined, sooner or later, to be taken [and is] probably doomed to a companionship with the exiled Bader Khan Bey". Already "His famous fortress at Julamerk is now occupied by a Turkish garrison."[699]

In the campaign against Bedirkhan, some Kurds became mercenaries and joined with the Turkish army to attack their own people.[700]

5.11 More elements of Bedirkhan's Kurdism

Besides establishing a just administration and building a strong Botan army, Bedirkhan demonstrated his allegiance to Kurdism in other ways. Bedirkhan habitually dressed in a distinctly Kurdish style and embraced the Kurdish way of life. It appears that he tended to place the interests of Kurdish people above the Ottomans and if asked to do something against Kurdish interests would, without hesitation, refuse.

For example, from Stevens' report, it is clear that Bedirkhan was a Kurdish Pasha and attempted to serve Kurdish people. It seems that Bedirkhan consciously noticed that there were people watching them. In other words, Bedirkhan and *Mir* Saifadin were aware that they

---

[698] Noel, Major E. M. (1920). Op. cit, p. 53.
[699] Cochran (1849). "Letter from Mr Cochran, December 21, 1848", *The Missionary Herald*, Vol. XLV, No. 5, May, 1849, p. 161.
[700] Safrastian, Arshak (1948). Op. cit, p. 51.

should be in Kurdish dress to show that they were different from Turks and other ethnic groups. Stevens observes that:

> "Both chiefs [Bedirkhan and Mir Saifadin a Kurdish chief] were handsomely dressed in the Koordish [*sic*] style, the variety and gaudiness of the colours imparting a very gay appearance. ....."

Bedirkhan in conversation with Stevens said that,

> "I have now dwindled down the simple Emir of Bohtan [*sic*], but with this I should be satisfied, if I knew that my Government appreciated services which I have rendered it. Before I obtained my present influence in Koordistan [*sic*], the country was insecure as it could possibly be; now a man may travel with safety all over it, with bags of gold on his head. I am a dependent of the Pasha of Mossul, but I am obliged also to attend to the wishes of the Pashas of Baghdad, Erzeroom and Diarbekir; and if I get too friendly with one, I am certain of making enemies of others. I am called a rebel, because knowing his treacherous character; I refused to visit the late Mehmed Pasha of Mossul, to whom I am indebted for getting a bad name at Constantinople. Compare the state of the people in my territory with that of those under Mossul and Diarbekir, and if their welfare is any consideration with the government, tell me candidly who serves the Sultan best, the Pashas of those places, or Bedr Khan."[701]

The above passage highlights Bedirkhan's desire to be a ruler of Kurdistan and to do his best for the Kurdish people. He was proud that his emirate was in a much better situation than the regions under the Ottoman Empire. The passage also alludes to conflicts of interest between different Ottoman rulers.

The letter from Sir Stratford Canning to Bedirkhan shows Canning's regard and respect for Bedikhan as a leader. He praises Bedirkhan for his "acts of justice and humanity" and conducts "highly appreciated by my government and nation" and refers to him as a "sincere friend".[702] Of course, the question of how far Canning personally held such views and how far such words might be the words of sweet-tongued diplomacy is a matter for debate.

---

[701] FO 195/288 The Consul of Moussul's report of a visit to Bedr Khan, Moussul, July 10th 1844. Enclosed in Sir Stratford Canning's dispatch No. 169 of 1844.

[702] FO 78/2699 Sir Stratford Canning to Lord Aberdeen, No. 129, Constantinople, May 22nd, 1845, enclosure No. 10, Sir Stratford Canning to Bedr Khan Bey. See appendix E for the letter.

5.12 Kurdism in *Lawik* following the Botan Emirate

The exploits of Bedirkhan swiftly became popular and were used by Kurdists. Abdulfatah Yahya [703] published the texts of two *lawiks* (Kurdish folkloric songs), passed down through oral tradition dealing with the Bedirkhan revolt, and its suppression by the Ottomans. Whilst the use of such oral sources may always be problematic[704], he established clear linear descent of these texts from singers active around the time of the revolt.

Life in Botan was reflected in Kurdish literature, especially in folk songs. Many *Lawikbêj* (lawik singer) who were living under Bedirkhan devoted their *lawik* to express their sense and feeling towards the Kurdish ruler and praised, describing the Ottoman army, as the force of an enemy.

One *lawik* which has great fame in Cizire, Hakkari and Badinan is the "*lawik* of Bedirkhan" which tells the story of Botan's resistance against the Ottoman army in 1847. The *lawikbêj* here appears as a Kurd who makes differences and comparisons between the significant rule of Kurdish Pasha, his simple guns and other war equipment with powerful Ottoman forces and the oppressive intentions of the Ottoman administration.

Wesman Paşa kuçik bab,
destê babê têlî, mîrê Bota, şêrê Kurda,
bi te nayê te girîdanê.[705]

Osman pasha the son of a dog
You cannot defeat the *Mir* of Botan who is the lion of the Kurds
You cannot capture him and imprison him.

Then the lawikbêj says:

---

[703] Yahya, Abdulfatah Ali (February 1985). *Botan wa al-Botaniyin wa al-'Ghniya al-Kurdiya al-Ta'rikhiya*, Arabic text, Botan and Botanians and historical Kurdish songs, Karwan, Monthly cultural magazine in Kurdish and Arabic languages, No. 29, pp. 154-167.
[704] Portelli, A. (1985). "The Peculiarities of Oral History", *History Workshop Journal*, 12 (1), pp. 96-107, 1981; J Vansina, ed Oral Tradition as History, Oxford.
[705] Yahya, Abdulfatah Ali (February 1985). Op. cit, p. 159.

Le me tê dengê topan u cibexan u le peyme tê.

Heyfe bo mixabina dilê me dimînê.

Kuçikê koşterê Romya

ketine şarê Cizîrê Bota.[706]

We are hearing the boom of cannons from behind

It is sad for us

That the Ottoman army

Now occupies the city of Cizire of Botan (Cizire was the capital of Botan)

The above verses which were repeated eight times as a chorus, show that the Turkish troops were regarded as occupiers.

Here it could be argued that the song conveys a sense of strong Kurdish consciousness and that the *lawikbêj* (folkloric singer) had a concept of Kurdism, which he extrapolated in a political sense. Kurdish intellectuals identified the combination of his words, and their meaning, in his consciousness to serve the idea of Kurdism.

Thus the attack on Botan and other parts of Kurdistan nurtured the idea of Kurdism and helped Kurdists to promote their nationalist thoughts. It could be understood that Kurdish songs and Kurdish language influenced the establishment of a discourse of Kurdism. The main point realised here is that Kurdish *lawikbêj* made clear a distinction between Kurds and Turks, without necessarily making a direct attack on the Sultan and Ottoman Empire.

One stanza speaks of the weakness of Othman Pasha, Commander of the Empire, in confronting the Botan Kurds. It points out that he was obliged to ask for reinforcements from the Ottoman garrisons in Mosul and Baghdad.

The fifth verse tells how, after occupying Cizire the capital city of Botan, the *Mir* ordered his commanders to attack the Ottoman army and kill soldiers and their commanders.[707]

---

[706] Ibid.
[707] Ibid, p. 157.

Mîr Bedirxan be sê denga kira gazî,

Hesenê Hewîrî Tahîrê, Meymo Samîyê Lutî,

Şemoyê Dêrşewî:

Wesman paşa seknî Cizîra Bota,

bi ṟojê eskerê xo kom dika,

bi şevê berela dika, ta ser ṟêza gunda.

Ev şev min divê bavêna ser ordiyê

Wî kuçik babî.

Bibṟin serê topçîy u qumandara.

De lo lo lo, lo lo[708]

Mîr Bedirkhan was praised by three famous men

Hasane Hawire Tahiri, Maimo Sameye Lute,

and Shamoya Dershawe.

Osman Pasha resided in Cizire.

During the daytime he would collect his troops

At night, he freed his troops until they reached the villages

Tonight, we should attack the Ottoman camp which

Belonged to that son of the bitch

And kill the gunners and their commanders

Long life! Long life!

In the final verse, the *lawikbêj* recounts how Bedirkhan was captured by the Ottoman army and the end of the Botan Emirate, telling how Zeyneb Xatun, the wife of Bedirkhan Pasha, went to see Othman Pasha and asked him to not chain Bedirkhan Pasha's hands.[709]

There is no doubt that historical events have strong links with the rise of proto-nationalism and nationalism. Consequently, in the event of attacking the Botan Emirate by the Ottoman army, it could be seen how Kurdism consciously transformed the reality of an event into a linguistic and literary representation.[710]

---

[708] Ibid, p. 157.
[709] Ibid, p. 158.
[710] Firro, Kais M. (2009). *Metamorphosis of the Nation (al-Umma)*, Sussex Academic Press, Brighton, p. 4.

"Qehremanê dastanê *Hemê Mûsê yê bi bernavê Bavê Nûrê*" hatiye nasîn li deşta Sirûcê, ligel hevalên xwe êrişê dibe çadira Osman paşa, weha di wê berhemê de mêrxasiya wî hatiye numakiri":

There is another heroical *beyt* entitled *Bavê Nûrê* wich was written in *Deşta Sirûcê* where they attacked tent of Ottoman commander Othman Pasha.[711] The following verses of the *beyt* are about the feelings of dislike held by the Kurds towards the Ottoman army and its commander:

Li eskerê nezamê qewimandin,
Attack the headquarters of the Ottoman army

....

....

Gihabû derê çadira Osman-paşa rimek li topçî da,
He went to the entrance of the tent of Othman Pasha, the artillery was fired

Ser topçî peyabû, serê topçî jêkir di ber topêda,
Hemê Mûsê approached the artillery man and chopped off his head
Lê çibikim rima bavê Nûrê şikestibû di laşê topçîda
What can I do, when *bavê Nûrê* attacked, the arrowhead broke in the body of the artillery man.

Şahid û şûdê bavê Nûrê gelek hene,
There are many witnesses about bavê Nûrê

Dibê:- heya niha jî tekelikê topê bê xuyî mane di deşta Sirûcêda,
They said the remnant of the artillery still exists in Sirûcê plain

These verses reflect the general opinion of the Kurdish people towards Bedirkhan as for them, he represented the Kurdish people serving as a unifying factor in the promotion of Kurdish nationalism in the war against the Ottomans. The *lawikbêjin* singing these verses promoted Kurdism and praised Bedirkhan and his rule. After his demise the verses served as

---

[711] Jalil, Jalili (1985). *Zargotina Kurdê Sûrîae*, Akademya RESS, Ulma Instîtûta Rojhlatzaniyê, Erevan, p. 27. See appendix F

important memoirs of a time when the idea of Kurdism prevailed and today are considered important in the historical legacy that was bequeathed by Bedirkhan.

5.13 Legacy of Bedirkhan

The defeat of Bedirkhan and the collapse of his administration in the Botan Emirate was a disaster for the Kurdish people. However, the event did not bring a long peace and stability to the Ottoman Empire in its relation with its Kurds. On the Kurdish internal affairs front, Kurds prepared to unify and they stood for another confrontation with the empire. On the other hand, it became clearer to non-Muslim Kurdish elements, such as the Christians, that Botan rule was far better than the Ottoman statute.

Bedirkhan had aroused a sense of unity and resistance among Kurds. After his defeat, the Ottomans could not establish an administration easily; people opposed direct rule from Constantinople.

It did not take long before Kurds under Yezdan Şêr (1830-1875), son of *Mir* Seyfedin Bedirkhan's brother, rebelled against the Turks in 1854-5. His influence spread in Cizire and beyond.[712] This meant that the Empire could not collect tobacco tax in Cizire.[713] To date, Kurdish resistance in northern Kurdistan against the Turkish state has resulted in serious confrontation around the Kurdish struggle for recognition.

It has been argued that Bedirkhan was a Kurdish "nationalist". Although he may have fought to maintain power, administrative and otherwise, he managed to do so within Botan, and especially with the Kurdish people. For instance, although he may not have been nationalist in the strictest sense of the word, he was able to help local governors to govern and keep Kurdish land.[714] His family, although mostly employed by the Ottomans, also carried on his Kurdish legacy and maintained their Kurdish roots. Two of his children published a Turkish-Kurdish newspaper named *Kurdistan* in Cairo, Geneva and Folkestone in England, the first newspaper to be published in the Kurdish language in (22nd April 1898).[715]

---

[712] Lobdell (1855). "Mosul: A letter from Dr. Lobdell", *The Missionary Herald*, Vol. 51, April 1855, pp. 111-4.

[713] Marsh (1857). "Mosul: A letter from Mr. Marsh, Setember12, 1856", *The Missionary Herald*, Vol. 53, January 1857, pp. 53-7.

[714] Ozoguz, Hakan (August 2001). "Nationalism and Kurdish Notables in the Late Ottoman-Earl Republican Era", *International Journal of Middle East Studies*, Volume. 33, Number 3, p. 398.

[715] Ibid.

Bedirkhan's image of security and economic prosperity remains a powerful symbol of the continuing code on which he built his fame among the population in general. In retrospect, Nestorians under his rule had a better life compared to the rule of the Ottomans. Nestorians were from twelve villages with inhabitants of nearly three thousand persons, and ten other villages in neighbouring areas. They were convinced that their economic life was better under Bedirkhan than under the Ottoman Empire. These people told missionaries that

> "In Bader Khan Bey's day, our taxes were far less than now; though he cursed our religion, and forced us to work for him on Sundays and feast days. Those Turks take the very bread from our mouths, and still cry, 'Give, Give.'"[716]

Furthermore, fifteen years after the collapse of Bedirkhan's emirate in Botan, still there were people waiting for his return; this might indicate that Bedirkhan shaped a sense of Kurdism and remained alive even after his defeat, or it could just mean that he inspired loyalty. Missionaries admitted that Kurds were seeking Bedirkhan's old and happy days. Missionaries from Kurdistan witnessed that:

> "the Koords were showing much more boldness since hearing of the death of the Sultan.....saying that they were just now rejoicing in the hope of the return of their favorite chief, Beder Khan. [*sic*]"[717]

Hajî Qdir-i Koyî the most paramount Kurdish nationalist and poet praised Bedirkhan's rule, describing him as a source of unity and a leader safeguarding the Kurds from the Ottomans. Hajî trusted his leadership and predicted that if Bedirkhan was removed from power, Kurds would suffer under the Ottomans. Here, he addresses Kurds in general in a way that suggests a sense of belonging to one people and one leadership. Hajî says:

Bedirxaniw le ser laçê lemewpaş
Le herlaêi detan hařn weku aş [718]

If Bedirkhan's family was removed
They [Ottomans] would smash you everywhere

---

[716] Coan and Rhea (1854). "Tour of MESSRS. Coan and Rhea through Koordistan", *Missionary Herald*, Nestorians, Vol. 50, March, 1854, p. 71.
[717] Walker, Augustus (). "Mission to Eastern Turkey- Diarbekir, Letter from Mr. Augustus Walker, August-September, 1861", *The Missionary Herald*, Feb, 1862, p. 57.
[718] Hajî Qadir Koyî (1969). *Diwani Hajî Qadir Koyî, Collected Poems*, Giwi Mukryani (Ed.), Third edition, Hewler Press, Hewler, p. 17.

Hajî Qadir understood well that survival of Bedirkhan Pasha and his power would prevent Kurds from being humilated by the Ottomans; he knew that Bedirkhan was a true Kurdish leader.

5.14 Conclusion

During Bedirkhan's era as *Mir* of the Botan Emirate, it is possible to recognise elements of Kurdism, through emerging perceptions of Kurdish self-unity. Bedirkhan and other Kurdish leaders under his influence understood that their unity around a sense of Kurdism was a cornerstone for their survival. Consequently, they joined together to establish a so-called "holy alliance" between themselves under the leadership of Bedirkhan Pasha, and they proved their loyalty to each other, and to him.

Another element of Kurdism was the sense that power held should be exercised. Bedirkhan presented himself as the true Kurdish ruler of the emirate. (See appendix C for his use of the term Kurdish). Hence, Bedirkhan was keen to improve the Botan Emirate on all levels. He promoted the establishment of a strong Botan Kurdish army, recruiting soldiers from all tribes and other religions without discrimination. Nestorians, Armenians and Yezidies were among those serving in his forces.

Bedirkhan always tried to take opportunities to extend the Botan Emirate, and to implement "Kurdism" over his people. Thus he implemented law and order everywhere and meted these out equally amongst the population. At the height of his power, Bedirkhan tried his best to keep Botan free from direct intervention by the Ottoman Empire. Using the word "Kurdistan" during Stevens visit, Bedirkhan emphasised the Kurdish identity of both himself and his emirate. His choice to wear distinctive Kurdish dress indicates Bedirkhan's pride in the distinct Kurdish customs of his own people.

Bedirkhan built alliances within Kurdish society in order to bring to his aid the powerful tribes and their leaders. To stabilise his reign he tried to build solid political foundations. He also sought to establish a strong army and gunpowder factories to supply its needs.

He paid attention to establishing mechanisms of security and justice. Moreover, he desired to improve his people's economic and social wellbeing. In this way he managed to bring Kurdish Muslims and non-Muslims together; as many Armenians and Yezidis took part in his administration and backed his resistance against the Ottoman Empire. His main ally was Nurullah (the Amir of Hakkari) who, in the beginning, had a good relationship with the Nestorians, especially with Mar Shimun, the Nestorian patriarch.

During the period of Tanzimat, the influence of the European powers over Ottoman affairs increased dramatically. As in other parts of the Empire, European states and American Christian societies went into Kurdistan. One result of this was to drive a wedge between Kurds and Nestorians who had been living together relatively peacefully for centuries.

The missionaries supported the Nestorians at the expense of the Kurdish emirates. When Bedirkhan sought to gain retribution on the Nestorians, both American and British missionaries did whatever they could through diplomatic channels to influence the Porte to attack the Botan Emirate and to bring it down. British diplomats from London, Istanbul, Mosul and other places, played a crucial role in compelling the Porte to send troops against Bedirkhan of Botan. Consequently, the emirate was destroyed. The centralisation policy of reform became a brutal lever against Bedirkhan's Kurdism.

The Kurdish people and their Mirs had an excellent relationship with missionaries until the Kurds realised that many of the missionaries were acting against their interests. In particular, the Nestorians were emboldened to establish some form of autonomy, and began to despise their Kurdish neighbours. The missionaries had ambitions to make Christianity the predominant religion in the region.

Bedirkhan contacted other Kurdish leaders to persuade them to unite for the sake of the interests of Kurdish people, regardless of their division between the Ottoman and Persian empires, underscoring his belief in Kurdism. He left behind a rich legacy of Kurdish folklore, poetry and song. He tried very hard to build good relationships with the British diplomats in Istanbul and with their consulates in Ottoman Kurdistan. However, he failed to understand both the international politics and the political purposes of foreign commissions and dealt with them inappropriately. Bedirkhan made several serious mistakes which diverted him away from his key ambitions. Unintentionally, he became the victim of his own wrongdoings.[719]

---

[719] For a cogent summary of these events see Eppel, M (2008). "The Demise of the Kurdish Emirates", *Middle Eastern Studies*, Vol. 44, No 2, March 2008, pp. 253-257.

Today, Bedirkhan has an esteemed reputation amongst Kurds and his family is considered an important Kurdish dynasty, with people looking to Bedirkhan as a paramount Kurdish leader (Judie, 2006; Bruinessen, 1992). At the beginning of Bedirkhan's reign, the idea of Kurdism had not been realised in any concrete sense, however, during his reign, it was nurtured through his energy to establish a Kurdish army and better international relations. By the end of his reign and his exile, his sons continued to follow his example and continued to realise his aims. The legacy of his reign is of major importance in the development of Kurdism, both within and outside of Kurdistan.

Chapter Six

The Development of Kurdism in the Baban Emirate 1800-1850

6.1 Introduction

This chapter analyses how the Baban Emirate functioned and played a crucial part in the development of Kurdism. The use of the Kurdish language in literature, especially poetry, by many writers and poets, such as Mawlana Khalid Naqishbandî, Ali Berdeşanî, Nalî and Salim, became an important factor in establishing the foundations not just of Kurdish identity, but of an entire school of Kurdism represented in the classical school of Southern (Soranî) Kurdish literature. Other domains of the usage of Kurdism will also be discussed, such as the political nature of Kurdish dynastic administrations and the attitudes of both Abdulrahman Pasha and Ahmad Pasha. The primary focus here will be upon literature. The significance for Kurdish identity of the late Baban Emirate was that both modern standard Soranî Kurdish and modern enlightened Kurdism can be said to have developed and continued there. As such, it played a central role in the consolidation of Kurdish identity, paving the way for the emergence of modern Kurdish nationalism. The way that language and culture in Baban appears to have reflected Kurdism will also be explored.

Various key figures and events, during the first half of nineteenth century, had a significant impact on the Kurdish issue in Baban. This chapter will discuss how external forces, especially Persia, both contributed to, and hindered, the development of Kurdism in Baban. Thus, ways in which internal, regional and international factors caused the Baban pashas to fail in their ambition to maintain Kurdish influence at home, ultimately preventing them from the promotion of Kurdism, will be illuminated.

Through discussing historical events and rivalries of the emirate, the constant drive of Baban *Mirs* [princes] to stress their ethnic and geographical distinction will be demonstrated. Ways in which Baban *Mirs* retained their independence or autonomy within the geopolitical context they found themselves in, planning for military strength to resist foreign aggression and establish good ways of ruling to ensure the continuity of Kurdish power and culture, will be explored.

In 1784, Silêmanî[720] became the capital of the Baban, developing steadily into a cultural centre of the emirate. From this moment, its rulers can be perceived to have thought more broadly about Kurdish affairs. Their efforts helped precipitate the shaping of a pre-national identity that, in due course, helped mould Kurdism among the Baban dynasty and intellectuals under their influence.

The widespread use of the Silêmanî dialect for writing amongst scholars and in mosques all over the Baban Emirate, alongside the flowering of an indigenous poetry, helped to establish Silêmanî as the written standardised 'Kurdish' language in most of Southern Kurdistan. The Kurdish dialects and their grouping remains an area for further study, beyond the scope of this thesis. Scholars differ as to how the dialects should be grouped. In general, the Kurds residing in the northern parts of Kurdistan call themselves *Kurmanj* and their dialect *Kurmanjî*, whilst the southern Kurds call themselves *Kurd* and their speech *Kurdî*.[721] Silêmanî, Sanandaji, and Mukriyani are closely tied sub-dialects of Southern *Kurmanjî*. Of the two major dialects of Kurdish, the northern one is usually called Kurmanjî and the southern one is called Southern Kurmanjî or Soranî, although it is spoken much more widely than the emirate of Soran.[722]

This chapter examines how the Emirate contributed to the formation of Kurdish national discourse. In particular, it considers the role of Abdurrahman Pasha who, at the end of the eighteenth and the beginning of the nineteenth-century, played a critical role in strengthening the Baban emirate. His measures kept Ottoman rule at a distance, at least for a time.

After the death of Abdulrahman Pasha in 1813, the rivalry between his sons, the pashas Mahmud and Silêman badly affected Kurdish affairs. This opened an opportunity for the Ottomans and Persians to penetrate further into Baban. Until 1850, Silêmanî was ruled by the Baban, a Kurdish family descended from Feqê Ahmad. Later that year, Abdullah Pasha of Silêmanî, the last *Mir* of Baban, was called to Baghdad by Abdi Pasha, the Pasha of Baghdad (1848-1850) and was replaced by an officer of Kurdish origin.[723] Shortly afterwards, the

---

[720] The standard spelling now a day is Sulaimaniyah. Various spellings have been used by English travelers and colonial administrators in Kurdistan and Iraq. I use the traditional historical Kurdish name and spelling: Silêmanî.

[721] However, both *the terms Kurdi* and *Kurmanjî* have been used interchangeably. See Hassanpour, Amir, (1992). *Nationalism and Language in Kurdistan, 1918-1985*, Mellen Research University Press, San Francisco, p. 19.

[722] Fu'ad, Dr Kemal (1971). "Zarawekani zimani Kurdi", Kurdish text, The dialects of Kurdish language, *Zanyari, General Scientific Kurdish Magazine*, No. 4, p. 19. Hassanpour, Ibid, p. 21. Kreyenbroek, Philip G. (1992). On The Kurdish Language in Kreyenbroek, P.G. & Sperl, S., *The Kurds: A Contemporary Overview*, Routledge, London and New York, pp. 68-83.

[723] Nawwar, Dr. Abdulaziz (1968). *Ta'rikh al-Iraq al-Hadith*, Arabic text, The history of new Iraq, Dar al-Katib al-Arabi liltiba'a wa al-Nashir, Cairo, p. 119.

Turkish General Ismael Pasha took up his place as a governor of Silêmanî.[724] The centralisation policy of the Ottoman Empire which aimed at bringing local people under the central government ended, in 1850, the semi-autonomous existence of the Baban Emirate. With its demise, the period of Kurdish principalities ceased.

The Emirate survived until 1850. Its relative longevity may have been attributable to its geographical isolation, but equally, also to the fact that the Baban Emirate had reasonably strong forces and a strong, popular base. In comparison to the other two emirates, its history and politics were most influenced by Persia, its location being just inside the Ottoman-Persian frontier.

6.2 Establishing a new Capital: From Qeĺa Çolan to Silêmanî

In 1669, the city of Silêmanî was built by on an ancient site, by Baba Silêman (1663–1675), taking his name. The capital city was later moved to Qeĺa Çolan from Mawet, where it remained until 1784.[725] From this time, Silêmanî became significant in 1783–4, when Ibrahim Pasha who envisaged a new, modern capital city for his emirate, agreed to transfer the capital of the Baban Emirate there.[726] This new location was more favourable, as it offered more opportunity for the *Mir* to expand his authority, enabling the city to become a centre for politics, trade and culture. Over time it became famed for its mosques and schools; especially in terms of the Kurdish scholars who taught there.

Qeĺa Çolan consisted of a municipal building for the conduct of the Emirate's affairs; as well as castles for pashas, and merchants. A new library was established by Silêman Pasha (1750-1764), which became well regarded and contained some six-thousand rare Arabic and Persian manuscripts. It was built by sending librarians on a grand tour to places as far apart as Cairo, Mekka, San'a in Yemen, Tehran and Isfahan.[727] During this Pasha's era, *medreses* were improved and most famous Kurdish Melas such as Sheikh Muhammad Wasim Sanandaji,

---

[724] Longrigg, Stephen Hemsley (1925). *Four Centuries of Modern Iraq*, The Clarendon Press, Oxford, p. 287.

[725] Wahbi, Tofiq (October 8th, 1973)., "Asl tasmiyat Qeĺa Çolan", Arabic text, The original name of Qeĺa Çolan, *Al-Taakhi newspaper*, Baghdad, No. 1454.

[726] Baba Silêman came from the Pishder district of the Baban tribe – Edmonds, C. J. (January 1935). "A Kurdish Lampoonist", *Journal of the Royal Central Asian Society*, Vol. XXII, Part I, p. 112. The Kurdish historian Muhammad Amin Zaki believed that Silêmanî was built by Ibrahim Pasha in 1784. Zaki, Muhammad Ameen (1939). *Terixi Silêmanî u wlati*, Kurdish text, *The history of* Silêmanî *and its surrounding*, al-Najah Press, Baghdad, pp. 89-90.

[727] Khal, Muhammad (1961). *Al-Shaikh Maruf al-Nodeyi al-Berziji*, Arabic text, *The Biography of al-Shaikh Maruf al- Nodeyi al-Berzinji*, Dar al-Tamadun Press, Baghdad, p. 12. Al-Qzilji, Muhammad, (1938). *Al-Taarikh masajid al-Sulaimaniya wa madarisiha al-diniya*, Arabic text, *Introduction of Sulémani's mosques and its schools*, al-Najaf Press, Baghdad, p. 23.

Mela Muhammad Ghazayi, Mela Ali, Mela Mahmud Qzilji and others taught in Qeĺa Çolan.[728]

6.3 Silêmanî: the new capital

By the mid-eighteenth century, the situation of the Baban emirate had improved politically, economically and militarily. This allowed it to gain more effective control over domestic and external affairs. The Emirate became more powerful and economically self-sustained. In the second decade of the eighteenth century, two exceptional factors emerged that raised the Baban Emirate to a higher eminence.[729]

Firstly, Khana Pasha of Baban had taken advantage of the anarchy during the Afghan invasion of Iran, to extend his authority from Kirkuk to Hamadan where Erdelan was included. Later, from 1719 to 1723, he became its ruler.[730] After four years in Sine (Sanandaj) the capital of Erdelan, he returned to Baban and left his son, Ali Khan, as the governor of Erdelan. Erdelan governed for six years until 1729, when Persia took it back.[731] Secondly, further consolidation was achieved when Soran was added to the Emirate in 1730, and then Badinan to Baban.[732]

There were a number of reasons for the move. Firstly, moving the capital at this time was done with the aim of extending the Baban Emirate's borders and influence within the region. Secondly, the move and treaty with the Ottoman Empire contributed to the stability in Baban. At this time, Baban was not paying taxes to the Porte. However, they did have to provide a military levy.[733] This treaty had two important impacts on the Baban Emirate. Primarily, it brought wealth to the Emirate by keeping more revenue in Baban. Almost as importantly, soldiers who came back to the Baban region had learned from their experiences and developed their knowledge of the administration of the Emirate. At the same time, Silêmanî had a very important economic position in Sharezur, being one of the most fertile plains in Kurdistan. This enabled some princes and officials of the Emirate to consider expanding their

---

[728] Al-Qzilji, Muhammad (1938). Ibid, p. 24.
[729] Hakim, Helkewt (1984). "Chand sarnjeki saratayi darbarai drustbuni shari Silêmanî", Few Comments regarding building of Silêmanî, Kurdish text, *Hiwa magazine*, No. 2, May, p. 75.
[730] Rabino , H. L. (1911). *Confidential Report on Kurdistan*, Printed at the Government Monotype Press, Simla, p. 80–81. Longrigg, Stephen Hemsley (1925). *Four Centuries of Modern Iraq*, Oxford University Press, Oxford, p. 159.
[731] Rabino , H. L. (1911). Ibid, p. 81.
[732] Longrigg, Stephen Hemsley (1925). Op. cit, p. 159.
[733] Nikitine, Basile (1956). *Les Kurdes*, Imprimerie Nationle, Paris, p. 163.

rule over the wider areas by building a stronger army. Thirdly, the position of Qeĺa Çolan, the previous capital of Baban, so close to the boundary line of the Ottoman and Persian Empires, meant that Qeĺa Çolan was vulnerable to their depredations. The new capital was more defensible from the regional powers. Finally, Qeĺa Çolan was in a very unfavourable location, as it lacked decent water supplies and the land was poorly fertilised so the people often went thirsty or hungry.[734]

The shift of the capital to Silêmanî, from Qeĺa Çolan, realised the ideals of the Baban dynasty as a centre of culture, economics, and politics. Later, realising its new significance; many religious leaders [Berzinji Sheikhs] and professionals from various fields of expertise decided to gather and establish themselves there, embracing Silêmanî as their new capital.

Silêmanî acted as the centre for later development of Kurdish identity, through the attraction of many Kurds from various regions; such as Soran, Mukryan, Sine (Erdelan).[735] In addition, many people came to Silêmanî from different places within Baban itself. Subsequently, the town's reputation was enhanced by the establishment of good municipal facilities, such as baths, markets and mosques.[736] As Lieutenant Heude stated in his memoir of his journey from India to England, "It is remarkable for several handsome domes and mosques, and some prettily situated gardens along the banks of the rivulet…"[737] Heude also observed; "On the whole…it may be described as something superior to the generality of Asiatic cities; a considerable degree of cleanliness being preserved by sewers and other public conveniences…"[738]

From the beginning, Silêmanî had full public services, including a water project for the whole city and watercourse. Several preindustrial manufacturing industries were established, such as soap making, weaving, gun making, tanning. Some boroughs in Silêmanî still hold the name of those industries, including *Sabunkeran* (soap-makers) and *Debaxane* (tannery). All of

---

[734] Rich, Claudius James (1836). *Narrative of a Residence in Kurdistan and on the Site of Ancient Nineveh; with journal of a Voyage down the Tigris to Bagdad*, edited by his widow, Vol. I, James Duncan, London, p. 119.

[735] Mela Karim, Muhammad (1981). "Aqidai Kurdi Mawlana Xalidi Naqishbandî", Kurdish text, The Kurdish Creed of Mawlana Xalidi *Naqishbandî*, *The Journal of Iraqi Academy- Kurdish Corporation*, Volume 8, p. 201.

[736] Soane, Ely Bannister (1969). *To Mesopotamia and Kurdistan in Disguise*, Reprinted, University Press Amsterdam, Amsterdam, p. 185

[737] Lieutenant William Heude (1819). *A Voyage up The Persian Gulf and a Journey Overland from India to England in 1817* Longman, Hurst, Rees, Orme, and Brown. London. p. 207.

[738] Ibid.

these industries needed teams of workers and produced more than the need of Silêmanî; surplus was sent outside of the Baban Emirate and Silêmanî became a trade centre.[739]

This plan to build a city, and the founding of schools and sponsoring of poets and scholars, had an immense impact on Kurdish identity in the beginning of the nineteenth century. Silêmanî has become a symbolic icon in Kurdish thought since it has become a capital of Kurdish culture. Furthermore, establishing public services, improving essential manufacture and building an army were all important aspects of the city. To illustrate the importance of Silêmanî as a city, it is worth citing Antony Smith on the impact of cities on the development of administration: "City planning forms hierarchy (civil, military and religious) …that so frequently provide us with clues about thoughts, feelings and attitudes of communities"[740] and "relating otherwise diverse phenomena into a picture of the factors and dimensions that comprise 'ethnic identity.'"[741]

6.4 Role of Silêman Pasha and the expansion of Baban

After Silêmanî became a capital, the Baban Emirate expanded further. The ruler Ibrahim Pasha (1783-1789) became known as 'the Pasha of Kurdistan'.[742] The people of the Emirate became more confident. The Kurdish people, their rulers and in particular the intellectuals hoped for a brighter future as they looked forward to a more advanced and developed emirate. After Ibrahim Pasha had died, Abdurrahman became Pasha of Baban (1789–1813). He was a renowned scholar who had built a mosque and *medrese* (Islamic school), honouring his name in Silêmanî. One of the great Kurdish poets, Nali taught there in the 1840s.[743]

Abdulrahman Pasha wrote a foreword for a manuscript of *"Sahih al-Bukhari"* within the Baban Library in Silêmanî in 1797.[744] Here he used the word "Kurdistan" to delineate the territorial boundaries of his emirate. He was probably the first leader of any Kurdish administration to use this term. He described the extent of his dominions as situated from

[739] Rasul, Dr Izzaddin Mustafa (1971). *Sernjê le zmani edebi yekgrtui Kurdi*, Kurdish text, A glance about united Kurdish Language, Salman al-A'zami Press, Baghdad, p. 28.
[740] Smith, Anthony D. (1999). *The Ethnic Origins of Nations*, Basil Blackwell, Oxford, p. 14.
[741] Ibid.
[742] He is given this name in Mignan, Captain R. (1839). *A Winter Journey through Russia, the Caucasian Alps, and Georgia*, Vol. II, Richard Bentley, London, 1836, p.31. Rich associates his name with 'Kurdistan, too. Rich, Claudius James, (1836). *Narrativ of a Residence in Koordistan and on the Site of Ancient Nineveh; with Journal of a Voyage Down the Tigris to Bagdad, and an Account of a visit to Shirauz and Persepolis*, edited by his widow, Vol. I, James Duncan, London, p. ix.
[743] Al-Khal, Sheikh Muhammad (1961). *Al-Sheikh Ma'ruf al-Nodehi al-Barzinji*, Arabic text, Al-Tamaddun press, Baghdad, p. 26.
[744] The manuscript of this book has been kept in the private library of Jelizade which is one of the most famous scholarly families in Southern Kurdistan for over two hundred years. Melai Gewre special collection in Koye, Southern Kurdistan of Kurdistan Regional Government.

Mosul to Baghdad and from there to Sanandaj [Sine] in Persian Kurdistan.[745] This demonstrates that Abdulrahman had a sense of the political geography of his emirate, and the Kurdish lands as a whole. It could be argued that the Pasha believed Baban to be part of Kurdistan and associated one with the other, using the terms interchangeably. This indicates the Pasha's sense of Kurdish identity. In conclusion, although Abdulrahman Pasha recognised the authority of the Ottoman Porte, and cannot be described as wishing to be truly independent of the Ottomans, he did not wish to be subject to the influence of any other regional power. His aim was to manage the affairs of his people without interference from any third party.

6.5 Abdurrahman Pasha and his Political Plan

On his ascent to power in 1789, Abdurrahman Pasha intended that Baban would be completely free from the influence of any other Pashalik. To keep his emirate secure and to advance its interests, he knew that he should serve the interests of both the Kurds and the Ottomans. His sense of Kurdishness could be interpreted as a loyalty to both Kurds and the Ottoman Empire.

As Claudius Rich noted;

"…He was willing to pay any annual tribute that the Porte might require, regularly and in ready money, at the capital, provided he should be secured from obeying any other orders than those of the Sultan...." [746]

For Abdurrahman Pasha, peace and stability could only be brought between the Ottomans and Kurds by peaceful agreement. Therefore, he started to establish peace and security in his country as a foundation for the progress of stable government. This was observed by Fraser, in 1838, during his travels in Kurdistan. One of his informants reminisced that:

"In [his] days you might have walked with jewels on your head and gold in your hand from one end of the Pashalic to the other. From Serdeşt to Kifri, from Koye to Bana, and no one would have asked you where you were going."[747]

[745] Muhammad, Mas'ud (1973). *Hajî Qadri Koyî*: On the life and works of the Kurdish poet Hajî Qadiri Koyî, Published by Kurdish Academy, Baghdad, p. 260. See also Muhammad, Mas'ud (1973). *The Journal of the Kurdish Academy*, Vol. I, Part I, p. 383.
[746] Rich, Claudius James (1836). Op. cit, Vol. I, p. 96.

His reputation for loyalty to the cause of Kurdish autonomy was lasting. Another tale, recounted by Rich, told of Abdurrahman Pasha's refusal of an offer from the government of Baghdad, because "were I to transfer my power to Baghdad, my own prosperity would be increased, but it would ultimately be the ruin of the family of the Bebbehs [Baban]."[748] This is a very clear indication that the Pasha had a strong conception of Kurdism, or family honour, which he was not ready to forfeit for personal gain.

6.6 Development of the Military under Abdurrahman

Despite the fact that Abdurrahman Pasha was never reluctant to pursue a policy independent of his nominal Sultan, he faced many hindrances. One of these was the concern that an alliance between Muhammad Pasha of Koye and the Pasha of Baghdad would be detrimental to Kurdish interests, particularly as at the time they had good relations.

During 1805, Abdurrahman Pasha fought bravely against the Ottoman army of Kuchuk Sulaiman [pasha of Baghdad] near to Derbendi Bazyan to defend his rule over the Baban Emirate. However he was defeated, partly because he did not have the full support of his clan which instead backed the Turks against him. Rich, who observed the battle, whilst travelling through the region, later in a narrative described the unfolding events:

"[Abdurrahman Pasha] placed here a wall and gate and three or four pieces of cannon, two of which were planted on the height in order to fire upon the Turkish camp below; and vain would have been Sulaiman Pasha's attack on this pass, had not a Kurdish chief called Muhammad bey [*sic*], a son of Khalid Pasha who was united with the Turks, led a division of the Turkish troops and auxiliary Koords [*sic*] up the mountain, by a pass only known to some Koords, and which had been neglected as impracticable, so that Abdurrahman Pasha found his position turned, and his guns on the height pointed against himself. He was then obliged to retreat, and the wall was razed by the Pasha of Baghdad, who afterwards advanced to Sulimania."[749]

---

[747] Fraser, J, Baillie (1840). *Travels in Koordistan, Mesopotamia, &c., including an account of Parts of those countries hitherto unvisited by Europeans. With sketches of the character and manners of the Koords and Arab tribes,* Volume I, Richard Bentley, London, p. 180.
[748] Rich, Claudius James (1836). Op. cit, Vol. I, p. 97.
[749] Rich, Claudius James, (1836). Op. cit, Vol. 1, p.59. Soane, Ely Bannister (1969). Op. cit, p. 329.

Abdurrahman Pasha paid attention to fortifying the Kurdish forces by establishing an artillery service for his army; also, along with other Kurdish leaders, he was forced to give military assistance to the Pasha of Baghdad as and when it was needed. Furthermore, at a time when Abdurrahman Pasha endeavoured to secure his rule over his principality, in order to defend his homeland, he deployed his artillery to strengthen and fortify all the passes around his territory [one of these was Derbendi Bazyan] to defend the Baban emirate against Ottoman aggression.[750] During the reign of Abdurrahman Pasha, the Baban emirate reached the highest level of its power and influence over Baghdad. By 1810, Baban had become a significant force in the area because Abdurrahman Pasha was strong enough to deny obeisance to the Pasha of Baghdad. However, Abdurrahman Pasha was deeply troubled, as various rivals in the ruling family tried to challenge his reign. Many times during his era[751], his rivals sought assistance from outsiders in Persia or of the Baghdad Pashalik.

By 1810, Sulaiman Pasha (of Baghdad) had become very weak due to consequences of the problems he had within his Pashalik. This meant the Ottoman Porte decided to remove him. Thus, when an envoy was sent to implement this decree, Sulaiman was reluctant to stand aside. To maintain power, he tried in vain to benefit from the support of local forces. Unfortunately for him, Abdulrahman Pasha (of Baban) had previously had difficulties with Baghdad's pasha; so during this decisive time, he decided to take the Ottoman's side which helped them to depose the Pasha of Baghdad.[752] The Kurds hoped his replacement would be someone who would behave less aggressively towards them.

This rivalry came to its crescendo after his death in 1813. This brought negative consequences for the fate of the Baban emirate which in turn affected the Kurdish struggle for retention of autonomy and influence on the one hand and the way Kurdism was perceived on the other. The dispatches of Claudius Rich to the East India Company provide an almost unique commentary on this affair.[753] As he put it:

"On the 5th October 1810 an attack was made by the Courds at the instigation of the Ottoman Porte, who had issued an order for the deposition of the [Sulaiman] Pacha of

---

[750] Rich, Claudius James, (1836). Ibid, p. 55.
[751] His era lasted for a span of 24 years
[752] Gazetteer of the Persian Gulf, Oman and Central Arabia, (1986). Lorimer, J. G, prepared by, Vol. I, (HISTORICAL) Part I, Chapters VI-IX, Archive Editions, p. 1309.
[753] Bruinessen. Martin van (1992). *Agha, Shaikh and State: The Social and Political Structures of Kurdistan*, notes that "virtually the only source on the condition of the emirate in the early nineteenth century is Rich, who stayed a long time in its capital", p.172. Rich could only comment on affairs from the perspective of that capital.

Bagdad, but to which order he had refused to submit—upon the army of the Pacha, which terminated in his defeat and death on the same day...."[754]

It is clear from this that Abdurrahman Pasha was now the dominant military and political force in the area. He could only have achieved this pre-eminence by developing the administration and resources of Baban to a point where they exceeded those of his neighbours. Rich later offered an account of the engagement to his superiors:

"On the 5th October, in the morning, the Pacha [*sic*] encamped at some little distance from the town with all the troops he could collect; about the hour of afternoon prayer, 2pm, the Reis Effendi advanced, and the action commenced by the Courds [*sic*] charging the Pacha's army; they were, however, completely broken by the Pacha's artillery; but this advantage was not followed up:..."[755] The reason why the advantage was not pressed is telling, "...the carriages of the guns were found to be old and unserviceable, and they were dismounted by their own fire..."[756]

It is clear that such inadequacies of the administration of Reis Effendi had precipitated the collapse of his technological superiority. Consequently: "The Courds rallied" and they now had an advantage; "they were greatly superior in numbers to the Turks."[757] Also, "The Pacha's [*sic*] army was weakened and dispirited by the desertion of a large body of Courds who were on his side, and of whom great hopes had been entertained."[758]

It is uncertain from Rich's account whether those fighters who left the field of battle simply returned home, or whether they joined their fellow Kurds: in all probability, elements of both happened. However, it is possible that Reis Effendi had relied on Kurdish fighters for a significant proportion of his forces. According to Rich:

"Thus terminated, at the age of twenty-four, the life and reign of Solyman [*sic*] Pacha, a man of a warm affection and actual good principles. His faults were such as proceed from extreme youth, and would have been corrected by age and experience. Since his

---

[754] Precis Containing Information in Regard to the First Connection of the Hon'ble East India Company with Turkish Arabia, (1874). Calcutta, p. 106. The British Library, London.
[755] Ibid, p. 106.
[756] Ibid.
[757] Ibid.
[758] Ibid.

reconciliation with me he has ever been the strongest and most sincere friend of the British, and I fear it will be long ere the Residency is so well situated."[759]

When the question of a successor for Baghdad arose, the Babans' influence was brought into consideration. Ra'is Effendi suggested that Abdulrahman Pasha of Silêmanî should become Pasha of Baghdad, but being proud of his Kurdishness the offer was refused by him. Rather than being under the influence of the Ottomans in Baghdad, Abdulrahman preferred to directly serve his people. Thus, he said that "It is true, said he that I should become a vizir of the first rank; but one draught of the snow-water of my own mountains is worth all the honours of the empire."[760]

An East India Company Report later noted:

"The Ottoman Government appointed Abdoolla Pacha [*sic*] of Baghdad [some time in December 1810], in succession to the deceased 'Sulaiman'. The new Pasha addressed a letter to this Government…, intimating his having been raised to that dignity by the Sultan, and stating it to be his earnest desire that the most friendly relations should exist between himself and the British Government…"[761]

The wording of this letter indicates that there was some confusion, in the writer's mind, about the viewpoint held by the Company and also those of the British Government; one which was not always absent from the Company's representations when pursuing its interests. The report also noted that:

"This letter was replied to in a communication from Mr. Governor Duncan on the 20th March 1811 congratulating the new Pasha on his accession to that dignity."

It did not take long for the Company's new friend to attack Abdurrahman Pasha, who had apparently been seeking some sort of accommodation with Persia. The report continued:

---

[759] Ibid.

[760] Rich, Claudius James (1836). Op. cit, Vol. I, p. 97.

[761] Precis containing information in regard to the first connection of the Hon'ble East India Company with Turkish Arabia, (1874). Op. cit, p. 106.

"In a letter dated the 2nd June 1812 Mr. Rich stated that the Pacha of Bagdad had received a *firman* from the Sultan directing the deposal of the 'Courdish [*sic*] rebel Abdulrahman Pacha,' in consequence of his having by his intrigues with Persians rendered himself entirely independent of his immediate superior the Pacha of Bagdad, and that His Excellency had accordingly marched with a force towards Courdistan.[*sic*]"[762]

To the surprise of Rich the expedition was not disastrous for the report adds that:

"In a further letter, dated the 24th of the same month (June 1812), Mr. Rich stated that the Pacha (of Bagdad) [*sic*] had on the 18th of the same month obtained a most signal and unexpected victory over Abdulrahman Pacha, the effect of which would, he entertained no doubt, lead to the entire subjection of 'the Courdistan'[*sic*] to the pacha [*sic*] of Bagdad, by which that Pachalik [*sic*]would acquire a strength and respectability it had not possessed for the last ten years, and would in reality become the most powerful territory under the Porte."[763]

Consequently, the Baban Emirate, after some time, was subject to interference from the Pasha of Baghdad; particularly, as it was not possible for Abdulrahman Pasha to hold him back for a considerable duration.

6.7 Abdulrahman Pasha's Will and His Kurdism

In 1813, Abdulrahman Pasha became ill. To write his will, he convened a gathering of all his sons, brothers, and Baban's notables. He filled this document with illustrations of his sense of Kurdishness. He spoke of his wishes for Baban's geo-political future. He was keen for his policies to be maintained: "…first; you all should keep my advice especially those which regarded political issues…"[764]

---

[762] Ibid.

[763] Ibid. Also see Gazetteer of the Persian Gulf, Oman and Central Arabia, (1986). Vol. I, (HISTORICAL) Part I, Chapters VI-IX, Op. cit, p. 1310.

[764] Cited in Nazim Beg, Husien (2001). *Ta'rikh al-Emarat al-babaniya*, Arabic text, *The History of the Baban Emirate*, translated from Turkish, Shukur Mustafa and Muhammad Mela Karim, Mukryani publisher, Hawler, p. 284. This document is cited by Muhammad Amin Zaki (1939). *Ta'rikhi Silêmanî u wlati*, Kurdish text, The history of Silêmanî and its surrounding districts, Al-Najah Press, Baghdad, pp. 62, 67, 69, 70. idem; A Brief History of Kurds and Kurdistan, Baghdad, 1931. The text was preserved by Hussain Nazim Beg, the clerk of the last Baban pasha Ahmad Pasha of Baban. The manuscript is in the possession of the Iraqi Kurdish scholar Muhammad Mela Karim and it is originally in Turkish. It was first translated into Arabic and published by Shukr Mustafa and Muhammad Mela Karim in 2001. The Kurdish historian Muhammad Amin Zeki has made a good use of this source in his historical writings. {Ref: Shukr Mustafa and Muhammad Mulla Abd-al-Karim: Ta'rikh al-Amarat al-Babaniyah, Arbil, 2001}. See appendix G.

He talked about his successor, stressing on several occasions the importance of not appointing anyone of those gathered as governor of Baban: "…I would not appoint any one to become the governor of Silêmanî [the capital of the emirate] … if I put one of you in this position, it would be unfair, and I have always tried to be just…" He was particularly concerned about his reputation, even after his death, and that the most appropriate person would be selected to succeed him, stating:

"if I appoint any of you, I will be responsible for any bad things done by that person …. I have made my own mistakes and do not wish to perpetuate them any more after my death. Therefore, my successor is in the hand of princes and notables; you should discuss the matter and find a well qualified person."[765]

Abdulrahman Pasha asserts that the decision as to who would govern Kurds should be arrived at by counsel amongst Kurds themselves, not through his personal will or interference from an outside force. By this and other political initiatives, Abdulrahman Pasha moved towards creating a fresher sense of Kurdishness. It could be suggested, in the light of this, that Kurdish consciousness was generated amongst a new generation of Kurdish politicians and intellectuals, who would later reject Turkish direct rule over Kurds.

He emphasized that whoever became the *Mir* of Baban should, like him, maintain concern to empathise with and preserve order amongst the people, and maintain their essential Kurdishness:

"He should be bound by religion, he must be committed to his "love of his people"[766] (country, or people's land) and love it, apart from those two, he must be generous. On the other hand, about other princes, they must desist from creating discord among themselves, but they should compete with each other to give a better service to unity and glory of the "qaum" singular (nation or people), keeping "aqwam" plural (the nations or peoples') interests first who ever are in power… I beg you all, you should be just and do your best to implement it over all subjects and be kind-hearted with them, and you should

---

[765] Nazim Beg, Husien (2001). Ibid, p. 248.

[766] It is interesting to consider how in translating Abdulrahman Pasha's original Kurdish words, recorded in a Turkish manuscript, into Arabic and then English may allow subtle changes to his intended meaning. For instance, the Arabic word "watan" may be translated both as "country", but also as "fatherland" or "people's land", which all have different nuances of meaning. The Arabic word "qaum" may be translated on the one hand as "nation", but also as "people".

respect scholars, devotees, elderly and princes. In short, you should know yourselves and do your best for your people."[767] See appendix H for full version.

Arguably, Abdulrahman Pasha was aware of the ideas of 'country', Kurdish people, self-government and collective consciousness. He called for togetherness among princes and Kurdish people as well. Through such unity, he emphasized that Kurds would achieve their goals. He therefore insisted upon unity and asked Baban's princes and notables for justice and its implementation among people. This was therefore a vision of the whole people, not just the ruling families' repository of glory.

6.8 After Abdulrahman Pasha: Mahmud Pasha's Struggle for Alignment with Regional Powers

British observers kept a close eye on events in the area, knowing that a Kurdish Pasha could exercise a choice of allegiance in any struggle against a rival dynasty. Mahmud Pasha of Silêmanî formed an alliance with the Persians whilst he was still nominally under Ottoman rule.[768] However, he maintained some independence, due to his initiation of innovations in the reform of Baban's military a force which he managed to marshal liberty from the Ottoman control.

It is clear that despite his independent action, he was constrained by the mores of the society that he governed; as Campbell observed:

"The oppression of Mahmud in his own country and the disgust conceived by the Kurds against the innovation of their chief, particularly in consequence of his attempt to introduce European discipline and form a standing army together with the intrigues of his brother Silêman Bey induced the people to revolt."[769]

This discontent led to Mahmud's removal from power, enabling Silêman to seek control. Yet this was far from being the end of matters, as once again when he sought help, as before, his request for assistance was sent to the Persians, not the Ottomans. The request was acknowledged, albeit at a price.

---

[767] Ibid, p. 284-5.
[768] IOR, L/PS/10/266 Summarised in Foreign Office; *Turco-Persian Frontier; Zahab 1639- Erzeroum 1847.* pp.55-6
[769] IOR L/PS/9/91From Campbell the Assistant in charge of the British Mission in Persia to Chief Sec. 30th September, 1830 , p. 349.

"Both [brothers] appealed to Abbas Mirza who finding the popular feeling so strongly pronounced in favour of Silêman, agreed to confirm him in the government provided he would engage to pay within a specified time the sum of ten thousand tomans … This sum Silêman engaged to pay before the stipulated period."[770] Monteith later asserted that instead of this money being paid as taxation it was given for rights of pasturage:

6.9 Silêman's Ascendancy to Authority

In consequence, Silêman managed to wrestle power from Mahmud Pasha, but his ascendancy did not stop hostilities completely. Persia allowed Mahmud to take up refuge and reside "…on the frontier adjoining the former Government."[771]; even under Persian captivity, he was "free to carry out intrigues within Soolimaneaeh" [*sic*]. Early in the following spring; he organised an incursion into Silêmanî, as he could still associate with the neighbouring chiefs. He gathered "…an Army composed chiefly of Bilbas Kurds …"[772] The foray was defeated, with considerable loss of life; and he fled back to the safety of Persia.

Meanwhile Silêman was having some troubles of his own. He had failed to fulfil some obligations to the Ottoman Turks, possibly because Mahmud's intrigues had stalled him:

> "…the time had now arrived when [he] ought to have discharged the arrears of his tribute and though he gave assurances that he was collecting the money and would have had it collected by the prescribed time had he not been disturbed by the attempt of Mahmud…"[773]

This proved extremely serious for him; as many of his backers withdrew their support, in favour of the deposed Mahmud: "…still the friends of the latter at His Royal Highness's Court induced the Prince to declare that Silêman having failed in his engagement had forfeited his authority and that Mahmud was to be reinstated."[774] Yet, Silêman remained as stubborn as ever. This occasioned a battalion of infantry and cavalry to be sent against him; forcing him to retire to Kirkuk (in the Turkish territories).

---

[770] Ibid, pp. 349-50.
[771] Ibid, p. 350
[772] Ibid.
[773] Ibid.
[774] Ibid, pp. 350-1.

The issue of Mahmud resurfaced, when the Persians came to his aid. They used the disorder as a pretext to enter Silêmanî. Yet the Kurds were not keen on any imposition of a ruler, like Mahmud Pasha, preferring one from within their own ranks.

"Mahmud Pasha who accompanied the Army is still, it is said, so unpopular that it will be impossible to reinstate him in authority and it is thought probable that his Royal Highness will find it indispensable to the tranquillity of the tribe to give it a chief from his own family."[775]

6.10 The Appointment of Abdulrahman Pasha's Successor

Finally in 1813, a decision was made about who to appoint as Abdulrahman Pasha's successor. Mahmud Beg[776] was installed by a council of Kurdish princes, religious men and tribal chiefs as the new ruler of Baban. However, he still needed to have this appointment ratified by the Pasha of Baghdad, which duly followed.[777] However, all was not well in the Baban camp. After a while, three uncles of the Pasha from his father's side, namely Abdullah Beg, Ahmad Beg, and Omer Beg, sent their followers to Kirkuk, and left their nephew behind to go themselves to Baghdad.[778] This indicated there was conflict and chaos amongst the ruling family of Baban, and within time this brought more disorder and unrest to the emirate. Ensuing weakness now provided the Persians and Ottomans with an opportunity to interfere in Baban affairs.[779]

6.11 The Effect of the Appointment of Said Bey as Pasha of Baghdad: son of Sulaiman Pasha "The Great"

On 16th March 1813, Sa'id Bey (the son of Sulaiman Pasha the Great) entered Baghdad: he was twenty one years old and had no public experience. Considering him unsuitable for leadership, the Sultan issued a *Farman* (decree) and appointed Dawood Effendi (later

---

[775] Ibid, pp. 351-2.
[776] The son of Abdulrahman Pasha, the late Pasha of Baban.
[777] Kirkukli, Shaikh Rasul (1413). Dawhat al-Wizaraa fi Taarikh Waqaea Baghdad al-Zawraa, Arabic text, The Umbrella of Ministers in the Event of Baghdad, translated from Turkish by Musa Kazim Nuras, al-Sharif al-Razi publisher, Qum, p.262. Zaki, Muhammad, Amin (1939), Op. cit, p. 131.
[778] Ibid, p. 263.
[779] Zaki, Muhammad, Amin (1939), Op. cit, pp. 131-2.

Dawood Pasha) as acting Pasha of the city. As the Sultan sensed possible disorder, the *Farman* without delay was sent to Baghdad, arriving in Baghdad on June 30th.[780]

The Effendi was described as mild and his personality contributed to widespread disruption throughout the Baghdad Pashalic. Thus, he was rapidly deposed as his posting had the opposite effect to the Sultan's intentions. In order to regain control, in November 1816 Sa'id Pasha was promptly replaced by Dawood Effendi. To effectively govern on behalf of the Sultan, the new Pasha of Baghdad was given complete authority.[781]

It was difficult for a small emirate such as Baban (Silêmanî) to remain semi-independent with two strong, powerful neighbours. Yet the Baban Pasha strove hard to preserve the integrity of his emirate, whilst keeping a distance from the neighbouring Ottomans and Persians.[782] However, due to the geographical position of Kurdistan, the Kurds were never allowed to act wholly as they wished.

6.12 The Effect of Baban's Geographical Position on its Political Status

Although the Baban Emirate was relatively peaceful, other regional powers did not wish it to continue in such conditions. In 1820, Mahmud Pasha [the ruler of the Baban emirate] explained the situation to Claudius Rich who recalled, "…the Turks, insisted that he should neither serve nor pay Persia; and yet Turkey was neither able nor willing to defend him."[783]

Rich judged that Mahmud Pasha was "…inclined to the Turks from religious prejudices…" as he was Sunni, not Shiite. In Rich's words, Mahmud Pasha said,

> "…[the Ottomans don't] deserve it…[as] their political conduct is blind, arrogant, and treacherous. [Thus] with a little prudence and conciliation, [it would be possible with] skilful application to [appeal to the] *Sunite* feeling of the bigoted Koords; [particularly as they] detest the Persian sect…"[784]

---

[780] Gazetteer of the Persian Gulf, Oman and Central Arabia (1986). Volume I, (Historical), Part I, Chapters VI-IX, Archive Editions, Buckinghamshire, p. 1312.

[781] Precis Containing Information in Regard to the First Connection of the Hon'ble East India Company with Turkish Arabia, (1874). printed at the Foreign Department Press, Calcutta, p. 108.

[782] For a summary of events in Baban during these years, based largely on Rich; see McDowall, David, (2000). A Modern History of the Kurds, I. B. Tauris Publishers, London, pp 34–6.

[783] Rich, Claudius James (1836). Op. cit, Vol. I, p. 71.

[784] Ibid, p.72.

Matters were complicated as each power in the region jockeyed for position, and Rich felt unable to unpick the ebb and flow of the manoeuvres:

"...There is at present a game going on, the intricacies of which it would be difficult thoroughly to unravel; but it is evident that it is a kind of *ruse contre ruse* affair. The Pasha of Baghdad is endeavouring to cheat the Pasha of Koordistan [*sic*] and the Shahzadeh of Kermanshah—while the Shahzadeh is cheating both the Pasha of Baghdad and the Pasha of Koordistan;[*sic*] ..."[785]

6.13 Kurdish Relations with the Dominant Empires

Throughout the history of two dominant regional empires, the Kurdish principalities' problem was a source of complexity and difficulty, which they seemed incapable of resolving. General William Monteith in Persia on the frontier, later emphasized how the Treaty of Gulistan in 1813[786] had failed to prevent instability on the border; since it failed to define the "...respective limits of the Persian Kurdish State of Sine [Erdelan] and Shaherazur, of Karachulan [*sic*]" . This meant the Kurds still made "...constant eruptions on Persian villages..."; moreover, many of those districts which fell within Persian limits had refused to submit to rule by them.

Monteith observed how the chiefs of Erdelan and Baban still "...enjoy sovereign power within their own limits..." Although there were limits to their freedom, as the powers expected them to supply "troops in case of war when they likewise furnish some money and provisions..." The Ottomans and Persians maintained a levy over them for if they failed to provide this assistance, they would hit them with taxation, as these provisions should be considered "...more as a free gift than a tax..."[787]

One sees here how the peace of Kurdistan remained subject to disturbance by their powerful neighbours. Yet the Kurds themselves did not remain idle spectators whilst two larger

---

[785] Ibid.

[786] The Treaty of Gulistan which assured Russia possession of Georgia and other districts who had previously owed suzerainty to the shah, which was brokered by the United Kingdom. Gazetteer of the Persian Gulf, Oman and Central Arabia, (1986). Volume. I, (Historical), Part II, p. 1876.

[787] IOR L/PS/10/266 Turco-Persian Frontier, Zahab 1639-Erzerroum 1847, Appendix D, p. 50.

empires struggled over their territory. At times they were capable of taking the initiative themselves, and throwing off external domination.

"The inhabitants of these districts refused to acknowledge the authority of his Highness Dawood Pasha on a late occasion, when a force under Mahmud Bey a fugitive Kurdish Prince was sent to enforce their obedience, subsequent to the abandonment of Silêmanî by Silêman Pasha, at the price of the invasion of this Assyrian Pashalic by the Persian troops in support of the cause of his brother Mahmud."[788]

6.14 Ahmad Pasha of Baban (1838–1844)

Ahmad Pasha was a statesman who wanted to develop the Kurdish identity through making Baban a strong local authority. He created an army independent of the Ottoman Empire. According to Felix Jones,

"he foresaw the advantages of a regular force, and in a few months after his investiture succeeded in overcoming the scruples' of his clansmen and subjects so far as to persuade them to lay by the dress of their ancestors, and equip themselves in the garb of the regular troops of the State. In a year he had raised and disciplined, according to European tactics, a respectable force."[789]

In 1838, Captain R. Mignan (of the Bombay Army) after visiting Silêmanî, the centre of Kurdistan, wrote that "the government of Silêmanî is administrated by a pasha, who was by birth a Kurd, subject to neither Turk nor Persian."[790] To maintain his independent authority he depended on establishing a competent military force.

To achieve this, Felix Jones recorded that, within a year of his accession the Baban ruler – Ahmad Pasha, had "...raised and disciplined, according to European tactics, a respectable force..."[791] Muhammad Amin Zaki later described Ahmad Pasha as very brave, tough and intellectual, with a commitment to strengthening his army on the new system.[792]

---

[788] Ibid.

[789] Felix, Commander Jones (1848). *Narrative of a Journey through Parts of Persia and Kurdistan*, London, pp. 81-2. British Library, London.

[790] Mignan, Captain R. (1839). Op. cit, Vol. I, p. 285.

[791] Felix, Commander Jones (1848). Op. cit, pp. 81-2. ORW. 1986.

[792] Zaki, Muhammad Amin (1939). Op. cit, p.158.

6.15 Skirmishes at the frontier that affected the Baban Emirate

By 1844, the Kirmanshah frontier looked, to the British Agent, Major Rawlinson, dangerous and unstable. Tensions there had led some members of the Kurdish tribe of Sinjabi in Kirmanshah, to murder a high-powered chief. It was thought that the culprits responsible for the crime would attempt to "…cross the frontier and seek refuge in the mountains of Silemenieh…" [sic]. In any event, orders were issued by Nejib Pasha of Baghdad to all the frontier authorities, including Ahmad Pasha of Silêmanî. The orders aimed to prevent confrontation between the two neighbouring powers, by refusing asylum to criminals, in any of the Ottoman territories.[793]

It was believed by Rawlinson, this edict might be difficult to enforce.[794]

"…is impossible in many parts to define the line of the frontier; [and], the Kurdish Elyaut [tribes] have been accustomed … …to pasture their flocks in winter in the Persian plains and …at present [are] encamped in considerable numbers far in advance of the line, which by … liberal interpretation of her rights can be assigned to Persia as a boundary; and [...] the subservience of Suliemanieh to Baghdad is by no means of that definite."[795]

In order to monitor the situation, Rawlinson sent one of his officers, Lieutenant Colonel Farrant,[796] to the border. After he had spent some time on the Ottoman-Persia frontier, he sent a despatch to Rawlinson in Baghdad stating that:

"It appears that the refugee tribe of Sinjabi had consented after much discussion to retire within the Persian boundary and they moved from the Turkish territory …[when they clashed with the]…townspeople of Khanakin & several lives were lost upon either side before the combatants could be parted."[797]

---

[793] IOR L/PS/9/14 Rawlinson H., the British Political Agent in Turkish Arabia to Secret Department, Baghdad, No. 1 of 1844, January 25th 1844.

[794] IOR L/PS/9/14 Rawlinson H., the British Political Agent in Turkish Arabia to Secret Department, Baghdad, No. 1 of 1844, January 25th 1844, p. 2.

[795] Ibid, Pp. 2-3 [4v-5]

[796] For a brief biographical note on Farrant see; http://indiafamily.bl.uk/UI/FullDisplay.aspx?RecordId=014-000113365

[797] IOR L/PS/9/14, Rawlinson, H. to Secret Department, Baghdad, March 26th 1844, Op. cit, op. 11-11v.

Still a major issue that lay unresolved was an "…anxiety to establish a right of interference…" in the region of Persia:

"…Ahmad Pasha being known at present to be somewhat disaffected towards Nejib Pasha of Baghdad, or whether the Erdelan's Chief has really, as he pretends, fled his protection from the displeasure of his own Government, I am not yet accurately informed…"[798]

6.16 Conflict over the Frontiers

Rawlinson observed a lack of trust in the Kurdish leadership by Baghdad:

"The other evil also, if not removed, is deprived in some degree of its dangerous consequences; for as I found that it as impossible to re-establish confidence between Nejib Pasha of Baghdad and his subordinate at Sulimaneah…"[799]

At the time, Baban posed a very serious problem for the Ottomans especially for Baghdad. Yet the biggest threat for the Baban emirate did not come from the Ottomans, but from Russia who had sent troops against the Kurdish district of Silêmanî. In a despatch by Justin Shiel to Viscount Palmerston dated May 25th 1840, it is stated that:

"the Russian troops who were dispatched against the Kurdish district of Soolemaniah which name is also applied to the principal town [there], have forced the actual Chief, whose claim to exercise authority is however, I believe contested and not acknowledged by the Turkish government to pay the Azerbaijanian Govt. a sum of money, and have pillaged a number of the villages belonging to that Chiefship."[800]

The major problem of borders occurred because for part of the year the Silêmanî Kurds [also known as the Jaf Kurds] would move their cattle to pasture grounds on land situated in the Persian territories. For this privilege, the authorities stipulated a fixed rent. Yet the Silêmanî Kurds often failed to fulfil this obligation:

---

[798] Ibid, Rawlinson, H. to Secret Department, Baghdad, March 26th 1844, Ibid, pp. 11v-12.
[799] IOR L/PS/9/14 Rawlinson H. to Secret Department, British Residency, Baghdad, No. 8, October 26th 1844, p 25[39].. British Library, London.
[800] IOR L/PS/9/115 Shiel to Viscount Palmerston dated, Erzerum, May 25th 1840, p. 159. British Library, London.

"...This rent was always ill paid, often entirely withheld and forces were sometimes employed to compel the Kurds to fulfil their engagement. It is not unlikely that at this moment Persia may have just claims against Soolemaniah [*sic*] on this account."[801]

Some Kurds, however, viewed matters differently. This is made clear in a comment by Baillie Fraser; as early as 1840 he observed that Kurds perceived themselves as constituting a people:

"Koords themselves, are not ill pleased to see a power of their own nation arising in a quarter which will act as a counterpoise with the government of Azerbaijan, and induce it to treat them with more consideration, or give them a support to fall back upon, in case of continued and extreme severity from their Persian rulers."[802]

6.17 Najib Pasha of Baghdad (1842–1847)

The second problem, which occurred in 1842, was that Najib Pasha replaced Ali Rida Pasha of Baghdad.[803] This new Pasha, unlike his predecessor, was particularly keen to impose Ottoman sovereignty throughout the empire. At this time the Ottomans, following European lines, arranged their administration into various departments.[804]

Rawlinson recognised Silêmanî faced some difficulties over territorial claims of the two regional powers; stating: "Suleimanieh may perhaps at no distant period be subject to some disturbance, as I think an attempt will be made to break upon the almost independent government of the Kurdish Pasha."[805]

6.18 The Reinstatement of Mahmud as Pasha of Silêmanî

Persian interference over Kurdish affairs continued. In particular, their support for the reinstatement of Mahmud Pasha as ruler of Silêmanî (Baban) was noticeable. Matters were

---

[801] Ibid, pp. 159-60.
[802] Fraser, J, Baillie (1840). Op. cit, p.119
[803] IOR L/PS/9/13, Lt. Col. R. Taylor to Secret Department, No. 12, Baghdad, 24th May, 1842, p. 48
[804] Ibid, H. Rawlinson, P. A. Turkish Arabia, Baghdad, 26th, December, 1843, p. 246.
[805] IOR L/PS/20/FO49/1 "Extracts from Correspondence relative to Turco-Persian Boundary Negotiations", Part I: 1843–1844. p. 147

not helped by Persia garnering support from the Kurdish camp; the chief Wali of Sine had given them his backing.[806]

A letter sent from the brother of the Wali of Erdelan [the Wali of Sine] to the governor of Bane ordered that in all districts: "Governors and the people of the country shall assemble its own Cavalry and meet in the Camp (of the Wali) with the triumphant train in the plain of Marboozan".[807] Justin Shiel believed this announced: "…their determination to re-establish Mahmood Pacha [*sic*], who had been displaced by the Turkish Government in the Pachalic of Sulemaniah [*sic*]."[808]

In 1842, the Sultan of Persia, in support of Mahmud Pasha, marched a large force to the frontier of Sharezur in Baban country. Other forces advanced from different directions: a). The Ouroman [Hewraman] tribe was sent to take possession of Kirkuk and Helebje; b). On the other side, the districts of Kizilja were occupied by Reza Quli Khan himself; c). Being preoccupied Reza Quli Khan sent his representatives to seize Alan and Siweil.

One can see from the observations of these British representatives that there was a long and consistent struggle by Kurdish administrators to operate independently of their nominal overlords. It is true this was often achieved by playing one off against another in a struggle for power. However, throughout these tribulations the brief existence of a Kurdish capital in the early years of the 19th century facilitated an environment for Kurdish scholars to begin the expression of their own identity. This is especially important to bear in mind as we turn to the activities of the major literary figures of the time.

The above section has touched upon some military and political aspects of Kurdish pashas of Baban which aimed at strengthening their authority and local self-rule. These political steps were important to develop the political and thus administrative aspects of Kurdism which in their turn provided a convenient political and social environment for the growing of Kurdish literature and culture as will be shown in the following section.

---

[806] IOR L/PS/9/13 Extract of a Letter by R. Taylor, P. A. Turkish Arabia to HM Ambassador at the Porte, dated Baghdad, 1st June, 1842, p. 58.
[807] IOR L/PS/9/122 Translation of a Letter from the Brother of the Wali of Erdelan to the Governor of Bane, written Thursday 25 Safer 1258- April 6th 1842, pp. 525-7.
[808] Ibid, p.518

6.19 Kurdism in Literature and Language under the Baban Emirates

After Silêmanî became the capital city of the Baban Emirate in 1784, alongside Turks and Persians, Kurdish scholars started to use the Kurdish language for written works. Kurdish dialects were also used in mosques all over the emirate.[809] This benefitted the Kurdish people; so that over time, Kurdish became the language of preference over Turkish and Persian. Such 'linguistic proto-nationalism'[810] undoubtedly helped to promote the sense of national distinctiveness among the elite Kurdish strata. As Hassanpour puts it, "Kurdish poets did not view literary creation as an end, or simply as an aesthetic endeavour. For them literate traditions, together with statehood, were the hallmarks of a civilised and sovereign people."[811] Indeed, according to other commentators, "It is normally the creative intellectuals, especially the poets, who take the first step of using the mother tongue in their work, thus endowing it with the power of becoming a collective identity symbol."[812]

A cultural and educational renaissance occurred in Baban, after Silêmanî had become its capital, in 1784. For the first time, new movements sprang up amongst Kurdish scholars and poets within the region. From them a set of ideas emerged which contained nationalist tendencies, thus paving the way for a Kurdish literature to develop. These were later being reflected in numerous literary contexts. It was observed by Soane that a multitude of poets were resident in Silêmanî, during the eighteenth and nineteenth centuries, "who have contributed in verse, to the literature of Kurdistan generally in Kurdish."[813]

Abdulrahman Pasha had spent some time in the Erdelan Emirate. When he became Pasha in 1789, he decided to make his own court in Silêmanî. He called upon writers and poets to use the Silêmanî dialect as his court's cultural language. The first, who wrote a Kurdish poem during Baban era, is reputed to be Ali Berdeşanî.[814] Berdeşanî's poems were political and he devoted his work for the Kurdish interests, as will be shown below.

---

[809] Rasul, Dr Izzaddin, Mustafa (1971). *Sernjê le zmani edebi yekgrtui Kurdi*, Kurdish text, Salman al-A'zami Press, Baghdad, p. 30.

[810] Smith, Antony D. (1993). *Nationalism and Cultural Identity*, Nevada ed, p. 90.

[811] Hassanpour, Amir (1996). The Creation of Kurdish Media Culture, in Kreyenbroek, Philip and Allison, Christine, edited by *Kurdish Culture and Identity*, Zed Books Ltd, London, p.49.

[812] Blau & Suleiman (1996). *Language and Ethnic Identity in Kurdistan: An Historical Overview*, in Suleiman (Ed) Language and Identity in the Middle East and North Africa, Curzon, London, p.154. They follow Smith, 1991, in their ascription of initiative to the 'creative' middle classes. Whilst one is tempted to suggest parallels with the 'Ossian' compilation of Thomson, perhaps a better analogy is with the 18thc Gaelic verse of Alexander MacDonald. See also, in passing, the brief comments by PG Kreyenbroek *on the Kurdish Language* in Kreyenbroek and Sperl (1992). (Eds) *The Kurds*, London, pp. 71-2 The poem is not referred to by Hassanpour, Amir, (1992). Op. cit, pp.82-3.

[813] Soane, Ely Bannister (1979). Op. cit, p. 389.

[814] Rasul, Dr Izzaddin Mustafa (1980). *Jiyan u barhami sha'rani Kurd*, Kurdish text, Life and works of Kurdish poets, Baghdad, pp. 40-77. Blau, Joyce (1996). Kurdish Written Literature, in Kreyenbroek, Philip and Allison, p. 22.

6.20 *Beyti Abdulrahman Pashai Baban*-The ballad of Abdullah Pasha of Baban

Ali Berdeşanî was one of the well-known Kurdish public poets praised by Hajî Qadri Koyî.[815] It's not known exactly when Berdeşanî lived; one writer asserts that he died around 1838-9.[816] He is credited with being a *beytbêj* [817] and a poet in the Baban court during the governorship of Abulrahman Pasha, Silêman Pasha, and Ahmad Pasha. This would place him there sometime between 1790 and 1840. The modern editor of the *beyt* Dr Izzaddin Mustafa Rasul, who is a well known scholar, believes the author to have been alive in 1838 or 1839.[818]

Berdeşanî is widely believed to have recorded the heroic poem in his own words, drawing upon common folkloric poems of the time. Berdeşanî recorded a *Beyti* (tale) about Abdulrahman Pasha of Baban (1789-1813) entitled *Beyti Abdulrahman Pashai Baban* (The ballad of Abdulrahman Pasha of Baban). There are a number of variants, as one would expect of an orally transmitted text. The first modern edition was published by Oskar Mann.[819] Another was edited by Muhammad Tofiq Wirdi,[820] and the most recent was collected by Abdulhamid Husseini who published it in 1981.[821] This heroic ballad reflects a reasonably contemporary view of the events taking place during the rule of Abdulrahman Pasha. It is tentatively suggested that this may offer insight into opinions of a poet who was a witness of what he described.[822] He begins in a conventional way by thanking God, setting out the subject of his praise:

Azm Alî Berdeşanî

---

[815] Hajî Qadri Koyî (1969). *Diwani Hajî Qadri Koyî,,: Complete Work of Hajî Qadri Koyî*, Giwi Mukryani, collected and edited by, third edition, Hawlêr Press, p. 111.

[816] Rasul, Dr Izzadin Mustafa (1980). Op. cit, p. 52.

[817] *Beytbêj* is some one who sings an epic or ballad whether it is in poetry or prose. Some professional beytbêj was very important in Kurdish society and had a respected position amongst the Kurdish emirates courts and with many Kurdish notables. Important part of Kurdish folk literature was preserved through the memory of *beytbêjs*. For example Oscar Mann's collection was recorded from a few numbers of *beytbêjs*.

[818] Rasul, Dr Izzadin Mustafa (1980). Op.cit.

[819] Mann, Oskar (1975). *Tuhfayi Mudhaffariyyah*, introduced, collated and set into Kurdish letters by Hemn Mukryani, Kurdish Academy Press, Baghdad. This version is 96 verses, pp. 342-348. I mostly use as my base text the 1981 version of Abdulhamid because it is a more 'complete' text than the others with 324 verses.

[820] Wrdi, Muhammad Tofiq (1962). Folklori Kurdi, Kurdish text, Kurdish Folklore, Part. II, Dar al-Tazamun Press, Baghdad, p. 3.

[821] Husseini, Abdulhamid (1981). *Beyti Abdulrahman Pashai Baban la zman Ali Berdeshaniyawa*, Kurdish text, Ballad of Abdulrahman of Baban in Ali Berdeşanî's words, Binkai Mela Awara Publisher in Europe. This version is the most completed one and contained 312 verses. Pp. 9-27.

[822] The use of ballad literature, in general, as a historical source is somewhat problematic. See for a good example of its judicious use Palmer, R. (1988,). *The Sound of History, Oxford,* also his *Touch on The Times*, London, 1974.. For a contemporary Kurdish perspective C. Allison Old and New Oral Traditions in Badinan in Kyeyenbroek and Allison (Eds) *Kurdish Culture and Identity*, 1996, pp. 28-47. Allison, Christine (2001). *The Yezidi Oral Tradition in Iraqi Kurdistan*, Curzon, Surrey.

Lengim nekeî le zubanî

Beytî dekem le diwanî

Medhî paşaî Kurdistanî[823]

I am Ali Berdeşanî

Oh God give me a fluent tongue

I am saying a ballad in the court of Baban

Praising the Pasha of Kurdistan

He emphasised that amongst Turkish and Shiite kings, he would opt for a Kurdish ruler.[824] Berdeşanî praises the fact that the Pasha of Kurdistan would not accept subjugation to a higher overlord and refuses to be a servant. He encourages his Pasha to use the power he has in order to achieve his aims.[825]

Berdeşanî was not just talking about the ambition and efforts of the Pasha to resist the interference of the Wali of Baghdad in the internal affairs of his emirate. He criticized the fact that he did not go and conquer Baghdad.

'Ew Abdulrahman paşaî Kurd

Be xow be leşkrî xurd

Paşa bu sehuikrd

heta Bexdayeî nebrd[826]

He was Abdulrahman the Pasha of the Kurds

Himself and his brave force

Made one mistake:

He did not take Baghdad.

He told his Pasha that he should ignore the Persian Shah and pay no attention to Ottoman Sultans. Instead he must do his best for his own country. He says:

---

[823] Husseini, Abdulhamid (1981). Op. cit, p. 10.

[824] Ibid.

[825] Ibid.

[826] Rasul, Dr Izzaddin Mustafa (1980). *Shi'ri Kurdi*, Kurdish text, Kurdish Poetry, Life and Works of Faqei Tairan, Ali Bardaşani and Bakhtiar Zewar, First Volume, al-Hawadith Press, Baghdad, p. 56.

Xom deçme pêş, leber loman
Xişle u şarî herwek çoman
dyare 'ecem naka boman
dest u bask u rimbî xoman [827]

I am taking the lead
It is our city and our jeweller
Persians will not do any good for us
We should trust ourselves through our arrows and muscles

The resistance of Baban to outside interference under Abdulrahman Pasha became a symbol for the Kurdish struggle for their identity and freedom. Here, Berdeşanî praised Kurdish struggle against their enemy and trusted that they were so strong that they would not be defeated.

Kêwî Gudrun nabin newî
Şêr leber 'askan narewî [828]

The summit of Magrun [mountain][829] would not bend
Lions never run away from deer

Berdeşanî expresses his fury against the powers that imposed their rule over the Kurds. He tells us that they were not acting as just rulers, because they were enemies. They destroyed every thing and killed poor people:

Serî danabun be xişt
Feqirî hemban le pişt
Çend kesî iftadeî kuşt

… … … …..

çend kesî kuştin jutêr [830]

---

[827] Ibid, p. 57.
[828] Ibid, p. 58.
[829] The Magrun mountain was about 20 miles north west of Silêmanî.
[830] Rasul, Dr Izzaddin Mustafa (1980). Op. cit, p. 60.

They [foreign armies] made bricks out of Kurdish heads

Those travellers, carriers,

many elderly and

peasants were killed by enemies.

Beyti Abdulrahman Pasha describes the story of the wars between the Baban emirate and the Ottoman Turks, and in particular the bravery of his Pasha. This might suggest Berdeşanî's loyalty towards Abdulrahman Pasha. At the same time, as a court poet, with a vested interest in pleasing the Pasha, public words might differ from privately held sentiments. Berdeşanî asserts that the Kurdish pasha was a brave man who could engage the world[831] ; he regretted that the pasha had not had an opportunity to achieve his aspiration.[832]

6.21 Mawlana Khalidi Naqishbandî Kurdî

Another scholar who emerged in Silêmanî was Mawlana Khalid Naqishbandî (1776-1826).[833] He established the Naqishbandî order which spread rapidly in Ottoman and Persian Kurdistan and in other parts of the Ottoman Empire such as Baghdad, Damascus, Anatolia and Istanbul and in Egypt as well.[834] In other words, Mawlana Khalid contributed highly to Naqishbandî development and the spread of its teachings in Kurdistan and beyond.

Mawlana Khalid was a unique *sufi* scholar among hundreds of students who were taught, educated and instructed in Delhi by Shah Abdullah Dihlavi, known as Shah Ghulam Ali, (d. 1240/1824). The exceptional position of Mawlana was confirmed by his master. Therefore, after a year staying with Shah Abdullah, Mawlana was told by his teacher to go back to Kurdistan. It was at this point that Mawlana asked his master to have *din wa dunya* {religion and world}which means apart from the judgment day he wanted to contribute and to do something for the world, the life of his countrymen and further. It was said that Shah Abdullah was so supportive towards him he prayed for him and gave the news that would be successful in his mission.[835]

---

[831] Mann, Oskar (1975). Op.cit, p. 343. Husseni, Abdulhamid (1981). Op. cit, p. 10.

[832] Mann, Oskar, (1975). Ibid, p. 344.

[833] Mudarris, Mela Abdulkarim (1979). *Yadi Mardan*, Kurdish text, Remembering the Great Men, Volume I, The Kurdish Academy, Baghdad, pp. 8,53.

[834] Al-Azzawi, Abbas al-Muhami (1973). *Mawlana Khalid al- Naqishbandî*, Arabic text, *The Journal of the Kurdish Academy*, Vol. I, Part I, Baghdad, p. 699.

[835] Mudarris, Mela Abdulkarim (1979). Op. cit, pp. 31- 32.

Mawlana Khalid returned to Kurdistan in 1811. On his way to and from India, Mawlana Khalid was confronted several times by Iranian Shi'a scholars and had heated discussions with them concerning different religious questions. He succeeded in all such confrontations.[836]

When Mahmud Pasha succeeded his father, Abdulrahman Pasha (d. 1813), he visited Baghdad and asked Mawlana to return to Kurdistan to give his assistance to improve Kurdish affairs. On the one hand, Mawlana made an important impact on the religious and political life in Kurdistan by spreading Naqishbandî widely all over Kurdistan. He was involved in political activities to bring unity among Baban dynasty members and encouraged them to back each other and not to be involved in negative ventures against each other.[837] This is an indication of his power and influence, and that this disunity was a real problem to him, one he probably thought weakened the emirate. On the other hand, Mawlana's *khalifas* (deputies) established strong centres and participated in spreading *tariqa*. In 1820, when James Rich visited Silêmanî he found that many Baban dynasty members admired him and said that Osman Bey told him that "almost all the principal Koords (*sic*) are his *murids* or disciples."[838]

There were many reasons for the rapid spread of the Naqishbandî order. It established a hierarchical system. Members were required to follow the rules of those in a higher position. A new *murid* [follower of the Naqishbandî sheikh] was linked to an older *murid* who, in turn, had links with *ser khatme* [the head of circle]. They were subordinate to a *khalifa* [a representative of the sheikh] who was also subject to a *pir* or *murshid* [the guide]. This was Mawlana Khalid himself.[839]

Families such as Nehri, Palu and Barzan who took the Naqishbandî *tariqa* [order] from Mawlana Khalid became main streams for Kurdish nationalism.[840] Thereafter, Kurdish identity was associated with the Naqishbandî *tariqa* and later also with Qaderiya (Barzinjis).

Mawlana's fame as a scholar and a Kurdish sheikh attracted many Kurds from Silêmanî, especially traders and skilled people, to become his followers. Later, some Kurdish groups

---

[836] Ibid, p. 27.
[837] Rich, Claudius James (1836). Volume. I, p. 148.
[838] Ibid, p. 141. For more information on *Naqishbandî* teriqe see: Bruinessen, Martin van (1992). Op. cit, pp. 222-228.
[839] Bruinessen, Martin van (1992). p. 224.
[840] Ibid.

and tribes such as Barzan, and Nehri entered the Naqishbandî order. Mawlana became well-known in Persian Kurdistan; Kurds as far afield as Hewraman, Meriwan, Sine and Mukryan, visited him in Iran and became his *murids*.

Famous Kurdish scholars from across Kurdistan joined his order,[841] including Mawlana's teacher, Sheikh Muhammad Qasim,[842] Well-known scholars from other regions of Kurdistan such as Shamdinan, Mardin, Urfe, Diyarbakir, Amedi and Bamerni entered his order. This order became a key element unifying Kurds from both sides of the frontier.[843]

As Mawlana Khalid's popularity increased, the Ottoman authorities grew cautious, especially when he sent some of his high ranking *murids* as representatives to Istanbul. As famous scholars became his followers, the Ottoman government decided to deport Mawlana's caliphs back to Silêmanî with instructions that they should not return to Istanbul.[844]

Socio-political factors also played their role in the rapid spread of the Naqishbandî order. Later, Mawlana Khalid became a model for political and social life in both parts of Ottoman and Persian Kurdistan. He was against all kind of oppressions. As a religious man, he wanted a just and fair government and he supported poor people. The traders, skilled people and labourers who worked in the buildings, caravans and caravansary of the new capital found their place among Naqishbandîs.[845]

Apart from being an Islamic scholar, he was a Kurdish thinker who called for unity among members of the Baban dynasty. Mawlana's respect and fame was so strong that his influence extended to the Baban ruling family as well. He tried to mend differences among the Baban princes and reminded them of their responsibilities towards the Kurdish people.[846] Mawlana Khalid tried to unite the Baban princes by asking them not to act against each other, as Persians and Ottomans were always attempting to gain influence over the princes for their own interests. In 1820, in the presence of Mawlana Khalid, Abdullah Pasha, uncle of

---

[841] These are some of them: Sayyd As'ad Haydari, Sayyd Sibkhatullahi Haydari, Sayyd Ubidullai Haydari, Mela Abdulrahmani Rojbayani, Mela Abdullai Jali and Sheikh Othmani Tawelayi, Sheikh Yahya Muzuri from Badinan who were the most famous Kurdish Melas at that time became Mawlanas murid. Ibid, p. 39-40.
[842] Muddaris, Mela Karim (1979). Op. cit, p. 33.
[843] His importance as a figure of unity is emphasized by Rich; *Narrative* pp 140-1; 148
[844] Al-Azzawi, Abbas al-Muhami (1973). Op. cit, p. 721.
[845] Hakim, Halkawt (January 1984). "Ab'ad zuhur al-Tariqa al- Naqishbandîya fi Kurdistan fi Awael al-Qarn al-Tasi' Ashar, Arabic text, The Ramification on the Apparition of the Naqishbandî Order in Kurdistan in the beginning of Nineteenth Century, *Studia Kurdica*, No. I, p. 59.
[846] Rich, Claudius James (1836). Op. cit, Vol. I, 1836, p. 148.

Mahmud Pasha, and his two brothers, Osman and Silêman, swore loyalty to Mahmud Pasha. The three took an oath on the sword and the Quran that "whatever letters might come either from them Persian or Turkey (Ottoman), they should open them at Sheikh Khalid's house and in presence of the whole party who then made the agreement."[847] He also advised Baban Pashas to remain just and do their best for the sake of their people.[848] Day by day, the reputation of Mawlana Khalid increased in Baban and beyond. Mahmud Pasha, the *Mir* of Baban, was jealous of him, and afraid of his growing power. Mawlana Khalid was aware of this and preferred to leave Silêmanî rather than to challenge the Pasha, for the sake of the Kurdish people's interests.[849]

Mawlana Khalid wrote eighteen books, including his poetic work in Kurdish, Farsi and Arabic.[850] This included a metaphorical poem that reflected feelings for his people and his internal anguish at missing his home town and family, which he wrote whilst in Delhi so that he could gain knowledge of the Naqishbandî order from Sheikh Abdullah:

Mewsimî idestu ma numid ez didarî yar
Alemê der 'eişu nuşu ma du çeşm eşkbar

... ...

... ...

bekrejoiy şud zahir çeşm rewan ez xunî dil
'aqibet krdem dwadix firaqî Serçinar
Xalida ger nistî diwaneî sehra newerd
Tu koja Kabul u Xezne u xakî Hind u Kendehar.[851]

Translation

It is Eid time and I am hopeless about seeing my beloved ones
People [here] are all happy, but my eyes are tearful...

....

....

---

[847] Ibid, p. 148.
[848] Muddaris, Mela Karim (1979). Op. cit, see Mawlana's letters to Baban pashas and princes, pp. 161-2, 165.
[849] Al-Khal, Muhammad (1961). Pp. 41-2.
[850] Muddaris, Mela Karim (1979). Op. cit, pp. 70-2.
[851] Muhammad, Mahmud Ahmad (1987). editor, *Ruhi Mawlana Khalid*, Kurdish text, Mawlana Khalid's Soul, al-Zaman Press, Baghdad, pp. 13-4.

My heart's blood is coming out from my eyes, like the stream of "Bekrejo" and Serchinar (rivers in Silêmanî – his home town), which both spring into two streams;

Tell me Khalid! If you are not passionate and crazy, where did you come from? What are you doing in Kabul, Ghaznin, and in the land of India and Kandahar?

In this poem, he expresses his feelings for his family and district, being one of the first Kurdish Scholars to do so. The poem is somewhat metaphorical; being in India, he feels as though he has left his soul with his land. He draws upon common imagery, making references to places in Silêmanî to which he feels tied.

In the title *Eqidey Kurdî-eqidey Mawlana* [Kurdish thought – Mawlana's thought] Mawlana expresses the Kurdish belief or Kurdish Creed.[852] It was a great step forward for Kurdish Muslim scholars to write in Kurdish. In particular, it was thought that Kurdish people should learn about everyday affairs, including religion in their own language. Mawlana's style of writing is very clear and could be easily understood by Soranî-speaking Kurds. Although Mawlana wrote his poetry nearly two centuries ago, the language can still be understood today by modern-day Soranî speakers.

Mawlana promoted justice and responsibility among the Baban dynasty. These two virtues are the most important elements for security and survival in government and the nation.[853] In an undated letter [854] to one of the Baban Mirs, he warned that the governor, responsible for the people, must rule according justly.[855] Mawlana Khalid was the first of the Kurdish scholars who selected "Kurdî" as his title; an act which can be viewed as indicative of his sense of belonging and Kurdish pride.

In conclusion, Mawlana Khalid's thought, which first emerged in Kurdistan, had the potential to develop and become a Kurdish interpretation of Islamic thought that could serve as an ideological basis for the formation of a wider and even national Kurdish identity. However, the political and social circumstances of the Kurds were not stabilised and developed enough to allow the systematic growth of such a Kurdish trend in Islamic thought when the Baban emirate weakened after the death of Abulrahman Pasha.

---

[852] Mela Karim, Muhammad (1981). *"Aqidai Kurdi Mawlana Khalidi Naqishbandî"*, Kurdish text, The Kurdish Creed of Mawlana Khalidi Naqishbandî, *The Journal of the Iraqi Academy- Kurdish Corporation*, Volume. 8, pp. 199-222.
[853] Mudarris, Mela Karim (1979). Op. cit, p. 161. Al-Khal, Sheikh Muhammad,(1961). Op. cit, p. 98.
[854] See appendix G.
[855] Mudarris, Mela Karim (1979). Op. cit, p. 161.

6.22 Nalî and other Baban poets

During the nineteenth century, the Kurds of the Baban Emirate produced a school of classical poetry, which, for a learned scholar, was equal to, if not more accomplished than, the poetry of their neighbours. This has inspired national pride for many generations of Kurds. Under Baban Emirate's administration, numerous poets, including Berdeşanî and Mawlana, began to flourish, at the court of Silêmanî and other districts.

Several distinguished Kurdish poets and scholars emerged; five of the most significant figures in Kurdish intellectual life during the century were in Baban alone. Apart from political, military and industrial revivals during the first part of the nineteenth-century, the question of language naturally emerged in the mind of the Kurdish poets. Kurdish language and literature began to take a great role in Kurdish society.

6.23 Nalî (1800–1873)

Mela Xidir Ehmed Şaweys (Nalî) was one of the greatest Kurdish poets in the classical Kurdish poetry. He may be considered to have played a major role in establishing Kurdish poetry in the Baban Emirate.[856] Major Soane, in his book *To Mesopotamia and Kurdistan in Disguise*, counted Nalî as the most famous poet of the country "the author of most of the various styles of poems that go to make up a complete 'Diwan' or, as it may be called 'set of Works.'"[857] For instance, a style of writing developed where the last word of each line of poem not only rhymed with previous lines, but began with a different letter of the Kurdish alphabet. It became an accepted convention to write poems around the themes of love, praise, battle, or about language and poetry itself.

Nalî lived at a crucial period of Kurdish history. Kurdistan was in a revolt against the Ottoman Turks. They were attempting to achieve greater self-rule; prompting them to define their cultural attributes within a framework of struggle against a foreign presence on Kurdish

---

[856] For more details see: Sejadi, Ela'din (1971). *Mêjuî Edebî Kurdî*, Kurdish text, The History of the Kurdish Literature, Second edition, Maearif Press. Nalî (1976). *Diwani Nalî*, Mudarris and Abdulkarim, Mela Abdulkarim and Fatih, Kurdish text, The Collection of Nali's Poetry, Kurdish Academy Press, Baghdad. Xeznedar, Dr. Marouf (2003). *Mêjuî Edebî Kurdî*, Kurdish text, The history of Kurdish literature, Vol. III, Aras Publisher, Erbil.

[857] Soane, Ely Bannister (1979). Op. cit, pp.389-90 On Nalî see also Edmonds, C. J. (1935). "A Kurdish Lampoonist", *Journal of the Royal Central Asian Society*, Vol. XXII, Part. I, January 1935, p. 113. It may be pointed out here that this a equates to an author's Complete Poetical Oeuvre, rather than a collection embracing their other writings. Or an 'anthology' of poetry in different styles.

soil and an aggressive foreign presence outside the borders.[858] Nalî well understood the Arabic, Turkish and Persian languages and cultures; particularly, as he travelled around both parts of Kurdistan, where he learnt about the Kurdish language and other affairs. However, his real achievement was that as well as being a scholar he was also a master of Kurdish language and a great poet. To this day *Diwan* (his Collected Work) is still read all over Kurdistan. Most important of all, was his role as initiator and originator of the Silêmanî dialect, laying down the foundation stone of the most beautiful classical poetry. His work is a corpus of verse that could stand alongside that of any other nation.

Nalî felt first and foremost that he was a poet of the Kurdish nation. He chose specifically to write in Kurdish, rather than choose from amongst the three languages, Arabic, Turkish and Persian, in which he was an expert. In so doing, Nalî helped to make the Soranî dialect the national language for Kurds, creating in the Kurdish mind a national discourse, which equated the Ottoman Turks with those things most disliked in the nation's consciousness. Turks were referred to as *gurig* [wolf or predator], thereby equating their rule with the draining of life from the Kurds. In his long poem which begins: '*Qurbanî tozî rêgatim 'eî badî xoş murûr*' [I sacrificed myself for your dust oh wind], Nalî asks if Kaniaskan was still a place for deers, or rather a place for the predatory Turks:

'*Êsteş mekani askye (Kaniaskan)
Yaxo buwe be mel'ebeyi gurig u lure lûr?*[859]

Is still (Kaniaskan) a place of deers?
Or has it become a place of wolves and their howls?

For Nalî and other Kurdish poets in the beginning of the nineteenth century, writing in Kurdish was an important basis for their Kurdism and indicated their love for their land and their people. Through their use of the Kurdish language, Kurdish poets expressed their loyalty to their nation and distinguished themselves from 'others'.

For instance, in a short undated poem, Nalî writes,

Teb'î şekkerbarî min 'eger Kurdî inşadeka

---

[858] For a brief comment on a similar process in central Europe see Breuilly, J. (1982). *The Sources of Nationalist Ideology*, Manchester, citing Frantisek Palacky, in J Hutchinson & AD Smith (1994). (eds) Nationalism, Oxford, p.107. Palacky's ideas were brought to English attention through the work of Thomas Masaryk.
[859] Nalî (1976). Op. cit, p. 187.

Imtihanî xoye meqsudî le 'emda wadeka[860]

My desire is running sweet, that is why I am writing in Kurdish

I would like to test myself that I can write my language

Nalî stresses that he meant to write in Kurdish, because he wanted to use Kurdish not other languages; he strove to test himself to create a new form of poetry in Kurdish.

Kes be elfazim neĺê xo Kurdiye xo krdiye

Her kesê nadan nebê xoî talibî me'nadeka [861]

Let no one chide me for writing in Kurdish

A sage looks for the profundity in Kurdish verse

In another verse of one of his *ghezels*, Nalî says of himself:

Muheqqeq meşrebî (Nalî) le şi'ra herweku (Xakî)

Xeyaĺî Kurdiye beytî serapa zulfî dutaye[862]

Nalî's poetic thoughts correspond to Kurdistan

His imagery is Kurdish; it can be read in several ways

It is clear from his verse that Nalî has great affection for Kurdish lands. His imagination is Kurdish; his verses, like the *beytî serapa zulfî dutaye* [plaits of his sweetheart][863] of which he writes, have two meanings. In the above verse we find a strong sense of Kurdism, Nalî telling us that his poetic style is Kurdish, his thinking is Kurdish, just as his motherland is Kurdish. Four significant elements of Kurdism can be isolated in Nalî's work: Kurdish language, Kurdish imagination, Kurdish people and Kurdish land.

He praises the elite Kurdish forces of the Baban Emirate:

---

[860] Ibid, p. 106.
[861] Ibid, p. 107.
[862] Ibid, p. 570.
[863] Ibid

Em taqime mumtaze kewa xaseyî şahin

Aşubî dilî memleket u qelbî supahin [864]

These shock troops are the Shah's particular men

Their characteristics are the heart of the army.

Nalî knew as a poet that language was one way to distinguish Kurds from others. He attains a high level of nationalist consciousness, by emphasizing that his poems have two meanings and therefore, may be interpreted in more than one way:

Muhaqaq maşrabî Nalî la şia'ra har wako xakî

Xayalî Kurdiya, baitî sarapa zulfî du taye [865]

For sure Nalî's way in poetry was as his land

His imagination is Kurdish; all his verses had two meanings

In this verse, Nalî directly connects his Kurdish thoughts, his imagination, and Kurdistan together.

Through the use of the Kurdish language, Nalî brought a new sensibility to the literature. This, in turn, left a positive residuum with all Kurdish people: he added many new political expressions to the Kurdish language. When he described his own people, he would use the most beautiful words; examples include *milleti Kurd* [Kurdish nation or people], *qelbi supa* [heart of army], *şari edil* [the town of justice], *dilî memleket* [the centre of the state], *şahi min* [my king]. [866] These appear to be Nalî's own expressions; apparently no equivalent expressions were used by previous Kurdish writers. In time, his new written 'dialect' naturally matured and replaced the Southern Kurdish Gorani used by the Erdelan court, in Sine and its surrounding districts.

Tab'î şekkerbarî min Kurdî eger inşadeka,

Imtihanî xoye meqsudî le 'emda wadeka. [867]

---

[864] Ibid. p. 370.
[865] Ibid, p. 570.
[866] Nalî (1976). Op. cit, p. 174-197.
[867] Ibid, p. 106.

When my kindest nature writes in Kurdish,

I look to myself, and, I write in Kurdish purposefully.

During the last fifty years of the Baban Emirate, its authority became Nalî's cherished ideal. He appears to express a deep respect and love for the ruling family in his literature written for them and for their princes, although it should be remembered that he would have had a vested interest in writing poems of praise, which might not necessarily reflect his own personal feelings. When Ahmad Pasha became an *emir* of Baban, Nalî expressed his loyalty towards him:

> *Ta felek dewreî neda, sed kewkebî 'awa nebû*
> *Kewkebî mihrî mubarek tel'etî peyda nebû.* [868]

> Until destiny took its round, hundreds of stars did not disappear,
> The star of the holy moon did not show its face.

He described the previous *emir* as the most just *emir* on earth, stating:

> *Qîsseî bêperde u kinayet xoşe: şahî min ke wa,*
> *'edilê bu qet 'edlî 'ew le dunyada nebû.* [869]

> It is nice to say without masks and metaphors that my Shah,
> Was so just, there was not any other justice on the earth.

The collapsing of the Baban Emirate became a turning point in Nalî's life and thoughts; he expanded the term of Kurdism to nationality by talking about Kurds as one people. Nalî analyzed the proper historical condition of the Kurds. He saw that when the Marib dam in Saba in Yemen collapsed in the sixth century, its waters washed away everything and left Arabs divided, different groups going their separate ways. Nalî described the situation of Kurds and Arabs without their own governments becoming occupied by others, writing,

---

[868] Ibid, p. 370.
[869] Ibid, p. 373.

Milletî Kurd u Ereb herdu yeke tefreqe bûn
Le jefaw u mihenî mulkî (Seba) w u Yemenî [870]

Both peoples Kurds and Arabs, each of them were one people
Sorrow and misfortune separated them

With the collapse of the Baban Emirate, Nalî left for Damascus.[871] There, in 1851, he wrote one of his most distinguished and longest political poems, which he sent to his close friend, Salim in Silêmanî, another remarkable poet:

Qurbanî tozî rêgetim eî badî xoş murûr,
Eî peykî şareza be hemu şarî Şarezûr. [872]

I sacrificed myself for your dust oh wind,
Who had knowledge and knew everything in *şarî Şarezûr*.

Nalî had heard so much of the terrible acts committed by the Ottomans against the Kurds that he was compelled to send an epistle to Silêmanî.[873] He said that it was impossible to compare peaceful Kurdish native rule with that of the Ottoman occupation, wondering if there was any possibility of a return to Kurdistan before Judgment Day.

Aye meqamî ruxsete lem beyne bêmewe,
Ya meslehet teweqqufe ta yewmî nefxî sûr. [874]

Is there any chance for me to come back?
Or is there no way until the day of resurrection?

Salim replied to Nalî with a long poem. This has come to be acknowledged as a significant piece of Kurdish literature, and will be discussed below.

---

[870] Ibid, p. 673.
[871] Ibid, p.175.
[872] Ibid, p. 174.
[873] See appendix H for more details.
[874] Ibid, p.197

6.24 Salim (1800–1869)

Salim (Abdulrahman Beg Muhammad Beg) was a member of a well-known family in the Baban Emirate, and closely connected with the ruling dynasty in Silêmanî. During the first half of the nineteenth-century, Ottoman Kurdistan was under continual attack from the Ottoman Empire. Pressure placed on Kurdish officials and intellectuals resulted in a wave of an awakening of nationalist sentiment. Salim was amongst the first of his generation of Kurds to challenge and oppose the use of Turkish and Persian languages. Salim became renowned for his nationalist thought and attitude, as illustrated in the following couplet:

> *Mehî Farsî zibanm guft şerhî halt gu,*
> *Witm jana belednim istilahî 'êwe min Kurdim.*[875]

> I was asked in Persian how I was
> I said, 'I don't understand your language, I am Kurdish'

Since both his audience and Salim himself would have known that he was more than capable of conversing in Persian, arguably these couplets were intended to affirm his Kurdishness. From the verse cited above, it appears that Salim believed in a common language as an expression of Kurdism, language and Kurdish feeling being interwoven. If Kurdism is a common feeling towards a distinct entity, characterised by unity that individuals express towards external affairs, then language may be regarded as a common tool to express that emotion. Thus Salim appears to have regarded the Kurdish language as the nation's soul, valuing it as a strong instrument distinguishing Kurds from Persians and Turks. By its use in literary expression, Salim promoted a means for uniting the Kurdish people. This was significant, as he wanted to assert the position of the Kurds and Kurdish language within the Ottoman's multi-ethnic and multi-lingual system.

During Salim's lifetime, the Kurdish language became a platform from which to call for a nation which would foster an individual's sense of association and affinity. To achieve this, Salim honed a new linguistic framework, promoting the original expression of Kurdish

---

[875] Salim (1972). *Dîwanî Salim*, Kurdish text, Complete Poetic Work of Salim, Kurdistan Press, Hewlêr, p. 8.

national sentiments, using phrases such as *mulki Baban* [the land of Baban-Kurdistan], *asiri Turkan*, [the prisoners of the Turks], and *Kurdziban* [Kurdish speakers], to name but a few.

Salim lived in a time of growing freedom and encouragement, for which the Baban Pashas had striven. At the same time, he saw the collapse and destruction of the Kurdish authorities at the hands of Ottoman Turks. In his poem *al-wida'* [Goodbye] dedicated to the downfall of the Baban Emirate; he expresses the positive characteristics of the authorities and of the Kurdish people. Simultaneously, his poetry attacks the Turks:

> *'el-wida' 'ei mulkî Baban 'el-wida'*
> *'el-wida' 'ei 'ehlî eiman 'el-wida'*
> *Wek asiri Turkman demben bezor*
> *'el-wida' 'ei şahî xuban 'el-wida'* [876]

> Goodbye oh land of Baban goodbye
> Goodbye oh truthful people goodbye
> The Turks are taking me by force
> Goodbye oh Shah of excellent people goodbye

Salim thought that the Baban state was the hope of the Kurdish people, describing that time as the 'Golden Age' of the Kurds, a time when they had everything: progress, cultivated lands, security, happiness, and education. In contrast, he saw the rule of the Ottoman Turks in Kurdish territory brought injustice, and the emergence of occupation, destruction, and suppression:

> *Ehlî Baban gryeken bo xanedan u agketan*
> *nimî, mehbus, nimî' meqtul, nimî menfikran*[877]

> Oh the people of Baban cry for your notables and your representatives
> Some of them imprisoned, some killed, some exiled

---

[876] Xeznedar, Dr. Marouf (2003). Op. cit, p. 143.
[877] Ibid, p. 146.

The poet then spoke in detail about the Ottoman Turkish invaders who tried to destroy the Kurdish soul and humiliate their people. He clearly understood that there was no affinity between the Kurds whom he saw as victims, and Turkish authoritarianism.

In many verses, Salim drew a clear picture about political, social and economic changes after bringing down the Baban Emirate by the Ottomans. In the following examples of Salim's verses, one learns that the Baban Emirate had an administration which was run by civil servants. When the Ottomans came to rule Baban, they destroyed registration books, to prevent Kurdish Baban from having similar authorities in future. He says:

> *Ehlî sadat u mela u Hajî bla şinken be soz*
> *Defteri ehlî weza'if dim 'mumen hekkran*[878]

> O Sadat, Mela and Hajî cry from your heart
> The registration book of civil servants was destroyed

From the *ehli weza'if* [people in employment], we understand that there were workforces in the Baban Emirate who worked in public service administrated by the Baban government.

In another verse, Salim clearly indicates that there was *Mejlisi Şura* [council of debate] in Silêmanî. Having a *Mejlisi Şura* in Baban was important in order to manage and administer to people well. Salim says:

> *Eskemil bênn qeraryanden le jêy axeleran*
> *Mejlisi Şura emêste xase bo esnafekan*[879]

> Bring chairs [bring new people] and put them instead of elite people
> Mejlisi Şura now is reserved for traders

The above verses give the impression that when the Ottomans controlled the Baban Emirate, they replaced all staff in the Kurdish administration with their own. In this way, the Ottomans brought down Kurdish self-government.

---

[878] Ibid, p. 148.
[879] Ibid.

In his riposte to Nalî's poem, Salim[880] expresses his regret for the Kurds' situation of being ruled by the Turks. Salim uses *shamal* [the breeze] as a metaphorical messenger, before discussing the destruction of Silêmanî and its subjects. Nalî has asked about many places, buildings, springs, schools, mosques, rivers, and graves, of particular interest when seeking to understand the sense of Kurdish identity at the time. We learn here of important places in Kurdistan from Nalî. the exile's perspective: *Şarezûr*, [the district of his birth] *Xakuxol* [the village of his birth], *Şiwesur* [a valley near *Cemçemal*], *Serçinar* [a river and a tourist sight near Silêmanî], *Bekreco* [a very fertile land and a canal which was built by one of Baban's Mir], *Silêmanî, Pirdi Serşeqam* [*Serşeqam* bridge, *Serşeqam* still is a borough in Silêmanî, *Dari Pirmesur* [Pirmesur is a saint whose shrine is in Silêmanî], *Şêx Hebas* [a saint from Berzinje family that situated in southern Silêmanî], *Kani Ba* [a tourist place near Silêmanî], Seywan [Silêmanî's graveyard], *Kani Askan* [a borough of Silêmanî, *Tancero* [a river near Silêmanî], and *Xaneqa* [Mawlana Khalid's mosque].

When asked if it would be possible to return to Kurdistan, Salim responded that it would not be safe to return whilst the Turks ruled, as they brought anarchy and disorder to the Baban. A number of verses reflect this sentiment.[881] For instance,

> *Lewsayewe ke hakimanî "Baban" bederkran*
> *Neidiwe kes le çehreî kes jewherî huner* [882]

> Since the Baban rulers were removed
> Nobody has seen any sensible behaviour (from Turks)

Salim suggests that there is no place for someone like Nalî amidst the presence of the Turks, whom he believes are the most brutal enemies in all humanity. Salim further emphasises that the Turkish occupation of Silêmanî is incompatible with any other occupation or aggressive power, viewing Turkish actions in Kurdistan as beyond belief.

---

[880] See Appendix I for more details.

[881] *Zistanî 'ewwelinbu, dṛa bergî "Şêx Hebas / Rumî 'ewende şume le şexiş deda zerer* [That first winter the "Shekh Hebas" graveyard was shattered/ Ottomans are so evil, they even destroy the cemetery] Nalî (1976). Op. cit, p.100.

şarêke piṛ le zulm u mekanêke piṛ le şin/ Jayeke piṛ le şor u wilatêke piṛ le şeṛ [Silêmanî is a town full of injustice; it is a place full of shed tears/ It is a position full of oppression; a land of war (because of Turkish actions)] Nalî (1976). Op. cit, p. 201.

Tu Xuda blê be hezreti "Nali", dexilibm/ Bem naweda qet neka be Silêmniya guzer [I appeal to you God, please great "Nali"/ In this terrible situation you should not approach Silêmanî] Nalî (1976). Op. cit, p. 201.

[882] Ibid, p.161.

6.25 Kurdî (1812-1850)

Mustafa Beg, son of Mahmud Beg, son of Ahmad Beg (Kurdî), was born and lived in Silêmanî; his poetry was first published in 1931 in Baghdad.[883] He was the youngest of the "Baban Triangle Poets", following the path of Nalî and Salim to develop further a literary pattern of rich Kurdish linguistic expression and Kurdish poetic literature. Mustafa Beg chose Kurdî as a nickname which reflected his sense of belonging to Kurdish people and proudly mentioned Kurdî at the end of all his poems.

One of Kurdî's most famous poems was his farewell addressed to Kurds. In this poem, Kurdî tied himself to his people. He expressed the wish that Kurdistan should be free from victims of injustice and oppression by strangers.

Ezizan min ewa ɽoyim le latan
Le mezĺuman beĺa coĺ bê wiltan
Ke eêwen padşay lutf u edalet
Be xiwa heyfe birenjênn gedatan
Eger ser bu, eger roh bu, eger diĺ
Hemu roiin, ciye eitr tematan [884]

My dears, I am about to leave you (to die)
In our land no one should be oppressed
While you [Kurdish people] are king of kindness and justice
You would not allow any poor person to be harmed
My head, my soul and my heart
All I had, I sacrificed them for you sake (if I have more, I would offer)

Furthermore, Kurdî wished to show his people that his personal life reflected their everyday lives. Anyone wishing to learn about Kurds may read about Kurdî's life. He was familiar with the Kurdish people's situation and through his poetic expression stimulated powerful Kurdish self-awareness.

---

[883] Kurdî (1931). Diwanî Kurdî, Dar al-Salam Press, Baghdad.
[884] Xeznedar, Dr. M. (2003) pp. 192-3.

Werin binwaɍne cawi piɍ le xwênm

Be tefsilat bibinn majeratan

Minm serkirdetan bo leşkri xem

Detirsim min biɍom bişkê supatan

Meĺên keĺki nebu ɍoyi jehennem

Serim qelxane bo tiry qezatan [885]

Come and look at my eyes full of blood

You can see in them, your full history

I am the leader of your sorrowful army

You might retreat, if I leave you

Finally, at the end of this poem, he concluded that he sacrificed himself two hundred times daily for poor Kurds and their *padsha* (kings), offered himself for the sake of Kurdish people. He said:

Ilahî min bibm ɍojî du sed car

Be qurbani geda u padişatan

Ewende ercu deka (Kurdî) ke car car

Biken yadi muhibbi bê ɍiyatan [886]

O my God let me, two hundred times daily,

Sacrifice myself for poor Kurds and their *padsha*

The only thing that (Kurdî) ask for is that from time to time

You keep me in your loving and true remembrance

6.26 Sheikh Reza Talebani (1835 – 1910)

One writer, who caught the attention of C. J. Edmonds, was Sheikh Reza Talebanî.[887] Edmonds noted that, "At the date of the British occupation less than seventy years had

---

[885] Ibid, p. 193.

[886] Ibid, p. 194.

[887] Edmonds, C. J. (1935). "A Kurdish Lampoonist", *Journal of the Royal Central Asian Society*, Vol. XXII, Part I, January 1935, pp. 111-123

elapsed since the extinction of Baban rule…most of the adult population must have heard at first hand….accounts of those spacious days of Kurdish independence."[888]

Sheikh Reza Talabanî in one couplet declares of them:

Ewen be heqiqet melikî milletî Kurdan,
Şaynî ziyaret bikrê xakî qedemtan.[889]

You are truly Kings of the Kurds,
You deserve the respect of all Kurds.

Sheikh Reza Talebanî looked back to the Baban era as a golden age, one when Kurds were free and prosperous with an emirate that cared for its population:

Wulati Baban/ The Baban Land

Le birmdê Silêmanî ke darulmulkî Baban bu,
Ne mehkumî 'ejem ne suxrekêşî 'alî Osman bu,
Leber qapî sere sefyan debest şex u mela u zahid,
Metafî keba bo 'erbabî hajet Girdî Seywan bu,
Leber taburî 'esker ŗê nebu bo mejlisî paşa,
Sedaî mosiqe u neqqaŗe ta 'eywanî keywan bu,
Drêx bo 'ew zemane, 'ew deme, 'ew 'esre, 'ew ŗoje,
Ke meydanî jridbazî, le dewrî kanî'askan bu,
Be zebrî hemleye Bexdaî tesxirkrd u teyhelda,
Silêmanî zeman, ŗastit dewê bawkî Silêman bu,
'Ereb enkarî fezlî 'êwe nakem, 'efzeln, 'emma,
Selaheddin ke dunyaigrt le zumreî Kurdî Baban bu,
Quburî piŗ le nurî 'alî Baban piŗ le rehmet bê,
Ke baranî kefî ehsanyan wek hewrî nisan bu,
Ke 'Ebdullah Paşa leşkrî walî Sineî şiŗkrd,
"Ŗeza" 'ew wexte 'umrî pênj u şeş tiflî debustan bu.[890]

---

[888] Edmonds, C. J. (1957). *Kurds, Turks, and Arabs*, Oxfors University Press, London, New York, Toronto, p. 57.
[889] Ghalib, Sabah (1974). "A Brief Study of the National Feeling of Sheikh Reza-i Talebanî", *Bayan Magazine*, Baghdad, No.14, p.7.
[890] Ibid, pp.6-8. Also see Edmonds, C. J. (1957). *Kurds, Turks and Arabs*, Oxford University Press, Oxford, pp.57-8. Sejadi, Ela'edin, (1971). Op. cit, p. 388.

I remember Silêmanî when it was the capital of the Baban,

Then subject to neither Persia, nor a slave of the Ottoman dynasty.

Before the gate of the rulers' palace, Sheikhs, Mullahs and the populace lined up,

Girdi-Seywan was the shrine for those doing business,

There were many fine battalions around the Pasha's court, guarding his chamber,

The sound of bands and drums rose to Jupiter,

Alas, for that time, that epoch, that age, that day;

When the tilting-ground was in the plain of Kanêskan,

With a shock of one foray he took Baghdad and chastised it,

Silêmanî of the time, if you want the truth, was the father of Silêman.

Oh Arabs! I do not deny your accomplishments, you are excellent, but

Saladin who took the world was from Baban Kurdish stock,

Let the bright tombs of the Baban dynasty be filled with God's mercy,

For the rain of their generosity, bountiful as the April showers,

When Abdullah Pasha routed the army of the Wali of Sine,

Reza was but five or six years old, a little boy of primary school.

Here Sheikh Reza Talebanî appears to associate virtues of military prowess, courage and generosity with the Babans and emphasizes their sense of Kurdish identity and autonomy. Sheikh Reza Talebanî, no doubt, wished to contrast present realities with earlier glories. Other poets such as Hajî Qadr i Koyî (1815-1897) and Mehwî (1830-1904) also further furnished this domain of Kurdish literature, building upon existing literary achievements.

6.27 Conclusion

Transferring the Baban Emirate capital to Silêmanî provided an opportunity for Kurdism to develop. In the first half of the nineteenth-century, Kurdish culture and language flourished. The successes and achievements of Baban pashas associated with their sense of patriotism and support for Kurdish culture provided the right conditions for the development of a discourse of Kurdishness, of Kurdish language, culture and Kurdish religious schools.

Abdulrahman Pasha was a statesman who tried his best to establish a foundation for a semi-independent Kurdish state. In this regard, he worked internally and externally. Internally, his deep respect for scholars, poets and writers was demonstrated by his promotion of the Kurdish language and literature within his domains. Externally, he fought to gain more political power to sustain and develop the Baban Emirate.

The spread of poetry, which flourished in his Baban Emirate, later helped to establish Soranî/Sothern Kurmanjî as a literary language. Many writers and poets were involved in the progress of literature. During the first half of the nineteenth century three writers, known as the 'Baban Triangle Poets', were particularly prominent: Nalî, Salim and Kurdî. These poets and other writers such as Mawlana Khalid possessed a high-level of national consciousness. They gave Kurdish literature and thought an important role.

Nalî and Salim were observers at the end of the Kurdish emirate, writing about the happiest time that the Kurds enjoyed. After the emirate was brought down, both poets saw the consequences of its collapse, observing how the Ottoman Turks used ruthless means against the Kurdish people.

The widespread use of the Silêmanî sub-dialect for writing amongst scholars and in mosques all over the Baban Emirate alongside the flowering of an indigenous poetry, helped to establish it as a standardised 'Kurdish' language. The sub-dialect of Silêmanî and three other sub-dialects, Sineyi (Erdelani), Soranî and Mukri (Mukryani), are closely tied together forming Middle Kurmanjî. Middle Kurmanjî is at the present time standardized in a written form called Soranî which could be found in the Southern (Iraqi Kurdistan) and Eastern (Iranian Kurdistan) Kurdistan. Soranî has been used constantly since Mawlana Khalid Naqishbandî through Nalî, Salim and Kurdî up to the present time.

Abdulrahman Pasha's struggle to obtain greater independence from the Ottoman regional powers was the first Kurdish movement at the end of the eighteenth and beginning of the nineteenth century to make a turning point in Kurdish politics. During his governorship, he gained advantages against Baghdad; indeed he played an important role in the nomination of a pasha for Baghdad in 1810. He managed to keep the Baban Emirate free from regional interference for more than a decade. During his reign the Kurds developed a strong feeling of

Kurdishness. On the other hand, they were aware that their pashas were disunited and hostile to each other and thus indirectly encouraged foreign interference in their affairs.

After the death of Abdulrahman Pasha, the rivalry between his sons Mahmud and Silêman pashas meant Kurdish affairs were badly affected. It gave an opportunity for the Ottomans and Persians to penetrate further into Baban. This period was crucial in Kurdish history; as the imposition of the Ottoman centralization did not pass swiftly and easily. Nor did the Kurds submit willingly; rather, they struggled very hard to maintain their local authority. Consequently, the Ottomans needed to resort to the use of their military forces to bring them under the authority of a central government. Eventually the Kurdish territories were subjugated, as Mahmud the Second's centralization policy started to come into effect.

The main reason for the end of the Kurdish Emirates was that the Kurds wanted to keep their semi-independence and therefore resisted the centralization policy. However, in the end, Kurds lacked sufficient power to challenge the centralising Ottomans. The individualism of the Baban Pashas was also a factor in the decline of the emirate. Finally the Kurdish Emirates, in general were somewhat precarious, given their geo-political situation; so the Kurds became trapped between the Ottomans and Persians, which the British coined as the "Eastern Question".

Abdulrahman Pasha's participation in the forming and encouragement of Kurdishness may be seen to this day. His character and his ambitions are still alive in Kurdish minds, and continue to be praised by poets, writers, politicians and historians.[891] There was no doubt that Kurdish princes were conscious of the Kurdish case and fully understood that Kurds were different from dominant Turks and Persians.

The 'sense' of Kurdism that found its expression in Abdulrahman Pasha's Baban, preceded the movement in the Ottoman lands towards the adoption of European Enlightenment based centralizations.[892] These sentiments formed a key element in the sense of Kurdish self-awareness that was to oppose these developing centralizations in the nineteenth century.

---

[891]Nazim Beg, Hussein (2001). *Ta'rikh al-Emarat al-babaniya*, Arabic text, *The History of the Baban Emirate*, translated from Turkish, Shukur Mustafa and Muhammad Mela Karim, Mukryani publisher, Hewlêr. Muhammad, Mas'ud (1975). Op. cit.

[892] These have been well documented by Hourani, *Arabic Thought in the Liberal Age*, Oxford University Press, London New York Toronto, 1962. Dawn C. E., *From Ottomanism to Arabism*, University Illinois Press, Urbana Chicago London, 1973. Khalidi, Anderson, Muslih, Simon (Eds) (1991). *The Origins of Arab Nationalism*, Columbia University Press, New York. Zeine, N. Zeine, (1973). *The Emergence of Arab Nationalism*, Third Edition, Caravan Books, New York, p.23.

In the Baban era, Kurdism developed significantly. It now contained various inter-dependent and mutually strengthening elements. There was an independent local administration with its own strong sense of national identity and distinction. Ethnic politics, independent military force, collective consultation, the sense of responsibility towards people and future generations, the flourishing of poetry in a standard written form of Kurdish language, the reflection of various national and cultural ideas and themes in the poets' writings, all helped to create a formidable body of national consciousness which led to the identification of Silêmanî as the capital city of Kurdish nationalism as well as Kurdish culture.

Chapter Seven

Conclusions

Finding the roots of Kurdism in politics, history, culture, language and literature is crucial for understanding Kurdish nationalism. Over the last thirty years, several studies have been published about Kurdish ethnicity, identity and nationalism, exploring significant issues going back to the last quarter of the nineteenth century. In this study, examples of three Kurdish emirates of the first half of the nineteenth century have been used to illustrate the workings of Kurdism. Political and social structures and ruling dynasties have been examined along with Kurdish language and literature in order to explore the historical relationship between Kurds and the Ottoman Empire and to understand the context within which Kurdish self-awareness has developed.

Kurds in western Kurdish territories, which were officially part of the Ottoman Empire, kept their emirate system which they had developed before the Ottomans came to Kurdistan. Since then, throughout three and a half centuries, until the middle of the nineteenth century, the Kurds considered themselves to be distinct from other groups living amongst and around them. This feeling of being a distinct group grew during Ottoman dominance, but the dominant powers of the time tried to suppress the growth of Kurdish influence. Despite this policy, Kurdism grew in the mind, thoughts, culture and language of the Kurdish people.

After the Battle of Chaldiran in 1514, the Kurds gained strong ground in the wars between the Ottoman and Safavid Empires. A number of different sized Kurdish emirates already existed, and maintained self-rule until 1850. At the beginning of the nineteenth century, there were changes in the relationship between the Kurdish emirates and the Ottoman Empire. Even before the *Tanzimat* [Ottoman reform], Kurdish consciousness emerged. The negative stance of the Ottomans, especially during the centralization policy against the local-rule in the emirate, helped generate and develop a sense of self-awareness amongst Kurds. It was the sense of being a Kurd and feeling distinct from other groups that made Kurds aware of their right to build up their own distinct culture by advancing their language and literature. In the first half of the nineteenth century, princes, politicians, scholars and poets, such as Abulrahman Pasha of Baban, Muhammad Pasha of Soran, Bedirkhan, Mawlana Khalid Naqishbandi, Nalî, Salim, Kurdî and others were symbols of Kurdism. They maintained

Kurdish self-rule and a legacy of Kurdism, by promoting Kurdish culture, language, literature, and Kurdish folklore.

Each Kurdish emirate contained a number of tribal confederations who supported the *mir* to rule and to sustain the emirate. Tribesmen were the main body of the emirate forces. Many *mirs* enjoyed support of tribesmen who were loyal to them rather than to the Ottoman Empire. It was upon this strong foundation that the Kurdish emirates made the Selim-Idris agreement with the Ottoman Empire. Accordingly, both sides had obligations towards each other. Kurdish dynasties were in charge of their local affairs and in return, they had to support the empire in its wars and contribute money both for *Zakat* (charity) and towards the central government. The Kurdish political system of emirate rule was hereditary; the Kurdish *mir* could not be removed by the central power.

The Kurdish *mir* who was in charge of the emirate, administered a much broader territory than the tribal leaders. The latter tended to have influence over a much smaller group of people, bound to them by blood relationships in some form or another. Crucially, a *mir* had to come from his dynasty and had to be blessed and appointed by the centralized power, whilst a tribal leader tended to be found or endorsed by local kinship networks. Furthermore, the ability of the *mir* was an important factor for the success of the Kurdish Emirate therefore, whenever a powerful *mir* appeared, the emirate flourished, strengthening itself and seizing more Kurdish territories.

The Kurdish *mirs* understood their society, and they manipulated the Kurdish community for their own benefit. Everyday affairs were run by Kurdish emirates with support from Kurdish tribes. The emirate system was wider, stronger and more systematic than the tribal system. Tribal leaders and chieftains were under the leadership of the pasha or head of the emirate. They were the power behind the emirates and responsible for providing the pasha with troops. They were also a source of revenue for the emirates.

Within the tribal system, each Kurdish tribe had its own structure and so the tribes were in some ways distinct from and independent of each other. At the same time, each tribe was part of the Kurdish semi-autonomous emirates which sought to defend Kurdish local rule. In the mid-nineteenth century, particularly through military reform and *Tanzimat*, the Ottoman Empire increased its influence over Kurdish tribes through land reforms.

The Kurdish emirates maintained their existence for centuries, and during that period they experienced many internal and external crises, playing an important role in establishing Kurdish cultural identity. Four main factors explained how the Kurdish emirates survived between the thirteenth and nineteenth centuries. Firstly, the nature of the Kurdish region was mountainous and isolated which allowed the survival of the emirates as they were far from the interests of the dominant powers of the region. Secondly, the Kurds would not accept direct foreign rule and resisted central authorities. Thirdly, Kurdish rulers considered that they had a hereditary and political legitimacy which came either from religion or from social and economic roots. Moreover, the Kurdish pashas had personality and charisma. Kurds respected the rulers of the emirates, followed them and fulfilled their orders. Without the emirate, both the Ottomans and Persians were not able to govern the Kurds. Finally, European powers were not yet interfering in the region, and did not perceive Kurds as obstacles to their interests. However, from the beginning of the nineteenth century, European governments especially Britain came to realize that the Kurds' strategic position posed a threat to European interests.

The *medrese* and mosque were to play an important role in the diffusion of Kurdism as many of the early Kurdish poets and scholars received their education there. The spread of mosques and *medreses* in Kurdistan may be seen as a clear indication that Kurds were interested in education and learning Kurdish language and literature. They promoted the growth of the idea of Kurdism among the *melas* and *feqês* which later had an impact on the local Kurdish population. Most of the larger *medreses* tended to be sponsored by the established Kurdish dynasties and local people. *Medrese* in Kurdistan produced *melas* for religious affairs, and played a key role in the emergence of Kurdish national awareness among Kurds in different parts of Kurdistan. Their main aim was to educate future religious leaders, but the *medrese* also became a centre for future political leadership.

Sharafkhan Bidlisi, who may be identified as the first proponent of Kurdism in the sixteenth century, transformed the idea of Kurdism in a very important qualitative way. Together with establishing a strong ground of Kurdish historiography, he provided a construction of what Kurdism means, bringing together as its elements, land (geographically identified), language (including variants of dialects), political power and administration. He also relates all these to one constant element with the Kurdish character and the ability of Kurds to match other peoples in terms of courage, knowledge and self-administration. It was Sharafkhan's self-awareness of being a Kurd, and his character and role as a scholar that made him proud of the self-rule of Kurdish emirates. For the first time, he defined the words Kurd, Kurdistan and Kurdish language as historical realities. Although he wrote his work in Persian, his content was consciously Kurdist.

The first instances of the use of Kurdish language in written poetry appeared after the Battle of Chaldiran. The first poets emerging in Botan at the end of sixteenth century included the pioneers Ali Harirî (1530–1600), Feqê Teyeran (1563–1641) and Melayê Cizîrî (1567–1640). They were influenced by Persian poetic traditions and classical norms, but they used the Kurdish language to incorporate elements of Islamic classical poetry developed by the Arabs and Persians. This was especially the case when they identified their feelings of Kurdish 'togetherness'.

Cizîrî used the word "Kurdistan", something which had not been done in poetry before. However, in general his poetry covered themes shared by Persian and Arab classical poetry, such as *ishq* (yearning love), wine and religious themes. Together with Ali Heriri and Feqê Teyeran, Cizîrî provided a precedent for Ehmedê Xanî to follow their pioneering paths. Xanî mentions Melayê Cizîrî's name (1567–1640) in his prologue. Ehmedê Xanî (1650-1706) clearly distinguished Kurds from other groups, and saw the Kurdish plight through their experiences of being dominated by the Ottoman and Persian powers. He called on Kurds to have their own king. Xanî's purpose was to create a literary collection in Kurdish to show that Kurds have their own language and literature. He also believed that the Kurds could be a great nation in their own right.

Since Xanî placed such a strong emphasis on fostering Kurdish unity, it is unsurprising that Xanî's legacy has had such as an important role and impact in promoting what may be described as the emergence of the first Kurdish nationalist and reformist intellectuals in the late nineteenth century and early twentieth century in the Ottoman Empire. He uses his whole reconstruction of *Mem u Zin* to make the Kurds feel proud of the distinctive characteristics of their Kurdishness.

Since the seventeenth century, Kurdish oral tradition, including *Dimdim* [epic] and later in the beginning of the nineteenth century, the work of *Beyti Abdulrahman Pasha of Baban,* has played an important role in promoting Kurdism within people's minds and hearts. The practice of sharing cultural folklore, *Dimdim,* was widespread among Kurds regardless of their dialects, sect and region. *Dimdim,* which has maintained its position as a key part of the oral tradition to this day, would appear to demonstrate the Kurds' admiration of its core messages. *Dimdim* has functioned as an inspirational paradigm for future generations, rather than being accurate in terms of historical detail. What it seeks to convey is 'feeling' and therefore we can see it as affirmation of what makes Kurds 'determined' to be Kurdish, a key element in the conveyance of 'Kurdism'. *Dimdim* reflects Kurdish struggle against and resistance to dominant powers.

From the sixteenth century to the mid–nineteenth century, the Kurdish emirates helped the Kurds maintain their autonomy. Relations between the Kurdish emirates, the Ottoman and Persian Empires were dependent on the attitudes of the latter two, and the Kurdish emirates struggled to retain their autonomy and maintain a balance so that there was no major conflict with the central powers. In the first half of the nineteenth-century when the very existence of the Kurdish emirates was questioned, with the only possible outcomes being either survival or collapse, the Kurdish emirates strongly resisted the centralising authority whose main aim was to bring them to capitulation and collapse.

In the conflicts between the Ottomans and Safavids, the issue was about the expansion of those two empires at the expense of the Kurds. Neither empire could endure such psychological stress from the heavy pressure caused by regular conflicts between them. These continual disputes sapped the strength of the powerful and the powerless in both states. The Kurds were caught in the middle and became the victims. This study has identified the political and cultural emergence of Kurdism towards a fuller state of political development in the early nineteenth century.

The case studies of the three emirates, Soran, Botan and Baban provide an insight into the development of Kurdism in terms of politics, language and literature. For example, during Muhammad Pasha's rule, the unrivalled position of the Soran Emirate enabled him to reorganise Soran's domestic affairs so that he could strengthen his grip on power, and enable him to raise followers to prepare for future struggles. Thus, the cornerstone of a Kurdish political administration could now be established. Local distinctions could be replaced with a wider Kurdish identity, which gave the Kurds in the emirate just one central authority and voice. Muhammad Pasha established the powerful security of calmness for his people.

Muhammad Pasha expanded the Soran Emirate primarily with his interests in mind; he seems to have failed to consider how his actions might have affected the regional interests of Ottoman and Persia on the one hand, and the interests of the British on the other. The Pasha of Soran did not realise how fragile his position was between various interests in the region. His military expansionist tendencies included campaigns against rival Kurdish Emirates, especially Baban and Botan. This suggests that Kurdish heads of emirates were not united around Kurdism, thus weakening the Kurdish position against outsiders. Despite this, the overthrow of the Soran Emirate did not lead to peace and stability between the Ottomans and the Kurds. The Kurdish people, especially the scholars, refused to conform to the centralization policy of promoted by Constantinople. It was only through military power that the Ottoman empire was able to enforce its policy on Soran and other Kurdish emirates. Here, the British policy implemented by ambassador Ponsonby in Constantinople and his representative Richard Wood, played a crucial role in bringing about the downfall of Soran. British policy pushed Muhammad Pasha to surrender to the Sultan's commander Rashid Pasha.

The use of Kurdish language and literature of the last period of the Soran Emirate was instrumental in developing Kurdism. The most famous Kurdish scholars in the Soran Emirate such as *Mela* Muhammad Ibnu Adam and Hajî *Mela* Abdullah Jelizade wrote in Kurdish. Ideas of Kurdish nationalism became an important ideological force for resisting occupation and calling for revolution and liberation. Hajî Qadiri Koyî became the most nationalistic Kurdish poet to give expression to these ideas in a language that could be understood by all sections of Kurdish society, from intellectuals to peasants. He developed the theory of nationalism as revolutionary, progressive and secularist. He clearly identified the goal of national unity of land, people and statehood as the only way for the liberation of his people and the revival of the past glories of the Kurdish nation. All the experiences and ideas learnt from Baban, Erdelan and Soran helped form the strong and passionate romantic nationalism that Hajî took to the Bedirkhans. Hajî was a political poet, connecting three Kurdish emirates together at least by literature, and writing for the sake of his people. Without hesitation, he called on the Kurds to establish their own state, take the path of revolution and acquire guns to achieve statehood. Hajî succeeded in establishing a united Kurdism in literary thought.

Certainly, we do not know exactly what was in Muhammad Pasha of Soran's mind regarding Kurdism, and whether he acted with Kurdish awareness or not. However, it is clear that he wanted to preserve his Kurdish feudal emirate. He supported Kurdish scholars and *medrese*. He built a strong army and established some sort of administration. In this way, Muhammad Pasha helped to generate a sense of Kurdish identity and loyalty amongst people, and a sense of Kurdish self-awareness which continued beyond the Soran Emirate.

The policies pursued by Bedirkhan Pasha helped in developing the notion of Kurdism in the Botan Emirate. Through the forging of alliances with other Kurdish leaders, Bedirkhan Pasha carved out an area of influence that left him in a position where he could begin to seek an autonomous area for Kurds. He can be seen to have attempted to maintain a degree of autonomy from the Ottomans. He pursued a number of administrative reforms and a modernisation of the army. All these served to strengthen his position as a leading power in the region. Kurdish people in Medyat, Merzan and Sert, were not under his government, but they recognised his authority. In other words, Bedirkhan managed to create an atmosphere and influence among the Kurds even outside of his region. The defeat of the Ottoman army in Nisib was taken as an opportunity by the Kurds to express their negative attitude towards the Ottoman Empire. Kurds wished for the Ottoman Empire to become weak, in the hope of gaining more rights and Kurdish self-rule. Bedirkhan had aspirations to have wider power than just his base in Botan. He knew that the Botan Emirate was a small portion of Kurdistan and he sought to extend his power over greater parts of Kurdistan.

With the *Tanzimat* and army reforms, the Ottomans intended to increase their power and influence over their disparate territories. However, the Ottomans' power was gradually being undermined. To re-establish their authority, they attempted to subjugate all the Kurdish emirates one by one. In this way, the Porte then added the emirate of Botan to the Pashalik of Mosul.

This stand, and other confrontations against the Ottomans, suggests that when Bedirkhan was powerful, he challenged the Ottoman Empire and considered Kurds to be distinct from other Ottoman peoples. This suggests that Bedirkhan was concerned to unify his people. Initially, he had no intention of harming the Christians; a pretext used by the Europeans, to topple Bedirkhan and the Botan Emirate. However, he did end up acting violently towards Nestorians, whom American and British missionaries encouraged to refuse Kurdish emirates rule. Bedirkhan massacred the Yezidis which has deeply damaged his reputation. Abolishing Kurdish rule was part of the centralization policy which was vital in restoring the Ottoman power in Kurdistan and other places.

Besides establishing a just administration and building a strong Botan army, Bedirkhan demonstrated his allegiance to Kurdism in other ways. Bedirkhan habitually dressed in a distinctly Kurdish style and embraced the Kurdish way of life. It appears that he tended to place the interests of the Kurdish people above the Ottomans. If asked to do something against Kurdish interests he would, without hesitation, refuse. Political life in Botan was reflected in Kurdish literature, especially in folk songs. Many *Lawikbêj* (*lawik* singer) who were living under Bedirkhan devoted their *lawik* to express their feelings and praise for the Kurdish ruler, describing the Ottoman army as the force of an enemy.

Thus, the attack on Botan and other parts of Kurdistan nurtured the idea of Kurdism and helped Kurdists to promote nationalist views. Kurdish songs and Kurdish language influenced the establishment of a discourse of Kurdism. Kurdish *lawiks* clearly distinguished between Kurds and Turks, without necessarily directly challenging the rule of the Sultan and Ottoman Empire. *Lawik* reflected the general opinion of the Kurdish people and the *Lawikbêj* therefore, promoted Kurdism and praised Bedirkhan and his rule. After his demise, the songs served as important memoirs of a time when the idea of Kurdism prevailed and today are considered important for Bedirkhan's historical legacy.

The defeat of Bedirkhan and the collapse of his administration in the Botan Emirate was a disaster for the Kurdish people. This event did not bring peace and stability to the Ottoman Empire in its relation with its Kurds. It became clearer to non-Muslim elements in Kurdistan, such as the Christians, that Botan rule was preferable to that of the Ottomans. Bedirkhan had aroused a sense of unity and resistance among Kurds. At the height of his power, Bedirkhan tried his best to keep Botan free from direct intervention by the Ottoman Empire. For example, he used the word "Kurdistan" during Stevens' visit, the British consul in Erzerum, emphasising the Kurdish identity of both himself and his emirate. His choice to wear distinctive Kurdish dress indicates Bedirkhan's pride in the distinct Kurdish customs of his own people.

Today, Bedirkhan has an esteemed reputation amongst Kurds and his family is considered an important Kurdish dynasty, with many Kurds looking to Bedirkhan as a paramount Kurdish leader. At the beginning of Bedirkhan's reign, the idea of Kurdism had not been realised in any concrete sense. However, during his reign, it was nurtured through his energy to establish a Kurdish army and better international relations. By the end of his reign and his exile, his sons followed his example and continued to realise his aims. The legacy of his reign is of major importance in the development of Kurdism, both within and outside of Kurdistan.

During the period of *Tanzimat*, the influence of the European powers over Ottoman affairs increased dramatically. As in other parts of the Empire, European states and American Christian organisations went into Kurdistan. One result of this was to drive a wedge between the Kurds and Nestorians who had been living together relatively peacefully for centuries. Even though Bedirkhan had reasons to stop the Nestorians' aggression, he made a crucial mistake in attacking them. The British also made a serious error by putting pressure on the Ottomans and encouraging them to destroy the Botan emirate, and for bringing Kurds into Northern Kurdistan under the direct rule of the Turkish yoke. The anguish of that event is still remembered by the Kurds today. English officials admitted that the American missionaries were responsible for creating tension and enmity between the two parties.

In the Baban Emirate, the transfer of the capital from Qeĺa Çolan to Silêmanî in 1784 was influential in inspiring the emergence of Kurdism. The Baban emirate, under Abdulrahman Pasha, took advantage of the Ottomans' difficulties and weaknesses in their internal and external affairs. The Kurdish pasha experienced wider authority and imposed his influence even on Baghdad, demanding to be under the direct influence of the Ottoman Sultan with no Ottoman official intermediary. This plan to build a city, and the founding of schools and sponsoring poets and scholars, had an immense impact on Kurdish identity in the beginning of the nineteenth century. Silêmanî has become a symbolic icon in Kurdish thought and a capital of Kurdish culture.

Abdulrahman had a sense of the political geography of his emirate, and the Kurdish lands as a whole. It is possible that the Pasha believed Baban to be part of Kurdistan and associated one with the other, using the terms interchangeably. This indicates the Pasha's sense of Kurdish identity. In conclusion, although Abdulrahman Pasha recognised the authority of the Ottoman Porte, and cannot be described as wishing to be truly independent of the Ottomans, he did not wish to be subject to the influence of any other regional power. His aim was to manage the affairs of his people without interference from any third party. His reputation for loyalty to the cause of Kurdish emirate was lasting. He refused the offer of becoming a governor of Baghdad because although it would increase his personal prosperity, he was concerned that it might ruin the family of the Baban. During his reign, a few Kurdish scholars and poets had started using Kurdish Soranî as a language for literature or as one which promoted Kurdish identity. Later on, the development of literature in the Soranî language provided a focus for Kurdish self-awareness, and this affected the development of Kurdish identity and its impact on Kurdish nationalism.

An emerging collective Kurdish self-consciousness may be observed where Abdulrahman Pasha asserts that the decision as to who would govern Kurds should be arrived at by counsel amongst Kurds themselves, not through his personal will or interference from an outside force. By this and other political initiatives, Abdulrahman Pasha moved towards creating a deeper sense of Kurdishness. It could be suggested, in the light of this, that Kurdish consciousness was generated amongst a new generation of Kurdish politicians and intellectuals, who would later reject Turkish direct rule over the Kurds. He emphasized that whoever became the *Mir* of Baban should, like him, maintain concern to empathise with and preserve order amongst the people, and maintain their essential Kurdishness. It could be argued that Abdulrahman Pasha was aware of the ideas of 'country', Kurdish people, self-government and collective consciousness. He called for togetherness among princes and Kurdish people as well. Through such unity, he emphasized that Kurds would achieve their goals.

Kurdish poets and writers also played an important role in the dissemionation of Kurdism through composing literature in their own language. For example,Ali Berdeşanî is reputed to be the first to have written a Kurdish poem during the Baban era. Berdeşanî's poems were political and he devoted his work to Kurdish interests. Likewise, Mawlana Khalid was a Kurdish thinker who called for unity among members of the Baban dynasty and he was the first to write prose in Kurdish. It was a great step forward for Kurdish Muslim scholars to write in Kurdish. In particular, it was thought that Kurdish people should learn about everyday affairs, including religion in their own language.
The poet Nali, writing in the first half of the nineteenth century, he felt first and foremost that he was a poet of the Kurdish nation. He chose specifically to write in Kurdish and through the

use of the Kurdish language, Nalî brought a new sensibility to the literature. This, in turn, left a positive residuum with all Kurdish people; he added many new political expressions to the Kurdish language. In time, his new written 'dialect' naturally matured and replaced the Southern Kurdish Gorani used by the Erdelan court, in Sine and its surrounding districts.

Salim, another great Kurdish poet towards the end of Baban emirate, thought that the Baban state was the hope of the Kurdish people, describing that time as the 'Golden Age' of the Kurds, a time when they had everything: progress, cultivated lands, security, happiness, and education. In contrast, he saw the rule of the Ottoman Turks in Kurdish territory brought injustice, and the emergence of occupation, destruction, and suppression. Salim suggests that there is no place for someone like Nalî amidst the presence of the Turks, whom he believes are the most brutal enemies in all humanity. Salim further emphasises that the Turkish occupation of Silêmanî is incompatible with any other occupation or aggressive power, viewing Turkish actions in Kurdistan as beyond belief.

Kurdî was the third of the "Baban Triangle Poets" with a sense of Kurdish self-awareness; he very proudly repeated his nickname in the last verses of his poems. He expressed his Kurdist view in highly emotional way, and thought himself and Kurdish people to be unified forever.

During the Baban era, Kurdism developed significantly. It now consisted of various interdependent and mutually strengthening elements. There was an independent local administration with its own distinct sense of national identity. Ethnic politics, independent military force, collective consultation, the sense of responsibility towards people and future generations, the flourishing of poetry in a standard written form of Kurdish language, and the reflection of various national and cultural ideas and themes in the poets' writings, all helped to create a formidable body of national consciousness.

Between 1800 and 1850, Kurdish language became a powerful symbol to distinguish Kurds from "others". Kurdish scholars made efforts to preserve and develop a written form of Kurdish, leading to the production of magnificent classical Kurdish poetry by Nalî, Salim, and later, Hajî Qadir and Sheikh Reza, amongst others. Kurdish intellectuals played a great role in leading the people and in strengthening a people's sense of Kurdish identity and belonging. The majority of Kurdish scholars and poets assisted the development of Kurdish literature, language and culture. Their work helped Kurds to develop a sense of a distinct identity from dominant groups. Kurdish scholars and poets also called to maintain Kurdish local rule within the framework of the ruling states. After the end of the Kurdish emirates, Kurdish poets and scholars expressed their anger towards dominant powers which they viewed as aggressors.

Although no single Kurdish emirate had absolute sovereignty over the whole of Kurdistan, some such as Soran, Botan and Baban in the first half of the nineteenth century, intended to modernise and urbanise society and extended their rule. The era of the emirates proved that Kurdish people were attached to their territories and to their ethnic identity. In Kurdistan, the principalities as territorial states did not progress to being fully established states. The collapse of the last three Kurdish emirates Soran, Botan and Baban was a set-back for Kurdish ambitions.

During the beginning of the nineteenth century, Kurdism did not fully grow into political nationalism. Throughout the first half of the nineteenth century, the first period of Kurdism occurred when Kurdish consciousness appeared among both politicians and intellectuals, with primary elements such as people (Kurds), land (Kurdistan), culture, language and literature.

Kurdism was a major factor in supporting the Kurdish emirates against Ottoman influence in Kurdistan, and laid the foundations of Kurdish nationalism in later periods, and paved the way for the emergence of Kurdish poets, writers and politicians. These years witnessed the earliest forms and expressions of Kurdish nationalism exemplified by both poets and politicians. Men such as Sayyid Ubeydullah of Nahri, Hajî Qadir Koyî, Bedirkhan's sons, Sayyid Abdulqadir of Nahri, Sheikh Mahmud Hafid and others, all became symbols representing Kurdism. Sayyid Ubeydullah of Nahri and Hajî Qadir Koyî influenced later intellectuals, such as Bekirkhans Babanzade Ismael Haqqi (1876-1914) and Abdullah Jewdet (1869-1932), who were influential in the twentieth century.

"Kurdism", as used in this study, denotes a self-consciousness and awareness of being a Kurd, and part of a wider group of Kurds. However, for the purpose of this thesis it has been necessary to define the term '*Kurdist*' as a person who identifies their own ethnicity as "Kurdish" and who promotes and expresses thoughts regarding the identity of the Kurds as a generalized term for the people living in the geographical area of the Middle East that has been known historically as 'Kurdistan'. In this sense both terms, Kurdism and Kurdist, indicate concepts of proto-nationalism and pro-active nationalism. It has been argued that there was a sense of Kurdishness amongst people in Kurdistan prior to the Ubeydullah Revolt of the late nineteenth century, particularly so in those areas known as 'Emirates' in the first half of the nineteenth century.

One of the greatest obstacles preventing the Kurdish emirate from fulfilling their ambitions and seeing their hopes materialise was the state of international politics at the time. In the first half of the nineteenth century, the imperialist projects of the European powers had unfortunate consequences for the destiny of the Kurdish people. European powers for their own interests wished to save the Ottoman Empire and therefore they put pressure on the Ottoman Empire to end the Kurdish emirates. Such policies led to the destruction of Kurdish self-governance. The suppression of the semi-independent Kurdish emirates resulted in anarchy and disorder in Kurdistan as the Kurds rejected direct Turkish rule. Although the Ottoman Sultan managed to destroy the Kurdish emirates and crushed the rebellions afterward, the Kurds did not acknowledge his authority.

There were two key factors which brought down the Kurdish emirates. Firstly, the Ottoman policy was to fight the Kurdish emirates one at a time. Therefore, control of Kurdistan by the Ottomans took longer to gain than any other part of the empire as the fight against the Kurds took longer. This situation was further exacerbated by the ferocity of the resistance put up by the Kurds against the Ottoman aggressors. Secondly, the Kurdish emirates were in conflict with each other, which resulted in a lack of unity between them.

Kurdish national identity took root over much of the region of Kurdistan and lasted for a considerable period of time. The three emirates of Soran, Botan and Baban under the leadership of the Kurdish *mir* shaped Kurdish identity and self-consciousness. However, the Ottomans and Persians used tough measures with the hope of terminating their existence and the European powers, due to their political purposes, never supported the Kurds.

The suppression of the semi-independent Kurdish emirates resulted in the creation of anarchy and disorder in Kurdistan as the Kurds were hostile towards direct Ottoman rule. Although the Ottoman Sultan managed to destroy the Kurdish emirates and crush the subsequent rebellions, the Kurds never acknowledged his authority. As part of their *raison d'etre*,

Kurdish leaders asserted their self-identity throughout the history of 'Ottoman' Kurdistan; their acknowledgement of Ottoman authority was dependent on this.

The Kurds were willing to support the Ottomans where this would allow Kurdish self-rule. Kurds shared Sunni Islam with the Ottomans and felt that the Ottoman Empire was their empire too, when it was not interfering with the Kurdish emirates. The resistance of the Kurds in Soran, Botan and Baban emirates, through to the first half of the nineteenth century indicates that Kurds wished to keep their Kurdism, their *mirs*, their culture, their land and their language. This desire led Kurdish scholars and poets to produce poetry about their resistance, regarding the Ottomans as strangers and enemies.

Finally, this thesis contributes to the study of Kurdish nationalism, exploring the concept of Kurdism in politics, language and literature in the late period of the Kurdish emirates. Drawing upon a range of well-known Arabic and English sources, but also upon lesser known English and Kurdish sources, some which have never been consulted for academic research before, this thesis explores the concept of Kurdism which has been found to have existed in thought since the beginning of the nineteenth century.

This study has raised a number of questions about the way in which Kurdish history should be viewed. It has been argued that the concept of Kurdism has prevailed since the late period of the Kurdish emirates as evident from the writing of pashas and *mirs*, along with scholars and poets of that time. To extend this research, it would be interesting to consult further sources held in British and Kurdish libraries, to examine the relationship between the Kurdish emirates in greater detail and to further explore the impact of European policy upon Kurdism during the first half of the nineteenth century. It would be of particular interest to explore Kurdism and Kurdish nationalism through Hajî Qadir's (1815-1897) eyes, Salim's Kurdism in the late period of the Baban Emirate (1800–1869) and Kurdism and nationalism of the Bedirkhan family after the destruction of the Botan Emirate. Lastly, the Kurdish emirate system may be regarded as a semi-autonomous force in Kurdistan. The destruction of the emirate system meant losing ground for developing Kurdish self-awareness and Kurdish statehood. It delayed the progress of the development of the Kurdish language and literature. It also created a gap in political administration which the Ottomans could not fill without paying a heavy price.